CLASSIC GERMAN COOKING

CLASSIC GERMAN COOKING

The Very Best Recipes for Traditional Favorites,
from Semmelknödel to Sauerbraten

LUISA WEISS
Photographs by Elena Heatherwick

TEN SPEED PRESS
California | New York

For Bruno

"Aua Aua" sagt der Bauer.
"Die Äpfel sind zu sauer.
Die Birnen sind zu süß,
Morgen gibt's Gemüs'."

CONTENTS

INTRODUCTION *1*   THE PANTRY *15*   EQUIPMENT *23*

BREAKFAST, SNACKS
& SPREADS *24*

SALADS *44*

SOUPS & STEWS *64*

VEGETARIAN MAIN
COURSES *88*

MEAT & FISH *116*

SWEET MAIN COURSES *168*

VEGETABLES, POTATOES
& DUMPLINGS *196*

DESSERTS *226*

BIBLIOGRAPHY *251*   ACKNOWLEDGMENTS *253*   INDEX *254*

INTRODUCTION

One recent morning in late spring, my family—my husband, Max, and our sons, Hugo and Bruno—and I drove southwest from Berlin, where we live, to Petzow on the banks of the Schwielowsee, one of Berlin and Brandenburg's three thousand lakes. We were there for a guided tour of Schlossgarten Petzow, a privately owned garden that had originally been created in the nineteenth century as part of a larger project that included a palace, a church, and a small village by three renowned Prussian architects and landscape designers, Karl Friedrich Schinkel, Friedrich August Stüler, and Peter Joseph Lenné.

We thought we were there to spend a few hours in a pretty walled garden; what I didn't expect was a history lesson that spanned from the Bronze Age to the reunification of Germany. Though after so many years in Berlin, I should have known that in any context here, history is never very far away.

After World War II, the occupying Soviet military expropriated the family that owned the garden, and it was divided into allotments for local villagers and refugees to grow food during the devastating hunger of the postwar years. Later, during the years of the German Democratic Republic, the garden became the site of an agricultural cooperative. After the fall of the Berlin Wall, the garden fell into disrepair. It became a dumping ground, with nearly a million kilos of garbage removed from it in later years, until the current owner, a wealthy West Berlin businessman named Klaus Kosakowski, bought it and set about restoring the garden's former glory.

It was Kosakowski who gave us the tour, proudly pointing out the efforts of the past twenty years: the beautifully crafted wooden hut for the beehives, the handmade bricks for the restored walls of the garden, the meticulously planned lines of sight throughout the garden to better contemplate the countless rosebushes and perfectly laid-out vegetable garden. Kosakowski also explained that during the multiyear cleanup of the gardens, excavators unearthed a Bronze Age–era holy site, which he decided to leave intact, an ancient clearing at the edge of all the manicured beauty.

A few steps farther and we were standing in front of a wizened elderberry tree. A small brass bell hung from one of its branches. Why the bell? Kosakowski explained that elderberry, known as Holunder in German or Holler in Austria, had been given its name by Germanic tribes who associated the tree with the goddess Hulda. She was rumored to inhabit the trees, shaking the branches free of their tiny white blossoms in spring, a storyline picked up by the Grimm Brothers' nineteenth-century fairy tale "Frau Holle." Since ancient times, elderberry trees have also been considered to be the threshold to other worlds inhabited by dwarves and fairies, Kosakowski solemnly explained, or maybe even the underworld. It was considered risky to fall asleep under an elderberry tree because you could end up trapped in the other world forever, and so, to avoid that, the bell was hung to keep drowsy visitors awake.

As we stood there listening to Kosakowski, everyone nodding thoughtfully about the elderberry tree, I thought about how emblematic this mixture of seriousness and whimsy is to Germany, and to German food, too. Germans are widely considered to be models of efficiency and solidity, their humor (and their food) stodgy and serious. And there is some truth to that. But believe it or not, this was not the first time that I'd been spoken to straight-faced about fairies in an otherwise unmagical context, and Germans can be far more carefree and twinkly-eyed than they are often given credit for. Butchers slip children slices of ham from the counter with a wink, older neighbors secretly place foil-wrapped chocolate Santas in the freshly polished childrens' shoes parked outside their apartment doors on the Eve of Saint Nicholas, and it is perfectly normal to serve children rice pudding or jam-filled pancakes for lunch. Pork, potatoes, and cabbage may be a large part of the traditional German diet, but so are the flavors of fresh milk and sour cheese, elderberries and red currants, mugwort and nutmeg, quince and pears.

The story about the elderberry tree stayed in my mind for a long time after our visit. I had grown up with the fairy tale of "Frau Holle," could still hear in my mind the rich timbre of the actress's voice who told the story on the recording I listened to as a child, but I had never known about elderberry's ancient history. Berlin's boulevards and parks are filled with wild

4 CLASSIC GERMAN COOKING

elderberry trees; their creamy disk-shaped umbels are spring's most delicious harvest. My friend Joan taught me how to gather the umbels, always careful not to shake off any of the fragrant pollen, and to macerate them with lemon before turning them into elderflower syrup. In various regions of Germany and Austria, the delicate umbels are dipped in a light batter and fried, then served with a gossamer dusting of confectioners' sugar. In late summer, after the umbels wither and dark purplish-blue berries appear in their place, they are gathered and turned into inky jelly or cooked down into compote, delicious with sweet, tender dumplings made with Quark.

Elderberry isn't the only food the Germans have been eating for millennia. The Roman historian Tacitus, writing in the first century CE, described the diet of Germanic tribes as consisting primarily of wild berries, game, beer (though he didn't call it that), and lac concretum, or solidified milk, which anyone living in Germany today might recognize as Quark, a fresh cheese that is still a staple of the local diet. In fact, when one contemplates traditional German cuisine today, with its braised venison, berry puddings, Quark spreads, and ever-present glasses of cold beer, it is remarkable how many of these ancient flavors are still at the table. Though one must also keep in mind the influence of poverty on the German diet; for most Germans for many centuries, porridges made from grains such as wheat, barley, and millet were one of the main sources of nutrition, and were mixed with little more than milk or lard.

Over time, geopolitical events from all four directions influenced the German diet. To simplify it somewhat: The northern spice routes via the Hanseatic League brought things such as cinnamon and cardamom to the German sweet kitchen; from the west came braised and roasted meat; from the south came noodles and dumplings; from the east came cucumbers, caraway, and paprika. Knights returning from the Crusades introduced saffron, pepper, and raisins. A particularly impressive example of culinary influence is from the French Huguenots who fled to Berlin and Brandenburg in the seventeenth century after the revocation of the Edict of Nantes. I once saw their contribution illustrated at an exhibit at Berlin's Märkisches Museum, which is devoted to the history of the city and surrounding region. A long table was filled with the foods those French Protestants introduced to Berlin—meat patties, asparagus, button mushrooms and porcini, carrots and cabbage, pears and apples, green beans and cauliflower, white bread and Mischbrot, which is a blend of white and rye flour bread. Even the cream puff! One shudders to think of what the average Berliner was eating before the arrival of the French.

And perhaps the most famous addition to German cuisine: potatoes. Today potatoes are such a part of German identity that a derogatory term for Germans by non-Germans is Kartoffel (potato) but potatoes weren't part of the German diet until the eighteenth century, when Friedrich II, king of Prussia, ordered Germans who were suffering under recurring famines to start eating the tuber of a plant that they had largely considered only decorative since its importation from Spain in the mid-sixteenth century. (It turns out they were cooking the tubers wrong.) Today, as a token of gratitude, visitors leave potatoes on the gravestone of Friedrich II in the gardens of his pleasure palace Sanssouci in Potsdam.

But perhaps more than anything, German cuisine reflects the influence of the Protestant Reformation as well as the trauma of constant, unabating hunger. As Wolfram Siebeck, an influential German food journalist, said to the *New York Times* in an interview twenty years ago, "It all started in 1618 with the Thirty Years' War, which devastated this country in a way that has never been repeated." Siebeck also believed that Germany was "never at a civilized level long enough for a refinement of eating to be realized."

Before I go much further, I should explain how I, a person of Italian and American parentage, have come to write not one but two books about German cuisine. (My first cookbook, *Classic German Baking*, was published in 2016.) I was born in West Berlin to parents from Philadelphia and Rome, respectively, who had moved to Berlin for an adventurous year. My father ended up staying for a decade; my mother has never left. When my father and I moved to Boston after my parents' marriage ended, I continued to visit Berlin regularly to see my mother and dear family friends. A year before the fall of the Wall, I moved to West Berlin to live with her and attended a bilingual Berlin public school. My life has always felt split between two places.

Fourteen years ago, I moved back to Berlin after a decade of working in publishing in New York and began working as a writer. I married my husband, a Berliner with roots in Saxony, whose family history is intertwined with the postwar division of Germany, and published a food memoir called *My Berlin Kitchen* (2013). In that book, I wrote about the German recipes that had come to mean so much to me, like the Quark soufflé with sour cherries that we ate for lunch on day trips to East Germany, the roast goose and braised red cabbage served each Christmas at my neighbor Christa's, the pickled herring salad thrown together in an unusual heat wave shortly after I moved back to Berlin, the savory stuffed cabbage I adored at my school cafeteria, and the sweet-sour red berry pudding called Rote Grütze that my friends Jürgen and Muck always served for dessert.

A few years later, in my next book, *Classic German Baking*, I wrote about the towering baking tradition of Germany (and Austria), gathering the ultimate recipes for everything from Schwarzwälder Kirschtorte (Black Forest torte) to Swabian soft pretzels, the best German Käsekuchen (cheesecake) to quintessential Brötchen (crisp white breakfast rolls). My goal was to help readers elsewhere understand the fundamental role that home baking plays in the lives of Germans and Austrians and to illuminate the culture through its recipes, from the canon of Christmas baking to the slabs of yeasted cakes available at every corner bakery.

With this book, I want to continue what I started with *Classic German Baking* by collecting the best and most emblematic recipes of everyday German and German-speaking home cooks in one book, but also explaining how German cuisine developed into what it is today. My goal is to capture the national favorites eaten across the land, as well as delicious regional discoveries that deserve a wider audience, and to canonize the recipes that every German will immediately recognize as a part of their culinary heritage. With this book, I also hope to illuminate German food culture, its rituals, rhythms, and traditions.

German food doesn't hold the same romantic allure as Italian or French food; indeed, food means something quite different to Germans than it does to their neighbors to the south and west. It's easy to poke fun at German food, which is riddled with clichés and lives up to quite a few of them. Many Germans have an inferiority complex about their traditional recipes, especially in comparison to their neighbors to the west and south, and are happy to publicly proclaim their preference for the cooking of other countries. And yet, to so many, German food is also the purest kind of comfort food. It is simple and hearty, the kind of cooking one turns to in the depths of winter to warm the very soul, the type of cooking that might not ever win a beauty award, but that will more than make up for it in terms of its power to nourish and comfort. In recent years, it seems like a rehabilitation of German food has been on the horizon, a recognition of all that it has to offer.

German food is also American food; more than forty million Americans are of German descent. From Texas to Minnesota, from Pennsylvania to Washington, many Americans hold a special place in their hearts for traditional German food such as Sauerbraten, potato salad, thick pea stew, and sausages of all kinds. German food is also Jewish food; what are matzo balls if not Knödel, latkes if not Kartoffelpuffer (to use just one of the dozens of names they sport in Germany), gefilte fish if not Fischklößchen?

Germans are particularly nostalgic about the food of their grandmothers, some of which is quite simple, like thin pancakes filled with applesauce or sticky potato dumplings served with brown gravy, some of which is more elaborate and now relegated to the occasional holiday meal, like a roast goose stuffed with prunes or braised beef rolls. In fact, if I had to pick any one word to describe German food, I think nostalgic is the word

I'd choose. Traditional German home cooking is old-fashioned; many of the recipes featured in this book have been made in some form or another for at least a hundred years or, in some cases, many more.

But one spoonful of a savory beef broth with ethereal snips of pancakes and minced chives will be enough to convince many of the staying power of traditional German cuisine, as will the toothsome chew of Swabian Spätzle under a cloak of caramelized onions and melted cheese. A plump cabbage roll in a savory gravy, served with a pillowy potato dumpling to pull apart with the tines of your fork, will satisfy in a way a salad never could. The same goes for the tradition of sweet main courses in Germany and Austria, like fruit dumplings rolled in toasted, buttered bread crumbs, eggy bread puddings layered with fruit, or thick pieces of a souffléd pancake caramelized in a pan and served with stewed plums, to name just a few. I hope that this book helps illuminate all these facets of German cooking and becomes a resource for home cooks, for people interested in central European foodways, and just a great collection of delicious, doable recipes that your family will love for years to come.

A note on the recipes I chose to include in this book: Classic German cooking spans an enormously wide breadth, with hundreds if not thousands of recipes to choose from. Each region in Germany has enough recipes to fill an entire cookbook. I had to be somewhat ruthless about the recipes included here, because I wanted the selection to be both traditional and appealing to twenty-first-century home cooks who don't necessarily live in Germany. I chose recipes that I thought were most likely to be attempted at home and of course included only my very favorite dishes. While I think I've managed to collect all the greatest hits and then some, there will inevitably be those who cry out for a beloved recipe that didn't make the cut. (Hamburger Labskaus, Kalbsleber Berliner Art, and Toast Hawaii, I'm looking at you.) My apologies in advance.

Last, if you are lucky enough to have a good German butcher near where you live or don't mind making mail orders—there are plenty of German butchers in the United States that have a robust online business— then be sure to befriend them and buy all their Aufschnitt (sliced, cured meats) for your fabulous German breakfasts. Buy their Bratwürste and grill them, then serve them with the cabbage salads and potato salads in this book. Buy their Weißwürste and serve them with sweet mustard and soft pretzels for a Bavarian breakfast. In Germany, sausages are always purchased at the store and then prepared at home with various side dishes, recipes for which are all here.

ABENDBROT

You will see many references to Abendbrot in this book, the German dinnertime meal of open-faced sandwiches. It is a tradition that was likely born out of the industrialization of German cities in the first quarter of the twentieth century. With more and more factories and places of work offering warm meals at canteens and cafeterias at lunchtime, there was no reason to cook a second meal in the evening. (However, West German housewives were expected to cook lunch for their children, whose school day traditionally ended at lunchtime, while in East Germany, where women were largely integrated in the work force, children usually ate lunch at school.) The evening meal consisting of buttered bread with some cured meat or smoked fish and a pickle alongside was more widespread in the north of Germany initially, but eventually made its way around the country, and stuck. For many decades and to this day, a majority of Germans eat "cold" at dinnertime.

The components of Abendbrot, which means "evening bread," start with bread—there are slices of dark bread, like rye sourdough studded with sunflower seeds or sprouted rye, or Graubrot or Mischbrot, which is bread made from a combination of wheat and rye sourdough. Then there is plenty of unsalted butter to spread thinly on each slice of bread, a selection of sliced cheese and cured meats, sometimes a chunk of liverwurst, or regional specialties like smoked fish in the north or Wurstsalat (ham salad) in the south, to put on the buttered bread. There is usually a plate of sliced cucumbers or tomatoes or some pickles to round out the meal. Abendbrot is always eaten open-faced, unlike American sandwiches. And typically, Abendbrot is prepared and eaten off individual cutting boards made of wood, porcelain, or plastic, rather than plates.

Unlike their neighbors to the south and west, Germans eat dinner relatively early, around 6:00 p.m. Abendbrot requires nothing much beyond assembly and this, combined with a reverence for good, nutritious, whole-grain bread and the idea that eating a lighter meal in the evening is better for health, has made it an integral evening meal.

THE PANTRY

APPLES

Long gone are the days when Granny Smiths and Red Delicious dominated the apple market. These days, it is easy to find dozens of different heirloom apple varieties at green markets and farms no matter where you live. So rather than call for a specific apple variety in any of the recipes, I urge you to use local apples that taste good to you. In the recipes that include apples in this book, I will tell you whether they should hold their shape in cooking or fall apart in a fluffy cloud, whether they should be crisp and juicy or sweet. Then you can choose the apples you like best.

BLACK PEPPER

Throughout the book, I call for freshly ground black pepper without a specific quantity, by which I mean that you should add as much or as little as you like. In my own home cooking, I rarely use black pepper at all, but I know that for many it is an essential part of every savory dish. (The exception is when I call for whole peppercorns.)

BOUILLON CUBES OR BOUILLON PASTE

When I call for vegetable or meat broth in recipes, you can use homemade broth (page 66), store-bought broth, or bouillon cubes or paste dissolved in water. Better Than Bouillon is my preferred brand of bouillon paste.

BREAD

Bread is the backbone of German cuisine. For open-faced sandwiches (Abendbrot) or breads to serve with spreads or at breakfast, you can look for sourdough breads, as well as sourdough breads made with rye that are as dark as possible and often studded with seeds. There are excellent quality artisan bakers all over the United States now. What will be harder to source is Brötchen, crisp white bakery rolls that Germans eat fresh for breakfast and, when stale, repurpose in a multitude of ways in everything from dumplings to bread pudding. (A recipe for them can be found in my previous book, *Classic German Baking.*) As an alternative, you can use any plain white yeasted roll, like Kaiser rolls. They should not be enriched (like Parker or dinner rolls, for example). Or you can use plain white sandwich bread.

BUTTER AND CLARIFIED BUTTER

The butter you use in these recipes should always be unsalted. If possible, you should use European-style high-fat butter. (American butter is lower in fat and flavor than German butter.) Some of the recipes call for clarified butter for frying, since clarified butter has a higher smoke point than regular butter and gives a delicious flavor to things like schnitzel and potato pancakes. You can find clarified butter at most good grocery stores, usually in the baking aisle or in the "international" foods aisle, or at Indian grocery stores, where it is labeled as ghee. My family eats buttered bread on a daily basis, so we keep our butter at room temperature in a covered butter dish for easy spreading. Throughout the book, when I call for butter at room temperature, I mean that the butter should be soft enough to cream with a wooden spoon.

CHERRIES

Preserved sour cherries are a staple in German cooking. Look for sour cherries that are jarred in sugared water (not syrup) in German or eastern European markets or in the "international" aisle of your grocery store. If you can find only frozen sour cherries, you can use those and increase the sugar in the recipe by a tablespoon or two.

CINNAMON-SUGAR

Cinnamon-sugar does a lot of heavy lifting in German cooking. It is the classic topping for Quarkauflauf, Eierkuchen, Grießschnitten, and Reicher Ritter. To make it, combine 1 part cinnamon to 4 parts sugar and mix well. It keeps well in the pantry. I always mix enough to keep for a while and store it in a small jar with a screw-on lid.

EGGS

The recipes in this book have all been tested with large eggs.

FARINA / SEMOLINA

German and Austrian cooking features a wheat product called Grieß that is used in dumplings and puddings and as a thickener for cakes. Soft wheat Grieß (Weichweizengrieß) is wheat farina, or Cream of Wheat, and is typically used for sweet dishes like puddings and cakes. Hard wheat Grieß (Hartweizengrieß) is ground semolina, made from durum wheat, and is typically used for savory dumplings and noodles. Look for coarsely ground semolina flour (for example, from King Arthur Baking Company).

FRESH AND DRIED HERBS

The most called-for fresh herbs in this book, by far, are flat-leaf parsley and chives. If you can, keep plants of them on your balcony or in your garden; both also do well in kitchens. These are of course easily found in grocery stores year-round. Mugwort, the traditional flavor for German roast goose, and summer savory are two additional herbs that I call for in this book and those will be harder to find. You can use dried summer savory in place of fresh, but mugwort will be tough; it's best to grow your own. Another herb that pops up frequently is marjoram. It's fine to used dried marjoram, which, much like dried oregano, stays fragrant.

FROZEN VEGETABLES

In Germany, frozen vegetables are high quality. In fact, my family prefers frozen green beans because they're more reliably tender and delicious (and never stringy!) than fresh, even local ones. As for spinach, I believe that frozen whole-leaf spinach is just as good as fresh spinach; it is arguably even better because it has already been washed for you. Is there any kitchen task worse than the onerous one of getting fresh spinach clean? The recipes in this book that feature spinach have been tested both with frozen spinach and fresh spinach; you can use whichever one you prefer. If possible, when using frozen, use whole-leaf spinach rather than chopped spinach. Frozen chopped herbs such as parsley and chives are also helpful to have on hand, if you can find good-quality ones, for topping soups or salads.

GELATIN

Several of the desserts in this book are made with gelatin. I call for leaf gelatin, also known as silver gelatin, which comes in small sheets and which I far prefer to powdered or granulated gelatin. Leaf gelatin must first be soaked in cold water, squeezed out, then melted in hot liquid, while powdered gelatin is first dissolved in water, then mixed into the dessert mixture. I find that powdered gelatin has a less ethereal mouthfeel and makes desserts too firm, while leaf gelatin imparts the loveliest wobble. Leaf gelatin can be found online and at specialty baking shops and at some well-stocked grocery stores.

GLUTEN-FREE FLOUR

In any recipe that calls for 3 tablespoons or less of all-purpose flour, you may substitute an equal amount of a gluten-free flour blend.

GROUND PAPRIKA

The Austro-Hungarian influence on German cooking means that ground paprika shows up frequently, either in large quantities in something such as Gulasch or as a sprinkling for color, like in Bratkartoffeln. Your pantry should be stocked with sweet paprika and hot paprika, ideally freshly purchased as it loses its fragrance relatively quickly, and ideally from Hungary. Do not substitute Spanish smoked paprika. Paprika turns bitter if it burns, so take care when adding it to a recipe—make sure the heat is low, that there is sufficient fat in the pan, and that you don't cook it for much longer than 30 to 60 seconds before adding liquid to the pan.

LEMONS

German and Austrian cooking and baking uses a lot of lemon zest. For this purpose, the lemons you use should be organic, if possible, and untreated. I rinse and dry my lemons before zesting them.

MILK

The recipes in this book have been tested only with whole milk. You can substitute reduced-fat milk, if necessary, but I do not recommend using skim milk.

NUTMEG

For freshness and flavor, I recommend buying whole nutmeg, available at any grocery store, and grating it as needed on a Microplane grater, which is why I specify the number of scrapes of nutmeg in the recipes that call for it. Whole nutmeg keeps for years, unlike ground nutmeg, which swiftly loses its flavor.

QUARK

Quark is a lean and sour fresh cheese that is a staple of German cooking. In Austria it is known as Topfen. Quark can be found commercially in the United States, but it is also easy to make at home with buttermilk. If you buy Quark, make sure it is unsweetened and unflavored. In Germany, Quark comes in three different varieties: full-fat (40% fat, sometimes also known as Sahnequark), low-fat (20% fat), and nonfat (Magerquark). Since the fat percentages refer only to the dry mass and Quark has a high water content, even 40% Quark has only about 10% fat. The recipes in this book were tested with both 20% and Magerquark, which can be used interchangeably. Therefore, to avoid confusion, I simply call for Quark throughout. A recipe for Quark can be found on page 30.

PLUMS

The typical plum used in German and Austrian cooking is the oval, dark-blue plum called Zwetschge (it has a variety of different spellings, depending on the region). In English, it is known as the damson plum or the prune plum and is in season in late summer. These plums, rich and tart, are excellent fruits for making compote or jam or can be baked in cakes and tarts, where they hold their shape beautifully. They also freeze well; if you can, pick your own, wash, dry, halve, and pit them, then freeze them to use all winter.

POTATOES

In Germany, potatoes are classified according to their texture once cooked. Festkochend ("firmly cooking") means they will keep their shape after cooking, making them good options for things such as salads, fried potatoes, or as boiled potatoes that you serve as a side. The equivalent elsewhere would be waxy, like Yukon Gold or Red Bliss. Mehligkochend ("floury cooking") are potatoes that are good for mashing or that can be crushed into fritters or batters. In the United States, they're known as starchy potatoes, like Russet. Potatoes in Germany are usually sold in 1 to 2 kilo sacks and a German home cook is rarely without potatoes in the larder. Which means that a home cook is rarely without leftover cooked potatoes, too. This cookbook includes several recipes for using up leftover cooked potatoes.

SALT

I tested all the recipes in this book with fine sea salt. (I use coarse sea salt for seasoning boiling water.) If you use table salt, you can reduce the quantities I call for by approximately half. Many cooks in the United States use Diamond Crystal Kosher Salt, which, according to *Bon Appétit* magazine, roughly converts from 1¼ teaspoons to 1 teaspoon of fine sea salt.

SAUERKRAUT

Sauerkraut is lacto-fermented cabbage and a traditional way to preserve cabbage. Though it is a relatively easy (and entertaining) project for home cooks, most Germans no longer make it themselves. In Germany, fresh Sauerkraut can be purchased by weight from vats at green markets, for example, or some larger grocery stores, or it can be purchased in cans, jars, or vacuum-packed plastic pouches. Although Sauerkraut can be eaten raw, most will cook it before eating, braising it with bacon, wine, or broth. You should be able to find it at well-stocked grocery stores or at German markets.

SOUR CREAM

German sour cream is looser than American sour cream and contains 10% fat, while American sour cream has about 20% fat. For the recipes in this book, that difference won't have much of an effect. However, I do want to explain why the US conversions will seem overly precise. In my conversion measurements, 1 tablespoon is 15 grams, ¼ cup of sour cream is 60 grams, ⅓ cup is 80 grams, ½ cup is 120 grams, ⅔ cup is 170 grams, ¾ cup is 180 grams, and 1 cup is 240 grams. But I developed the recipes using grams, so to keep the conversions as faithful to the original as possible, I had to get pedantic about tablespoons here and there. Mercifully, a touch too much sour cream is hardly a bad thing, and too little sour cream is easily remedied.

SPECK OR SCHINKENSPECK

One of the most frequently used ingredients in this book is Schinkenspeck or Speck, also known as bacon. Cured pork is one of the main flavorings of German cooking and is used in everything from soups and stews to build flavor to crispy toppings on fried potatoes or fish. Speck is made from cured pork belly and is quite fatty. In Germany, it is often sold vacuum-packed in thick slices for home cooks to chop up as needed. Schinkenspeck is made from cured pork leg (*Schinken* is "ham" in German) and is much leaner than Speck. In grocery stores in Germany, you can buy pre-chopped Schinkenspeck, which is very convenient. While you can substitute bacon for Speck, it is harder to find a substitute for Schinkenspeck. Because it keeps well, I think it makes sense to mail-order some from a German butcher or market, if you don't have one near where you live, and keep it in your refrigerator to use as needed.

EQUIPMENT

My home kitchen is stocked with an assortment of good-quality stainless-steel pots and pans of different sizes: small for melting butter or warming up small portions of food; medium for sauces, frozen vegetables, rice, or grains; and large for cooking soup, potatoes, noodles, and dumplings. I also have a couple of larger, heavy Dutch ovens made of enameled cast-iron that I use for braises, stews, and dishes that start on the stove and finish in the oven. I have a well-seasoned 10-inch / 25cm cast-iron frying pan that I use for fritters, eggs, fried potatoes, and pancakes of all kinds, and a cast-iron crêpe pan with very low sides for thin pancakes and Rösti. For casseroles, roasts, and other oven-baked dishes, I have an assortment of roasting pans in various sizes made of porcelain enamel, ceramic, and metal.

Other essentials include a couple of cutting boards and some heavy, sharp knives both large and small; a colander for draining larger items; fine-mesh sieves for soups, jellies, or puddings; a Microplane grater for lemon zest and nutmeg; a spider for removing dumplings or fritters from the pot; a box grater for cheese, potatoes, and onions; a food processor; an immersion blender; electric beaters; a bench scraper; and whisks, wooden spoons, and silicone spatulas of varying sizes. A hand-cranked poppy seed grinder is indispensable for grinding the topping for Germknödel, though a coffee or spice grinder will also do the trick. (A food processor will not.) A scale, dry and liquid measuring cups and spoons, and a selection of prep bowls in different sizes for mixing are also important.

A candy thermometer, a potato masher, and a cookie scoop are nice to have.

BREAKFAST, SNACKS & SPREADS

Germans are famous for their breakfasts. I've lost count of how many people over the years have mentioned their wonder upon experiencing their first real German breakfast, whether as exchange students or business travelers or tourists. To Germans, though, a table set with a basket of freshly baked rolls and sliced dark, seedy bread and a few platters of sliced cheese and meats, some jars of homemade jam and one of honey, not to mention a bowl or two of fresh cheese, perhaps flavored with freshly minced herbs or onions, a boiled egg for every eater, and some sliced cucumbers or cherry tomatoes or a pile of spicy radishes, is simply what breakfast is supposed to be.

This is, to be clear, the description of a weekend breakfast. Weekday breakfasts are usually a pared-down version and largely skew savory. Germans tend to regard French, Italian, or American breakfasts as too flimsy and sugary. Who can stay full until lunchtime on a bowl of corn flakes with milk, a cappuccino and a handful of cookies, or a croissant dipped in a café crème?

In recent years, breakfasts from other cultures have made inroads in Germany. Smoothies, oatmeal (called porridge), and pancakes appear on breakfast menus regularly. But I'd like to propose that German breakfasts start taking hold elsewhere. They are impressive and easy to pull together (the eggs are the only thing that requires cooking).

To prepare a good German breakfast, one starts by making rounds of the market and grocery store. Purchase a good assortment of cheese, which can be relatively local—like Gouda (which is Dutch), Emmentaler (which is Swiss), fragrant Alpine cheese such as Bergkäse (good substitutes would be Gruyère or Comté), and Harzer Käse, an extremely pungent specialty that is passionately adored by a subset of the German population and loathed by others—or imported. Typically, most of the cheeses should be sliced before serving, to facilitate being laid out on buttered bread, but of course some people serve cheese that you cut as you go.

Next, purchase a selection of cured meats such as cooked ham, liverwurst—an absolute must for any breakfast with German children—salami, and cured ham, too. There should be a minimum of two to three different jams on the table, ideally homemade, though purchased is of course permissible, and a pot of honey, for spreading on bread, sweetening tea, or drizzling over a portion of Quark. And don't forget the Nutella.

The bread should be freshly baked and varied—crisp rolls, sliced bread, pretzels, poppy-seed-spangled sweet rolls, they all have their place. Then set the table with a pretty tablecloth, cloth napkins, plenty of unsalted butter at room temperature, bright stems of candy-like tomatoes, cucumber spears or slices, fresh fruit such as grapes or cut-up melon, egg cups, some olives, even fresh juice. Little vases of seasonal fresh flowers plug the gaps. All that's left, at the end, is to boil the eggs and make the coffee (or tea).

And that's really the most wonderful thing about German breakfasts. There's hardly anything to cook. On weekends, when one wants to maximize every minute one has with loved ones at the table, it's elemental.

ZWEI EIER IM GLASS MIT SCHNITTLAUCHBROT

Soft-Boiled Eggs with Chives and Buttered Bread

SERVES 1

2 eggs
Salt and freshly ground
    black pepper
Unsalted butter
2 slices rye sourdough bread
    or dark seeded bread
Minced chives

My favorite German breakfast eggs are two soft-boiled eggs in a glass. Imagine a little juice glass with two peeled eggs in it, slightly wobbly on the outside and molten on the inside. You can salt and pepper the eggs to your liking, or add a knife-tip of butter; some people like to add a dash of Worcestershire sauce or Tabasco, too. Then you cut them up with a little spoon directly in the glass and eat them with triangles of thickly buttered dark German bread that is carpeted with minced chives. (Ideally, the layer of chives is so thick that you can't even really see the butter through them.) The combination of the tang of cultured butter with the delicate oniony flavor of chives on top of the malty, toasty flavors of the bread is so delicious alongside those warm, soft eggs. I love eggs in all forms, but this preparation is particularly German and particularly delightful. If I ever open a café, this will be the first thing on the menu.

1   Bring a small pot of water to a boil. Place the eggs in the boiling water and cook for 5 minutes for a soft-boiled egg or 7 minutes for a set white and jammy yolk. Remove the eggs and plunge them into a bowl of cold water and let them sit for a minute.

2   Carefully peel the eggs and place them in a small juice glass. Sprinkle with salt and pepper.

3   Butter the bread generously from edge to edge, then cover with a thick, even layer of chives. Eat the eggs with a spoon, taking bites of bread as you go.

BAUERNFRÜHSTÜCK

Farmer's Breakfast: Meat and Potato Hash

SERVES 3 TO 4

½ cup / 65g minced Speck
    or bacon, or leftover cold
    meat, diced
3 to 4 Tbsp vegetable oil, or
    as needed
2 small onions, diced
10 medium cold boiled
    potatoes, peeled and sliced
    ¼ inch / ½cm thick
Salt and freshly ground
    black pepper
3 or 4 eggs, one per person
1 to 2 Tbsp milk
1 to 2 Tbsp unsalted butter
½ tsp sweet paprika
½ tsp dried marjoram
Several scrapes of
    whole nutmeg
Handful of flat-leaf parsley,
    minced

Bauernfrühstück, or the farmer's breakfast, may be in the breakfast chapter, but it really can be eaten any time of day and is often served for lunch or dinner in Germany. It is a classic way to use up leftover potatoes and meat. It typically consists of a panful of fragrant fried potatoes with onions and bits of bacon or Speck, or small pieces of a leftover roast that traditionally would have only ever been served on a Sunday (der Sonntagsbraten is "the Sunday roast"), plus a few eggs scrambled to hold it all together. In Austria, a similar dish is called Tiroler Gröstl, but the eggs show up fried on top rather than scrambled underneath. Old Berlin cookbooks refer to this dish charmingly as Hoppelpoppel.

What's important about Bauernfrühstück is to get the ratio of potatoes to eggs right. (As my German husband told me the first time I attempted Bauernfrühstück at home with too many eggs: "You made a frittata!") The final dish should have about twice as many potatoes as eggs, which work mainly as a binder. You can use the Bratkartoffeln recipe (page 211), adjusted to however many boiled potatoes you have on hand, then calculate about an egg per person. But I like to add a bit more seasoning to my Bauernfrühstück than I do to Bratkartoffeln, like a dusting of ground paprika, a shower of dried marjoram, and several scrapes of nutmeg. They take this humble meal to the next level. (Whole caraway seed is also delicious here.)

Ultimately, this is a flexible dish and can be edited to your tastes. Serve with Gurkensalat (page 46), the pickled beet salad on page 48, or a sharply dressed green salad.

1   Place the Speck in a 10-inch / 25cm nonstick or well-seasoned cast-iron skillet over medium-high heat (if the pork is particularly lean, add 1 Tbsp of oil) and cook for about a minute, just until the Speck starts to get fragrant, then add the onions and cook, stirring occasionally, until the pork bits are crisp and the onions are well browned (don't let them burn), about 8 minutes. (If using leftover roast rather than Speck or bacon, start cooking the onions first, and after 3 to 4 minutes, add the meat and cook until it crisps up.) Scrape the mixture into a small bowl and set aside.

2   Wipe out the pan just to make sure there are no errant pieces of onion remaining and add 3 Tbsp of oil. Place back over medium-high heat and add the sliced potatoes, shaking the pan to distribute them evenly. Cook without stirring or touching the pan for about 5 minutes, then shake the pan to move the potatoes around. (You can flip them with a spatula, too.) Season with salt and pepper to taste.

3   Cook for another 10 minutes or so, periodically shaking the pan and flipping the potatoes, until they are golden brown and crisping in spots. While the potatoes are cooking, beat the eggs with the milk until completely smooth.

4   Add the butter, paprika, marjoram, and nutmeg to the potatoes and stir to combine. Toss the potatoes around so that the flavorings disperse, then scrape in the reserved meat and onion and toss well.

5   Pour the eggs into the pan and let them sit for a few minutes, then toss and flip so that the eggs mix with the potatoes and meat. Cook until just set, then remove from the heat.

6   Stir in the parsley, adjust the seasoning, and serve.

QUARK

Fresh Cheese

MAKES 2 TO 2⅔ CUPS /
500 TO 670 GRAMS,
DEPENDING ON HOW
LONG YOU DRAIN IT

8½ cups / 2L buttermilk

There may be no food more German than Quark, which is a fresh cheese with a decidedly sour flavor and was, according to Tacitus, probably eaten by Germanic tribes at least two thousand years ago. It can be eaten plain, flavored with fruit for dessert (page 31), flavored with onions and herbs to be eaten with potatoes (page 33) or potato pancakes, spread on bread for a protein-rich breakfast such as Kräuterquark (page 33), folded into batters for cheesecake, turned into tender dumplings (page 245), or made into delectable fritters (page 34). The importance of Quark to Germans and German food culture cannot be overstated.

It used to be unheard of to find Quark outside of Germany's and Austria's borders. In fact, some Germans that I know love Quark so much that they used to bring it with them when they traveled for fear of going without. But today some American producers make Quark, which you can mail-order or buy in select grocery stores if you live in the United States. And, mercifully, it is quite easy to make your own with buttermilk.

I owe this recipe to blogger Meeta Khurana Wolff's German grandmother-in-law.

1   Preheat the oven to 150°F / 65°C. Pour the buttermilk into a large baking pan and cover tightly with aluminum foil.

2   Place the baking pan in the oven and bake for 8 to 12 hours. When the buttermilk is ready to drain, the solids will have separated from the whey, either in soft clumps or in one uniform mass.

3   Place a fine-mesh sieve over a large pot and line the sieve with cheesecloth. Remove the pan from the oven, discard the foil, and pour the contents of the pan into the sieve. Let sit for at least 2 hours and as long as 5 hours, then pick up the corners of the cheesecloth and twist to squeeze out any residual moisture in the Quark. (You can discard the whey or repurpose it in smoothies or other recipes.)

4   The Quark can be refrigerated in an airtight container for several days or used immediately.

QUARKSPEISE

Creamy Fruit Quark

SERVES 2

1 cup / 250g Quark (page 30)
1½ Tbsp sugar
Heavy cream or milk, optional
½ to ¾ cup / 80 to 125g
    chopped fruit

It may seem silly to include a recipe for something so basic, but Quarkspeise is a beloved snack or simple dessert for so many Germans and feels like an essential piece in the puzzle of German food. Quark is thicker and creamier than yogurt, high in protein and low in fat, and adapts wonderfully to many different flavorings. The basic concept of Quarkspeise is to simply sweeten plain Quark with some sugar and add a few spoonfuls of fruit, like chopped fresh strawberries or chopped canned mandarin oranges. A big bowl of this basic formula regularly showed up at dessert-time at my children's kindergartens and at playdates at friends' houses. But of course, there are many variations. You can add flavorings like vanilla or cinnamon or toasted nuts. Fresh fruit is lovely, but canned fruit is also delicious in Quarkspeise. To turn it into something decadent, whip some cream and fold it into the loosened Quark before adding fruit. You can even layer it with crushed cookies and fruit to make a festive parfait. The recipe below is simply a guideline and can be easily doubled or adjusted to your tastes.

1   Place the Quark in a bowl and add the sugar. Whisk until loosened. If you like, you can add a spoonful or two of heavy cream to make a looser Quarkspeise. (Avoid adding too much or it will become soupy.)

2   Fold in the amount of chopped fruit you would like and serve.

KRÄUTERQUARK

Herbed Quark

SERVES 2 TO 4

1 cup / 250g Quark (page 30)

2 Tbsp heavy cream, milk,
    or whole milk yogurt
    (not Greek yogurt)

Juice of ½ lemon

½ tsp salt

Freshly ground black pepper

½ small red onion,
    finely minced

3 sprigs flat-leaf parsley,
    finely minced

Small handful of chives,
    finely minced

Sliced radishes, optional

Boiled potatoes or sliced
    dark rye or grainy bread
    for serving

Kräuterquark—Quark flavored with herbs and seasoned with salt and pepper—is a standard at the German table. It is often made for breakfast to be spread on dark and seedy bread. But Kräuterquark served with boiled potatoes (Pellkartoffeln, page 209), and traditionally then drizzled with some flaxseed oil, is an archetypal German meal: simple, economical, and nutritious. There are many ways to flavor your Kräuterquark—the basics are usually minced chives and parsley, but you can add any herb you like, really. The chives give it a delicate oniony hit, which you can augment with sliced scallions or minced onion to add a bit of crunch. Allium lovers can use all three!

To loosen the Quark a little as you mix it with the flavorings, I like to thin it with a little heavy cream or a bit of runny whole milk yogurt (Greek yogurt is too thick). I also like to stir in a squeeze of lemon juice to give the whole thing an additional hit of acidity. This recipe is easily doubled (or tripled).

1   Place the Quark in a bowl and whisk in the heavy cream. Whisk in the lemon juice, salt, and pepper.

2   Fold in the onion, parsley, and chives. Stir well. Set aside for 5 minutes to allow the flavors to meld.

3   Taste and adjust the seasoning. If desired, top with sliced radishes. Alternatively, you can julienne the radishes and fold them into the herbed Quark. Serve with boiled potatoes or spread on dark rye or grainy bread.

QUARKBÄLLCHEN

Quark Fritters

**MAKES ABOUT
18 FRITTERS**

¼ cup plus 2 Tbsp / 75g sugar,
    plus 1 cup / 200g for rolling
1 cup plus 3 Tbsp / 300g Quark
    (page 30)
2 eggs
Pinch of salt
½ tsp vanilla extract
Grated zest of ½ lemon,
    optional
Scant 1⅔ cups / 200g
    all-purpose flour
1 tsp baking powder
4 cups / 1L vegetable oil

Quarkbällchen, or Quark fritters, are tender and light fried orbs that are rolled in sugar and eaten as a snack. They're usually found at street markets and occasionally at bakeries. The batter is quite simple, with almost equal amounts of Quark and flour, not too much sugar, and a simple flavoring of vanilla (grated lemon zest is a wonderful addition; it goes well with the sour flavor of Quark). It's helpful to have a candy thermometer so you can measure (and keep steady) the temperature of the oil. And a small ice cream scoop with a spring mechanism will help keep your fritters round. If you don't have an ice cream scoop, portion the batter with soup spoons. If you don't have a candy thermometer, you can use the traditional method of putting the handle of a wooden spoon in the cooking oil to see if it's hot enough—you'll know it's ready for frying if bubbles form around the handle.

1   Place a cooling rack over a sheet pan. Place about 1 cup / 200g of sugar in a wide plate for coating the fritters. Set aside.

2   Place the Quark in a mixing bowl and whisk in the eggs. Then whisk in the ¼ cup plus 2 Tbsp of sugar, the salt, vanilla, and zest, if using. In a separate bowl, whisk together the flour and baking powder.

3   Switching to a wooden spoon, beat in the flour mixture just until well-combined. Don't overmix. Set aside.

4   Pour the oil into a medium pot and set over medium-high heat. Bring the oil to 350°F / 180°C. When the oil is at the right temperature, regulate the heat to keep the temperature steady. Using an ice cream scoop, scoop five fritters into the pot. Let them cook, turning once, for 3 to 4 minutes. They should be golden brown all over. If they are browning too quickly, that is a sign that the oil is too hot.

5   Using a spider or fork, remove the fritters carefully from the oil and place on the cooling rack just for a moment while you portion the next round of fritters and place them in the oil. While the second round of fritters is in the oil, roll the first batch of fritters in the bowl of sugar. Put the sugared fritters back on the cooling rack.

6   Repeat with the remaining batter and sugar.

APFELKÜCHLE

Apple Fritters with Cinnamon-Sugar

MAKES 15 TO 20 FRITTERS

½ cup / 100g sugar

1 tsp cinnamon

¾ cup / 100g all-purpose flour

¼ tsp baking powder

½ tsp salt

6 Tbsp / 80ml whole milk

1 egg

¾ tsp vanilla extract

3 or 4 medium apples

Juice of ½ lemon

2 cups / 500ml vegetable oil

2 Tbsp club soda or beer

Fine sea salt for sprinkling

Apfelküchle, or apple slices dipped in batter and fried, are a specialty of southern Germany. They're commonly served as an afternoon snack, which is why I put them in this chapter, though they can also be served for dessert with Vanillesoße (page 238) or a scoop of vanilla ice cream. To make them, you first prepare a batter that is like a thick pancake batter and leaven it with a touch of baking powder and some sparkling water or beer (the beer gives the fritters a bit more flavor). Peeled and cored apples are sliced into rounds, dipped in the batter, and then fried. Afterward, you can roll them in cinnamon-sugar or simply dust them with confectioners' sugar. They'll look like proto-doughnuts.

You should use apples that hold their shape when cooked and have a good balance of tart and sweet flavors. Two important pieces of advice that I implore you to follow:

1. Top the fritters with a sprinkle of fine sea salt just before serving.

2. Don't eat these straight out of the pan. They will burn the roof of your mouth and the textures will seem discordant. Toss them in cinnamon-sugar and let them sit for a bit before you eat, so that they are still warm but no longer scorching. The supple apple melds with the crunchy coating beautifully and the flavors just sing.

1　In a wide plate, mix the sugar and cinnamon until well-combined. Set aside. Put a paper towel on another plate and set aside.

2　In a mixing bowl, whisk together the flour, baking powder, and salt. Pour the milk into the flour mixture, crack in the egg, and add the vanilla. Whisk together briskly until creamy and well-combined and no lumps remain.

3　Core and peel three of the apples, leaving them whole, then cut each apple crosswise into ¼-inch / 1cm rounds. Place the apple rounds in a bowl and sprinkle with the lemon juice. Toss well. Keep the fourth apple to the side in case you have enough batter left at the end to use it.

4　Pour the oil into a shallow sauté pan (it should come up about an inch in the pan) and set over medium-high heat. Using a candy thermometer, bring the oil to 350°F / 180°C. Alternatively, you can test if the oil is ready when a

CONTINUED

wooden stick such as a chopstick or the handle of a cooking spoon is put in the oil and the oil fizzes and bubbles.

5   Pour the club soda or beer into the batter and whisk well to combine. Immediately place a few apple rings in the batter and turn around a few times to coat well. Pick up one at a time, letting the excess drip off a bit, then place carefully in the oil. Don't crowd the pan—I fry about five slices at a time, slipping them into the pan one after another. Cook until golden brown on one side, regulating the heat so that it stays constant, about 3 minutes, then flip and cook the other side for another 2 to 3 minutes. If you don't have a candy thermometer to measure the temperature, keep an eye out for signs of the temperature getting too high (for example, if the oil starts smoking or the fritters brown too quickly), and turn down the heat a little. When the fritters are golden brown all over, remove with a spider and place on the paper towel–lined plate. Let them drain while you put the next round of apple slices in the batter and then in the oil.

6   As soon as the next round of fritters is in the oil, immediately toss the freshly fried fritters in the cinnamon-sugar, turning them a few times. Put the finished fritters on a serving plate. Repeat with the remaining apples, batter, and cinnamon-sugar. If you have enough batter left over, prepare the fourth apple while your last round of fritters is frying.

7   When all the fritters have been coated with cinnamon-sugar and are on a serving platter, sprinkle a pinch or two of fine sea salt all over the fritters. Give them a few minutes to cool, then serve.

REICHER RITTER

Plum-Stuffed French Toast

MAKES 12 PIECES

4 eggs
½ cup / 125ml whole milk
Vanilla extract, optional
12 slices soft white sandwich
    bread
6 spoonfuls Pflaumenmus
    (page 39)
Clarified butter for frying
Cinnamon-sugar (page 16)
    for serving

In German, stale bread dipped in a mixture of egg and milk and fried in butter is given the charming moniker of Armer Ritter, or "poor knight." The legend is that the fried bread symbolized the shields that foot soldiers (poor knights; no horse!) carried in the fourteenth century. Armer Ritter skews plain and savory and can be made with stale white rolls or sliced white bread. My husband grew up eating Armer Ritter for dinner with sliced tomatoes. Older cookbooks, especially Austrian ones, mention cubes of Armer Ritter as Einlagen in beef broth.

You probably don't need a recipe for Armer Ritter, but what you need to know about is its fancy sibling, Reicher Ritter (or "rich knight"). Reicher Ritter has a thick layer of Pflaumenmus (page 39), or plum butter, in the middle of two slices of bread and, once fried, is served with a generous sprinkling of cinnamon-sugar. The combination of yeasty white bread, plum jam, and cinnamon-sugar on top is reminiscent of one of my favorite German treats, the plum jam–stuffed doughnut served for New Year's Eve and during Carnival. I think of this as a great afternoon snack, but this could also be a delightful breakfast or even a sweet dinner. (Many old Austrian cookbooks include a recipe for a savory Reicher Ritter stuffed with seasoned calves' brains instead of Pflaumenmus; this was apparently a special occasion treat.)

Your best bet here is sandwich bread, squishy and simple. I love to cut these diagonally before frying, so you can better see the inky line of filling, but you can of course keep them whole if you prefer. The cinnamon-sugar is nonnegotiable!

1   In a wide, shallow bowl, whisk the eggs together, then whisk in the milk until completely combined. If you want, add a dash of vanilla.

2   Spread six of the bread slices evenly with a spoonful of Pflaumenmus each. Top with the remaining bread slices and cut each sandwich in half on the diagonal.

3   Melt a generous knob of clarified butter in a nonstick pan or well-seasoned cast-iron pan over medium-high heat. Soak four triangles in the egg mixture, turning once or twice, then transfer the triangles to the hot pan. Fry for a few minutes on each side, until golden brown (turn down the heat if the bread begins to burn). Place on a serving platter and repeat with more clarified butter and more stuffed bread.

4   Serve hot with cinnamon-sugar sprinkled on top.

PFLAUMENMUS

Roasted Plum Butter

MAKES ABOUT 4
(8 OZ / 225G) JARS

4 lb / 1.8kg Italian
    prune plums, pitted and
    quartered
2 cups / 400g sugar
1 cinnamon stick
2 whole cloves

This is a wonderful recipe to start your journey into preserving. You simply mix pitted prune plums, sugar, and a few spices in a Dutch oven, and put it in a hot oven for a few hours, stirring only occasionally. When the cooking is finished, use an immersion blender to puree the mixture, making an inky-dark butter to spoon into dumplings (page 191) or use as a filling for stuffed French toast (page 38). It's also delicious on toast. Traditionally, Pflaumenmus, which is known as powidl (PO-veed-el) in Austria and lekvar in Eastern Europe, was made without sugar, but I add some to give potentially unpredictable fruit a bit of a lift and to give the jam a slightly longer shelf life.

A note on food safety: Sterilize your jars and caps. Pour the jam in when it is boiling hot. Screw the caps on tightly and turn the jars upside down. Let them cool completely and the jars will be vacuumed shut. This is the method used by countless European preservers over centuries and it is 100 percent safe. There is no need for a water bath. Because of the relatively low amount of sugar in the plum butter, once opened, it should be refrigerated and eaten within 1 month.

1   Place the plums in a large, heavy-bottomed, oven-safe pot. Add the sugar, cinnamon, and cloves. Stir well, cover, and let sit at room temperature for at least 8 hours or overnight.

2   Heat the oven to 350°F / 180°C. Put the pot, uncovered, into the oven and cook for about 2 hours, stirring occasionally.

3   Meanwhile, wash the jars and lids in very hot water with soap or wash them in the dishwasher. Set them aside.

4   When the plums have broken down and the liquid has reduced to a thick jam, remove the pot from the oven and fish out the cinnamon stick. (If you can find the cloves, fish them out, too.) Puree the jam with an immersion blender until smooth, then fill the sterilized jars with the hot puree and screw on the lids. (If you prefer a chunky jam, skip the pureeing and ladle the hot jam into the jars. This is called Pflaumenmarmelade; Pflaumenmus means the fruit has been pureed.) Immediately turn the jars upside down.

5   Let the jars cool completely before turning them right side up again and labeling them. Unopened, the jam will keep for at least 1 year.

OBATZDA

Bavarian Cheese Spread

MAKES ABOUT 1 CUP / 300G

1 wheel (250g) Brie or
    Camembert, chilled
1½ Tbsp / 20g unsalted butter
3½ Tbsp / 50ml heavy cream
1½ tsp sweet paprika
1 tsp whole caraway seeds
Salt and freshly ground
    black pepper
½ shallot, finely minced
Small handful of chives,
    minced

Obatzda, or Obatzter, is Bavarian dialect and roughly means "something mixed." Obatzda is a creamy, rust-colored spread made of mashed-up Brie or Camembert and given pungency from onions and caraway, typically served alongside astoundingly delicious fresh pretzels or dark rye bread, always with a freshly tapped mug of beer. Obatzda was originally developed to use up odd ends of cheese and has, over the years, become an essential part of the Bavarian Biergarten experience. There are about as many variations of the recipe as there are Bavarians, so you can fiddle with the flavorings as you like. Officially, one is only supposed to use Bavarian Weißbier as the liquid to loosen the mashed Camembert. Personally, I've had better luck with heavy cream. I like serving Obatzda with fresh soft pretzels or crusty bread and a big pile of crisp red radishes at the start of a meal, but it is also a very nice addition to the a weekend breakfast spread or if you're having Abendbrot for dinner. Ideally, serve Obatzda the day it is made, but any leftovers can be refrigerated for up to 3 days (note that it will deteriorate visually, however, and should be kept for family consumption only after the first day). The recipe is easily doubled.

1   Cut the rind off the cheese and discard, then place the cheese in a mixing bowl. With a fork, mash it until creamy, working in the butter and cream as you go. (The cheese will be somewhat lumpy, but try to get it as smooth as possible.)

2   Mash in the paprika, caraway, a pinch of salt and pepper, and the shallot. Adjust the seasoning to your taste.

3   Scrape into a serving bowl and sprinkle the entire top of the Obatzda with chives. Cover and refrigerate for an hour before serving.

LIPTAUER

Austrian Cheese Spread

MAKES ABOUT
1¼ CUPS / 350G

7 Tbsp / 100g unsalted butter,
    at room temperature
1 cup / 250g Quark (page 30)
½ tsp sweet paprika
½ tsp ground caraway
1 tsp mustard
½ tsp salt
Freshly ground black pepper
1 medium red onion, minced
2 large pickles, minced
½ bunch of chives, minced
Fresh pretzels or rye
    sourdough or dark seeded
    bread for serving

This powerfully seasoned Quark dip, a kissing cousin of Obatzda (page 40), hails from Austria. The Quark gives it an appealing sour flavor that is tempered by the sweet butter and array of flavorings. My Austrian friend Kathrin Kuna has lovely childhood memories of public swimming pools in Lower Austria, where children could order a portion of Liptauer with a glass of skinny pretzel sticks for dipping from the pool kiosk. Whether you serve this as a snack or as part of an Abendbrot spread, you can adjust it to your taste, fiddling with the quantities of flavorings until you get it just the way you like it.

1   Mash the butter in a bowl until soft, then mix in the Quark until the mixture is smooth. Stir in the paprika, caraway, mustard, salt, and pepper until well-combined.

2   Fold in the onion, pickles, and chives. Taste for seasoning. Serve with pretzels or bread.

ERDÄPFELKAS

Potato Cheese

MAKES ABOUT
2 CUPS / 700G

3 medium (about 300g total) starchy potatoes, like Russet

1 cup / 250g Quark (page 30)

½ cup plus 2 Tbsp / 150g sour cream

½ tsp caraway seeds

½ bunch of flat-leaf parsley, minced

2 small red onions, minced

½ tsp salt

Freshly ground black pepper

½ bunch of chives, minced

Sliced dark bread for serving

The last in a trio of spreads along with Obatzda and Liptauer, Erdäpfelkas (which is its Austrian name; it's also known more colloquially as Kartoffelkäse or Arme-Leute-Käse in Germany, poor people's cheese) is a savory mixture of mashed potatoes, Quark, and sour cream, flecked with herbs and onions, that is spread on bread for supper. While cheese might have been something out of reach for the very poor when this recipe came into being, Quark and potatoes were affordable and nutritious foodstuffs available to everyone.

The tradition of eating this is widespread in northern Austria and Bavaria. Opinions on flavorings differ; some think caraway is nonnegotiable while others don't care for it. You can fiddle with the seasonings as you like. And if you prefer to use scallions instead of onions, go right ahead. Erdäpfelkas is a lovely addition to the Abendbrot table or makes a very simple meal on a slice of deliciously dark bread. It will keep for up to three days in the refrigerator.

1   Place the potatoes in a small pot. Add enough water to cover by an inch and set over high heat. Bring to a boil, cover, lower the heat, and simmer until the potatoes are cooked through, 15 to 20 minutes. Drain the potatoes and as soon as you can handle them, peel them. Mash them until creamy with a potato masher or fork and set aside to cool.

2   Stir the Quark and sour cream into the potatoes until smooth. (There will be little flecks of potato throughout.) Stir in the caraway, parsley, and onions. Season with salt and pepper, adding more salt if you like.

3   Just before serving, top with the chives. Serve with sliced dark bread.

SALADS

It's easy to caricature German food as being stodgy and heavy, with an intense focus on meat. And there is truth to the caricature, since the deprivation of the postwar years gave way to a focus on meat as an indicator of prosperity in the latter half of the twentieth century. Salad usually just shows up as a little burst of color in a corner of a plate filled with meat and potatoes. But Germans haven't always eaten this way—in fact, for many centuries, one of the main sources of nutrition was gruel cooked with water or milk and maybe flavored with a bit of cured pork. Meat was expensive and, for the average German, largely out of reach except on holidays or special occasions. Potatoes didn't start being planted for food in Germany until the seventeenth century; it took until the nineteenth century for them to become widespread.

The earliest record of salad in Germany was during the reign of Charlemagne, who is known as Karl the Great in Germany, though it is unclear if lettuce was being grown for gustatorial or medicinal purposes at that point. In the Middle Ages, Hildegard von Bingen, the famed German mystic and medical practitioner, wrote that salad dressed only with the right mixture of herbs and vinegar could be advisable for human consumption. In the sixteenth century, salads began showing up with regularity in cookbooks, and by the nineteenth century, many different types of salad greens were being cultivated throughout Germany. In the Brothers Grimm fairy tale "Rapunzel," a pregnant woman cannot contain her craving for rapunzel, a salad green largely assumed to be lamb's lettuce. She begs her husband to steal some for her from the garden of a neighboring witch who, as punishment for the theft, takes the infant once she's born, names her Rapunzel, imprisons her in a tower, and . . . well, you probably know the rest.

In Germany, most people eat a hot meal at lunchtime and a cold meal at night. That cold meal, called Abendbrot, or evening bread, consists of open-faced sandwiches made on good German bread, with various sliced cheeses and cured meats to top it. It is a concept that takes some getting used to by people who move to Germany from elsewhere, and who may be used to eating warm meals in the evening. But when you think about it, it makes a lot of sense nutritionally and is a boon for working parents who don't want to come home from work and go straight into cooking dinner. Eating a warm cooked meal at lunch gives you plenty of time to digest it. Having dinner be more assembled than cooked is infinitely more relaxing than racing through the evening dinner prep.

To accompany the open-faced sandwiches, many families just offer a plate of cut-up vegetables such as peppers, cucumbers, tomatoes, and maybe some pickles. But most of the salads in this chapter are perfect accompaniments to Abendbrot. You can think of them as a step up from crudités—but just barely. These salads are the most archetypal in Germany these days. There are cucumbers and beets, potatoes and cabbage, and of course, a soft green salad made with herbs that will always make me think of Hildegard von Bingen.

GURKENSALAT

Cucumber Salad

SERVES 6

2 English cucumbers, peeled

1 Tbsp sugar

2 tsp salt

¼ cup / 60ml white
    wine vinegar

2 Tbsp vegetable oil

2 Tbsp minced chives or dill

This simple salad of thinly sliced cucumbers bathed in a sweet-sour dressing is a stalwart on tables across the land. It shows up as a side to hearty cuts of meat in restaurants, graces kitchen tables at dinnertime, and is a constant in Germany's lunch canteens. Gurkensalat can be made in winter as in summer, thanks to the ubiquity of hothouse cucumbers. Cucumbers are extremely popular in Germany; it's rare to find a household without at least one cucumber slumbering in the crisper drawer, ready to be cut up for the daily Abendbrot. The addition of sugar in the dressing might seem unusual, but German salads usually skew slightly sweet. Despite this, Gurkensalat is quite refreshing. I am partial to the delicate, oniony flavor of chives in my Gurkensalat, but some regions of Germany are more likely to include dill.

1   Thinly slice the cucumbers, either by hand or with a mandoline. The slices should be less than ⅛ inch / 3mm thick. Place in a large bowl.

2   In a separate bowl, whisk together the sugar, salt, vinegar, and oil. Add the herbs and stir.

3   Toss the dressing with the sliced cucumbers and serve.

CREMIGER GURKENSALAT

Creamy Cucumber Salad

SERVES 6 TO 8

2 English cucumbers, peeled

1 to 1½ tsp salt

½ cup plus 2 Tbsp / 150g sour
    cream

2 Tbsp white wine vinegar

2 Tbsp vegetable oil

Minced chives or dill

Freshly ground black pepper

This variation on classic Gurkensalat (page 46) includes sour cream in the dressing. Some versions use yogurt or cream instead, so feel free to play around until you find a mixture that you like best. I find the fat content and sour flavor of sour cream the nicest pairing. Creamy cucumber salad is particularly good when served with hearty Buletten (page 119), pan-fried fish, or a plate of crusty Bratkartoffeln (page 211). In Germany, both creamy and regular cucumber salads are considered great party food since they tend to hold up well sitting on a buffet table for a few hours.

1   Thinly slice the cucumbers, either by hand or with a mandoline. The slices should be less than ⅛ inch / 3mm thick. Place in a large bowl and toss with 1 tsp salt. Set aside for 15 to 30 minutes. Drain.

2   Meanwhile, in a separate bowl, whisk together the sour cream, vinegar, oil, chives, and pepper to taste.

3   Pour the dressing over the cucumbers and mix well. Taste for seasoning, adding more salt if necessary, and serve.

ROTE BEETE SALAT

Red Beet Salad

SERVES 4

1 lb / 500g red beets, raw or
  cooked
1 tsp caraway seeds
Pinch of sugar
Salt and freshly ground
  black pepper
3 Tbsp vegetable oil
3 Tbsp white wine vinegar or
  apple cider vinegar
Handful of chives, minced,
  optional

Much like the Gurkensalat (page 46), this simple, sweet-sour salad can accompany any number of savory dishes. One of my favorite market stands on Winterfeldtplatz in Berlin serves Swabian Maultaschen (page 155) with a dollop of warm potato salad (page 62) and a spoonful of this red beet salad alongside. It is also considered de rigueur to serve this salad with Königsberger Klopse (page 120). In my opinion, any rich, savory meal—like smoked fish, fried potatoes, or Tafelspitz (page 147)—benefits from a side dish of this pungently flavored salad.

If you have the good fortune of coming across fresh horseradish root, grate a few strands on top. It will take it to the next level. (Minced chives add a delicate oniony flavor, but they are optional.) Red beet salad is particularly easy to make if you have access to precooked beets, but even if you don't, you shouldn't let that stop you from making it. Like almost all the recipes in this chapter, beet salad improves with a bit of rest time. While red beets are traditional, you can substitute golden beets.

1   If the beets are raw, first cook them by placing them (unpeeled) in a large pot and covering them with cold water by an inch. Place the pot over high heat and bring to a boil, then lower to a simmer and cook, covered, until tender, 30 minutes to 1 hour. The time will vary depending on the size and age of the beets. Drain the beets, plunge them into an ice bath until cool, then peel off the skin.

2   Slice the beets, either by hand or with a mandoline, as thinly as possible. Place them in a serving bowl and add the caraway, sugar, salt, and pepper and then the oil, vinegar, and chives, if using. Mix well and set aside to marinate for at least 15 minutes and up to 1 hour. Serve.

KOPFSALAT MIT JOGHURT-DRESSING

Butter Lettuce Salad with Yogurt Dressing

SERVES 4 TO 6

1 large head of butter lettuce,
    Boston lettuce, or oak
    leaf lettuce
Scant ½ cup / 100ml low-fat
    or whole milk yogurt
2 Tbsp heavy cream
½ tsp sugar
2 pinches of flaky salt,
    or more as needed
Freshly ground black pepper
Small handful of chives,
    finely minced

I am half Italian, so I'm used to my green salads being full-flavored and punchy. Italian salad greens can be bitter and our dressing is zingy with vinegar or lemon juice. Traditional German green salad is, by contrast, a gentle hug. Sweet, tender butter lettuce is sauced with a creamy dressing made of yogurt, a bit of cream, salt and pepper, and chives. There's nary a drop of vinegar or lemon juice in sight. Nevertheless, it is delicious. The chives and salt give the salad the most appetizing yet delicate hit of flavor. It's wonderfully cooling in summertime. Unlike most of the other recipes in this chapter, this salad should be dressed immediately before serving; otherwise the lettuce will wilt.

Opinions vary greatly on the herbs in the dressing; I happen to think chives are best. Many German cooks insist on using a mix of dried herbs specifically blended for salad dressings. Some prefer dill. Low-fat yogurt has a nice sour flavor and thinner consistency than whole milk yogurt, so I prefer it here. But you may find you prefer the richness of whole milk yogurt. The dressing is flexible to your tastes.

1   Wash and dry the lettuce carefully and remove any brown spots. Tear into bite-size pieces. Set aside.

2   Place the yogurt in a salad bowl. Whisk in the cream, sugar, salt, pepper, and chives.

3   Just before serving, add the lettuce to the bowl and toss gently to coat. Taste a piece of lettuce and adjust the seasoning as desired. Serve immediately.

KRAUTSALAT

Shredded Cabbage Salad

SERVES 6 TO 8 AS A SIDE

1 small head of green cabbage
(about 2 lb / 1kg)
1 large yellow onion, finely
minced
1 tsp whole caraway seeds,
optional
⅔ cup / 130g sugar
1½ cups / 350ml apple cider
vinegar
½ cup / 130g vegetable oil
1 Tbsp salt
Freshly ground black pepper
4 cups / 1L club soda
⅔ cup / 3.5 oz / 100g minced
Speck or bacon, optional
Small handful of chives,
minced, optional

Krautsalat, tangy and refreshing, is a standard side salad in Germany. It's cheap, feeds a crowd, improves with time, and can be made year-round. Plus, it's a great foil to rich meat dishes. It took me a while to crack the recipe; eventually I got a hot tip from my friend Christie Dietz, a travel writer in Rheinhessen, who passed on a recipe similar to a popular one on Chefkoch.de, a German recipe site.

The key to the right texture is to marinate the cabbage in a mix of club soda and punchy dressing for at least 24 hours. The cabbage should be shredded super finely, either by hand or with a mandoline. The onion is nonnegotiable, but other flavors, like caraway (often paired with cabbage for its digestive properties) or bacon (typical in Bavaria) are up to you. The chives at the end add an aesthetic flourish. Krautsalat will keep, refrigerated, for a few days.

1 Cut the cabbage in half and cut out the core and discard. Discard any outer leaves. Shred very finely. Place the shredded cabbage in a very large bowl. Add the onion and, if using, the caraway seeds.

2 In a separate bowl, whisk together the sugar and vinegar until the sugar has dissolved. Whisk in the oil, salt, and pepper.

3 Pour this mixture over the cabbage. Then pour in all the club soda. Mix the cabbage well. Cover the cabbage with a lid that is smaller than the circumference of the bowl and weight it down so that the cabbage is entirely submerged in liquid.

4 Let the cabbage sit for 24 hours (this can be at room temperature).

5 Remove the lid and drain all the liquid from the bowl. Place the salad in a serving bowl.

6 If adding Speck, fry it up in a small pan for a few minutes until crisp. Drain the fat and mix the Speck into the drained salad.

7 Top with the chives, if desired, and serve.

KOHLRABISALAT MIT APFEL

Kohlrabi-Apple Salad

SERVES 4

2 small to medium kohlrabi

2 small crisp, sweet apples

Juice of ½ lemon

¼ cup / 60g sour cream,
    or more as needed

2 Tbsp apple cider vinegar

1 Tbsp whole-grain mustard

1 Tbsp vegetable oil

½ tsp sugar

Salt and freshly ground
    black pepper

Small handful of chives,
    minced

Small handful of flat-leaf
    parsley, minced

Although it's unclear where kohlrabi first originated, it is so closely associated with Germany that its German name, kohlrabi (cabbage turnip), is what it's known by in most other languages. I remember feeling thrilled when my CSA in New York City in the early 2000s started including kohlrabi in our weekly deliveries; its smooth, jade-colored peel and almost glassy flesh reminded me so much of home. But it was such a novelty that none of my other CSA members had ever heard of it or knew what to do with it!

My family mostly just eats kohlrabi raw—chilled, peeled, cut in half, then into half-moons—before dinner or while watching television. It's refreshing and appetizing . . . not to mention remarkable how swiftly one little bulb can disappear when prepared this way. (For cooked kohlrabi, see page 200.) But sometimes you need to dress up the humble kohlrabi a little, like in this shredded salad that combines the cabbage-y crunch of kohlrabi with sweet, crisp apples and a creamy, mustardy dressing. As in all German salads, there's a touch of sweetness to balance the savory flavors, and the combination of both parsley and chives is the essential finishing touch.

If your kohlrabi is sold with the leafy greens still attached, and if they are fresh and in good shape, you can shred them and add them to this salad (or save them to add to soup) for a bit of added nutrition.

1   Using a paring knife, peel the kohlrabi and cut away any woody bits. Cut in half crosswise, then cut each half into half-moons, and then cut those half-moons into small sticks.

2   Wash the apples but leave the skin on (you can peel them if you prefer). Core and cut into similarly sized pieces as the kohlrabi.

3   Combine the kohlrabi and apple in a serving bowl and pour in the lemon juice. Toss to combine.

4   In a separate bowl, whisk together the sour cream, vinegar, mustard, oil, sugar, salt, pepper, and herbs. Pour over the kohlrabi and apple mixture and toss. If you'd like a little more dressing, add another tablespoonful of sour cream. Let sit for 15 minutes to allow the flavors to meld and toss again before serving.

SPARGELSALAT

White Asparagus Salad

SERVES 4 AS AN
APPETIZER OR SIDE

1½ lb / 800g (about 10 fat
    stalks) white asparagus
¼ cup / 15g finely minced
    flat-leaf parsley
¼ cup / 12g finely minced
    chives
2 sprigs tarragon,
    finely minced
3 Tbsp best-quality olive oil
2 Tbsp white wine vinegar
¼ tsp salt

White asparagus season in Germany is world-famous. White asparagus, a protected food, has a fixed window of harvest—mid-April (the starting date depends on how spring progresses) to June 24, which is the final date each year, a matter of tradition. (Green asparagus is grown and harvested far longer, well into the summer.) During the season, market stands across the country groan under the weight of boxes of the prized spears, and restaurants feature white asparagus on special menus. It's most classically paired with Hollandaise (page 114), boiled potatoes, and thin slices of ham that is either cooked or cured, depending on the region, the salty ham a wonderful foil to the sweet, juicy asparagus. But depending on the region, local dishes—such as Kratzete (page 114), a simple pancake torn into bits and pan-crisped in Baden, or pan-fried plaice in northern Germany—are also traditional accompaniments to the asparagus.

This asparagus salad, which I included in my first book, *My Berlin Kitchen,* is best when made with very fresh white asparagus, which is thicker and larger than green asparagus and sweeter, less herbaceous, and more delicate. (When it's no longer fresh, white asparagus can taste bitter.) You can, however, make a pretty good salad with jarred white asparagus, usually found in Spanish specialty shops. (Do not substitute canned asparagus.) The salad tastes delicious right away but improves with a bit of rest. Time gives the plump asparagus a chance to soak up the herbal dressing, rendering it even more succulent. Peeling the asparagus gives the finished pieces a lovely, juicy texture. You can make this salad with green asparagus, too. It won't have the same silky texture, but it will still be delicious.

1   Break off the woody ends of the asparagus and peel the entire length of the stalks. Bring a large pot of salted water to a boil. Lower the asparagus into the water and turn down the heat so that the asparagus cook at a simmer for 13 to 15 minutes.

2   While the asparagus cook, whisk together the herbs, olive oil, vinegar, and salt. Set aside. When the asparagus are tender, drain them. As soon as they are cool enough to handle, cut them into 1-inch / 2.5cm pieces. Add the still-warm asparagus to the vinaigrette and stir gently to coat the asparagus. Let sit for at least 2 hours before serving.

BOHNENSALAT

Green Bean Salad

SERVES 4 AS A SIDE

1 lb / 500g green beans, fresh
    or frozen (look for "cut
    green beans")
Salt
1 small red onion or shallot,
    finely minced
3 Tbsp white wine vinegar
½ tsp sugar
Freshly ground black pepper
2 sprigs fresh summer savory,
    minced, or ½ tsp dried
3 Tbsp extra-virgin olive oil

My favorite home cook in Germany is American: Joan moved to Germany from the United States as a young woman in the 1950s. I was fortunate enough to grow up in Joan's and her husband Dietrich's orbit, and it was at their table that my love of cooking and baking was born. Through Joan, I have developed a deep affection for so many German classics, like Quarkauflauf with cherries (page 180), hearty Wirsingeintopf (page 86), or this simple green bean salad. In Germany, green beans are traditionally cooked and served with Bohnenkraut (literally translated as "bean weed," and known in English as summer savory). And Joan's bean salad, which makes an appearance each year at her legendary birthday picnics, is always mixed with fresh summer savory. Its taste, vaguely reminiscent of oregano, reminds me so deeply of her.

Individual portions of Bohnensalat are ever-present at lunch canteens, right next to the Krautsalat and sliced beets. I love the bright flavor and zingy dressing of this salad. And best of all, it is equally delicious with fresh or frozen beans, making it a godsend for busy cooks who need good salad recipes all year long (or who don't have time to top and tail fresh beans).

1   If using fresh beans: Top and tail them, then cut them into 1-inch / 2.5cm pieces. Bring a large pot of water to a boil, salt it, and cook the beans for 4 minutes. Drain them and plunge them into an ice bath for a few minutes. Drain and set aside.

2   If using frozen beans: Place them in a medium pot and add ¼ cup / 60ml water. Place over high heat, covered, and bring to a boil. Cook for 3 minutes, then drain and plunge them into an ice bath for a few minutes. Drain and set aside.

3   Place the onion in a serving bowl with ½ tsp of salt, the vinegar, sugar, pepper, and summer savory. Let sit for at least 5 minutes.

4   Whisk in the oil and add the beans. Toss well and adjust the seasoning to taste. Let marinate for at least 30 minutes before serving. The salad can be made up to 2 days ahead and refrigerated.

HERINGSSALAT MIT ROTE BEETE

Pickled Herring Salad with Potatoes and Beets

SERVES 2 AS A LIGHT
MEAL

¾ cup / 165g drained pickled
　herring pieces
1 large dill pickle, diced
2 medium waxy potatoes,
　boiled, peeled, and diced
1 small crisp, sweet apple,
　peeled, cored, and diced
½ cup loosely packed flat-leaf
　parsley, minced
1 tsp yellow or Dijon mustard
Salt and freshly ground
　black pepper
1 Tbsp white wine vinegar or
　apple cider vinegar
3 Tbsp extra-virgin olive oil or
　vegetable oil
3 small cooked red beets,
　peeled and diced

Herring features largely in northern German cuisine. Northern Germans are proud of their mighty little herring, whether pickled, matjes (salt-brined), fried (Brathering), or even suspended in aspic. A classic northern German salad combines matjes herring with apples, pickles, and red beets all chopped to the same size, then dressed with cream and served with Pellkartoffeln (page 209). I'm more partial to pickled herring, which is called Bismarckhering in Germany (theories for the association with the former chancellor abound, but none are definitive). My affection for it can be traced to my grandparents' lunch table in their Elkins Park, Pennsylvania, kitchen. Like many Ashkenazi Jews, my father's family loved pickled herring, a staple in Jewish delis.

In this recipe, I keep all the important parts of the matjes herring salad—the pickle, the apple, and the beets—but replace the boiled potato accompaniment with cubed potatoes in the salad and swap out the matjes for chunks of pickled herring. Instead of a creamy dressing, I use vinegar and oil, which feels like a better match, especially in the hot summer months when a cold, sweet-savory salad such as this one is just the thing for a sprightly meal. I like to eat this salad as soon as it's dressed, but you can make it in advance, and some even prefer its flavor after it's had a few hours to marinate. It keeps, refrigerated, for a few days.

1 　Cut the herring into bite-size pieces and place in a serving bowl. Add the pickle, potatoes, apple, and parsley.

2 　In a separate bowl, whisk together the mustard, salt, pepper, vinegar, and oil. Drizzle this over the herring and mix well to combine.

3 　Just before serving, add the beets to the bowl and fold in gently. Serve immediately.

NORDDEUTSCHER KARTOFFELSALAT

Creamy Potato Salad

SERVES 6 TO 8

2.2 lb / 1kg waxy potatoes,
  like Yukon Gold
1 Tbsp coarse salt
1 large shallot or red onion,
  finely minced
5 small pickles or
  8 cornichons, diced
2 tsp yellow or Dijon mustard
1 tsp salt
Freshly ground black pepper
½ cup / 115g mayonnaise
½ cup / 120g whole
  milk yogurt
1 Tbsp apple cider vinegar or
  white wine vinegar
1 Tbsp vegetable or olive oil
4 eggs, optional

German potato salads basically break down along geographical lines. Creamy potato salads are beloved in the north; vinegar-and-broth-dressed potato salads are classic in the south. Northern German potato salad will perhaps feel most familiar to American cooks, with its mayonnaise dressing, chopped pickles, and boiled eggs. But affections are usually quite split on potato salads, and as a mayonnaise skeptic, I used to avoid this kind of potato salad in favor of the other one (page 62). But my older son's favorite potato salad is a mayonnaise-based one, lightened with yogurt, that we buy from a local butcher shop on days when cooking is out of the question, and my younger son would eat mayonnaise with a spoon if he could. And so, in middle age, I have come around. If I had to choose between the two, I'd always be in the vinegary potato salad camp, but I'll admit that a dollop of this one—cool, crunchy, and creamy—next to a sausage or a Bulette (page 119) is very nice.

1   Scrub the potatoes, if necessary, and place in a large pot. Fill with cold water to cover by an inch. Add the coarse salt. Bring to a boil over high heat, then lower the heat, cover, and simmer for about 20 minutes, until tender. Drain and let cool just until easy to handle.

2   While the potatoes are cooking, place the shallot in a large serving bowl. Add the pickles. Add the mustard, salt, pepper, mayonnaise, yogurt, vinegar, and oil and stir until creamy and well-combined. Set aside to marinate.

3   If using, cook the eggs by bringing water to a boil in a small pot, then lowering in the eggs and cooking them for 7 minutes. Drain and set them aside to cool.

4   Peel the potatoes and cut them in half lengthwise, then into ½-inch / 1.3cm slices, dropping them in the dressing as you go. When all the potatoes have been peeled and sliced, mix the salad well to coat all the potatoes with dressing. The salad should rest for at least 30 minutes before serving, if possible. (If you are making the salad more than 30 minutes before serving, refrigerate it and bring it to room temperature before serving.)

5   If you're including the eggs, peel them, cut them into quarters, and arrange them on top of the potato salad just before serving.

SCHWÄBISCHER KARTOFFELSALAT

Swabian Potato Salad

SERVES 8 TO 10 AS A
SIDE, CAN BE EASILY
HALVED

4.4 lb / 2kg waxy potatoes,
   like Yukon Gold

1 Tbsp coarse salt

¼ cup / 60ml vegetable oil

2 medium yellow onions,
   minced

2 cups / 500ml beef broth

6 Tbsp / 90ml white wine
   vinegar or apple cider
   vinegar

1 Tbsp Dijon mustard

1 Tbsp salt

Freshly ground black pepper

Minced chives or flat-leaf
   parsley for garnish

In the recipe for Norddeutscher Kartoffelsalat (page 61), I said that southern German potato salad is made with vinegar and broth. But now that we're here, I would like to clarify between two southern German potato salads, namely the Swabian and the Bavarian. They're both made with thinly sliced waxy potatoes with a boiled dressing, but the Swabian version includes mustard, while the Bavarian eschews it (if you leave mustard out of the recipe below, hey presto, you've got yourself Bavarian potato salad). To add further texture and flavor, you can add a few thinly sliced pickles to the Swabian version, or fold a very thinly sliced cucumber into the Bavarian version.

Just to add one final option: For a classically Austrian variation, make the Bavarian version, and then, just before serving, fold in some washed and dried lamb's lettuce and top it with a drizzle of pumpkin seed oil. Scrumptious. These vinegary potato salads go exceptionally well with Wiener Schnitzel (page 142), simple boiled sausages, or Maultaschen (page 155), and they hold up fantastically well at party buffets and picnics (except the lamb's lettuce one).

1   Scrub the potatoes, if necessary, and place in a large pot. Fill with cold water to cover by an inch. Add 1 Tbsp of coarse salt. Bring to a boil over high heat, then lower the heat, cover, and simmer for about 25 minutes, until tender. Drain and let cool just until easy to handle or overnight.

2   When ready to make the potato salad, peel the potatoes and slice them ⅛ inch / 3mm thick. Place in a large bowl. The slices may fall apart, which is fine.

3   Place the oil in a sauté pan and add the onions. Cook the onions over medium heat until glassy and fragrant, stirring frequently, 8 to 10 minutes. Do not let them brown. Add the broth and bring to a boil. Whisk in the vinegar, mustard, salt, and pepper. Remove from the heat and immediately pour the hot dressing over the potatoes. Stir very well to combine. The potatoes will fall apart, but should not become entirely mashed. Let sit for an hour.

4   Stir again and adjust for seasoning before serving. Garnish with herbs.

SOUPS & STEWS

Soups and stews hold such an important place in German cooking that every grocery store in the country sells a bundle of fresh vegetables called Suppengrün, or "soup greens," consisting of a few carrots, a halved leek, a thick slice of celery root, and fresh parsley (and occasionally parsley root). Meanwhile, almost all meat sections carry meaty bones and stew meat, which are labeled as Suppenknochen and Suppenfleisch. While there are exceptions, a soup is usually served as a first course in small portions, while a stew is a one-pot meal. As with all aspects of German cuisine, there is always a hunger angle: Soup, a cheap source of calories and easily stretched to feed more eaters at the table, has long been an integral part of the German diet, not least since soup kitchens to feed the starving masses were instituted in the late eighteenth century throughout Germany. My friend Maja Welker, who assisted me on my previous cookbook, *Classic German Baking,* told me about an embroidered dish towel that hung over her grandmother's stove with the expression "5 sind geladen, 10 sind gekommen, gieß Wasser zur Suppe, heiß alle willkommen!" or "5 were invited, but 10 came, pour water into the soup, everyone's welcome!"

The word for stew in German is Eintopf, which literally translates to "one pot." Eintöpfe can be made from a variety of different ingredients, usually built on a base of sautéed Suppengrün, bulked out with legumes or starches, enriched with a bit of meat, and cooked until thick. Although one-pot stews were being made centuries ago, the term Eintopf was introduced to the lexicon around the time of the First World War, when military canteens began serving one-pot meals of thick pea stew or Gulaschsuppe. During the Third Reich, the Nazi government urged housewives to cook an economical Eintopf on Sundays instead of the traditional and more expensive Sunday roast, then donate the savings to the Winter Relief Charity, a party organization. Eintopfsonntage ("One-Pot Sundays") even became required of restaurants.

Today, no cafeteria or canteen, where many Germans eat their only hot meal of the day, is without an Eintopf on the menu on any given day.

For a culture in which much importance is given to having one warm meal a day, Eintöpfe are an ideal solution for busy cooks in our modern world. They're crowd-pleasing, especially when you throw in a few rounds of sliced sausages, they're cheap and filling, they improve with time, and they're difficult to mess up. And they're versatile—if you don't like legumes, make them with barley. If you don't like barley, make them with potatoes. When my older son attended a parent-run Kita, or daycare, the parents took turns cooking lunch for all twenty-one kids and their caregivers. When it was my turn, my go-to meal was always an enormous Eintopf with sliced sausages on the side to dot on top and lots of delicious bread. The pot always came home empty.

German soups are usually a more delicate affair. A small bowl of intensely flavored, clear beef broth is one of the best ways to start a meal and offers a good balance if you're having a proper German sweet dish for lunch. But it's also pure comfort, especially when laced with thin slices of pancakes or delicate squares of egg custard on a cold winter's day.

RINDERBRÜHE

Clear Beef Broth

MAKES ABOUT
9 CUPS / 2.2L

1 Tbsp vegetable oil

1 large onion, unpeeled
and halved through the
root end

About 1.1 lb / 500g beef bones,
rinsed and dried

1 thick slice beef shin
(about 1.1 lb / 500g),
rinsed and dried

10½ cups / 2.5L water

About 1.1 lb / 500g beef brisket

2½ tsp salt, plus
more as needed

2 bay leaves

2 tsp whole black peppercorns

1 tsp juniper berries, optional

10 whole allspice, optional

2 carrots, peeled and cut into
quarters

1 leek, root and dark green
part trimmed, cut into
quarters

⅓ celery root, peeled and cut
into chunks

1 parsley root, peeled and cut
into chunks, or a small
bunch of curly parsley,
optional

A well-made, richly flavored beef broth is the backbone of German and Austrian cuisine. One builds the base of flavor by searing an onion until golden brown, then adding beef bones and meat to the pot with water. Once those are well-simmered, carrots, celery root (which is more traditional in Germany than celery stalks), and parsley go into the pot. If you can find parsley root, use that instead of parsley, as it has a stronger, earthier flavor that helps balance the broth. Bay leaves, peppercorns, juniper, and allspice add subtle complexity of flavor.

Germans (and Austrians) hold both the flavor and clarity of the broth in high esteem. The pattern of the china plate in which the broth is served should be still visible through the broth's rich amber hue. To keep beef broth from getting cloudy, you must take the time to skim off the scum; during cooking the broth must simmer over very low heat—no roiling boil will do—and when the broth is strained, you must restrain yourself from pressing down on the bones or vegetables to eke out more flavor or liquid.

Beef broth is usually served as an appetizer, either with just a sprinkling of chopped chives on top or a variety of Einlagen, which roughly translates to "things to put in the soup." Einlagen can range from the beef that was cooked in the water to begin with (diced into elegant little pieces, of course) to tiny meatballs, from delicate dumplings made of semolina (Grießklößchen, page 72) to hearty liver dumplings, from thin strips of eggy pancakes (Flädle or Frittaten, page 69) to butter-toasted croutons. Even noodles technically count as an Einlage, as do thin slices of stale bread or soft pretzels.

If you mix a variety of Einlagen along with bits of meat and some vegetables in broth, you've got what the Germans call Hochzeitssuppe, or wedding soup, which differs slightly from region to region, and was traditionally served as a first course at weddings. Another name for the soup is Freud-und-Leid-Suppe ("joy-and-suffering-soup"), which refers to the fact that it was also served at funerals and other community occasions.

Any leftover beef can be served as a second course, sliced thinly, with a sharply flavored sauce such as Remoulade (page 108), Cumberland (page 138), freshly grated horseradish, or even just mustard. Or else make a salad: Thinly slice a red onion and cook some green beans until just tender. Slice the soup meat thinly. Whisk together 1 part vinegar to 2 to 3 parts oil with a spoonful of mustard and salt and pepper to taste. Toss the still-warm beans and sliced onion with the dressing, then fold in the sliced meat. Taste for seasoning, then mince some chives and strew over the salad.

CONTINUED

1   Place the oil in a very large pot over high heat. As soon as the oil is hot, place the onion, cut-side down, into the pan and let it sear for 2 to 3 minutes, until well-browned.

2   When the onion has finished searing, place the bones and beef shin in the pot alongside the onion and let sear for a few minutes on one side. Pour in the water and add 2 tsp of salt. Add the beef brisket, submerging it completely. Bring the water to a boil.

3   While the water is heating up, scum will rise to the surface. Using a spoon or spider, carefully skim off as much scum as possible and discard. This will help you produce a clear broth.

4   As soon as the water starts to boil and you have finished skimming the broth, lower the heat and cover. Simmer for 1½ hours.

5   After 1½ hours of simmering, add the remaining 1 tsp of salt, the seasonings, and the vegetables to the broth. Simmer for another hour.

6   After 1 hour, remove the meat from the pot and set aside. Pour the soup through a fine-mesh sieve. Do not press down on the vegetables or bones. If desired, you can reserve and cut up the carrots and celery root to serve with the broth. Discard the rest. The meat can be cut into small pieces and served in the broth or it can be served as a second course, thinly sliced.

7   Before serving, bring the soup to a boil again and adjust the seasoning to taste. Turn off the heat and proceed with whichever Einlage you choose.

FLÄDLE

Sliced Soup Pancakes

SERVES 4 AS A STARTER
IN BROTH

½ cup plus 1½ Tbsp / 75g
    all-purpose flour
¼ tsp salt
1 egg
¾ cup / 200ml whole milk
Butter for the pan
2 Tbsp finely minced chives

A great way to use up any leftover pancakes (page 181) you might have on hand is to cut them into strips and drop them into hot beef broth. Of course, you can also just prepare the pancakes fresh. This soup is eaten all over southern Germany and Austria. Flädle is the Swabian word for pancake strips; the Austrian word is Frittaten. (So Flädlesuppe or Frittatensuppe is the name of this dish.) Typically, this would be served in a small bowl as a first course, but a big bowl of this is a very nice dinner, too. You can substitute a gluten-free flour blend for the flour here.

1   In a large bowl, whisk together the flour, salt, egg, and milk until the batter is completely smooth. If you have time, let it sit for 30 minutes. Whisk again before cooking.

2   Place a knob of butter in a sauté pan and melt over medium-high heat. Pour in a ladle of batter and tilt the pan to create an evenly thin pancake. Cook until golden brown on one side, a minute or two, then flip and cook the other side. Place on a plate and repeat with the remaining batter, adding butter to the pan when needed.

3   When all the pancakes are cooked, roll them up tightly and slice into strips. Just before serving, divide the strips among soup plates. Top with hot beef broth and chives.

EIERSTICH

Egg Soup Custard

SERVES 4 AS A STARTER
IN BROTH

2 eggs
6 Tbsp / 90ml whole milk
¼ tsp salt
10 scrapes of whole nutmeg
Vegetable oil for the dish
2 Tbsp finely minced chives

Eierstich is a steamed egg custard cut into little cubes or any other shape you are partial to (you can even use little cookie cutters to cut out stars or other shapes). The combination of savory broth and smooth little bites of egg custard is a fortifying start to a meal or can be a very simple and comforting dish on its own.

1   Place the eggs in a bowl and whisk in the milk. Add the salt and nutmeg and whisk very well. The mixture should be a uniform color, with no streaks of egg or milk. Lightly oil a heatproof glass dish (I use a 5-inch / 12cm square one) and pour in the egg mixture. Cover tightly with aluminum foil and set aside.

2   Pour water into a lidded pan large enough to hold the egg dish, but only enough water to come halfway up the side of the dish. Set over high heat and bring to a boil.

3   As soon as the water boils, turn the heat down to low and carefully place the foil-covered egg dish into the simmering water. Cover the pan with a lid and cook over very low heat for 30 minutes. The custard will be tender but set.

4   Wearing oven mitts, carefully remove the egg dish from the hot pan and remove the aluminum foil. Using a thin, sharp knife, loosen the edges of the eggs, then carefully unmold them onto a cutting board. Cut into small cubes or other shapes.

5   Distribute the egg shapes and chives among the soup plates. Ladle over hot broth and serve immediately.

GRIEẞKLÖẞCHEN

Semolina Soup Dumplings

MAKES ABOUT
16 DUMPLINGS,
SERVING 4 TO 6 AS A
STARTER IN BROTH

1 egg

Unsalted butter, at room
    temperature

¼ tsp salt

15 scrapes of whole nutmeg

Coarsely ground semolina
    flour

2 Tbsp finely minced chives,
    optional

Grießklößchen (or Grießnocken / Grießnockerln in Austria) are little dumplings of semolina and egg lightly flavored with nutmeg. The dumplings swell as they poach, becoming tender and pillowy. If you see a resemblance to matzo balls, you're not mistaken. According to cookbook author Joan Nathan, German Jews first started adapting dumplings with matzo meal for Sabbath meals in the Middle Ages.

The traditional way to make these dumplings is to weigh one egg (without the shell), then use that weight to measure out the butter and semolina. This method gives such perfect results that I really do hope you will try it, and it also simplifies scaling the recipe up. If you do not have a scale to measure the egg and other ingredients, one large egg usually weighs around 2 ounces / 56 grams, so you can calculate 2 ounces / 56 grams of butter and ⅔ cup / 112 grams coarsely ground semolina. The mixture should hold its shape when rolled into balls.

1   Crack the egg in a small bowl and weigh the egg. Set aside.

2   In a separate medium bowl, place an equal amount in weight of butter. Using electric beaters, beat the butter until light and fluffy. Beat the egg into the butter, then season with salt and nutmeg. Scrape down the sides, then beat again briefly to mix.

3   Measure in twice the amount in weight of semolina. Mix until well-combined. Refrigerate for 10 minutes.

4   Bring a large pot of salted water to a boil. As soon as it boils, turn the heat down to low. Roll the mixture into 1-inch / 2.5cm balls with your hands. Alternatively, you can shape the dumpling batter into quenelles. Dip a small spoon in cold water, spoon out a portion of batter, then drag the spoon edge against your palm firmly to create a tightly packed quenelle. Drop the dumplings in the hot water as you work. When all the dumplings are in the water, regulate the heat so that the water just barely simmers. Cook for 10 minutes.

5   After 10 minutes, turn the heat off and let the dumplings sit in the hot water for another 10 minutes. Cooking the dumplings in water instead of the broth keeps the broth clear.

6   Using a spider, drain the dumplings and divide them among soup plates. Top with hot beef broth and chives (if desired).

GULASCHSUPPE

Goulash Soup

SERVES 6 TO 8

1 lb / 500g boneless beef
    shank or shin, cut into
    ½-inch / 1.3cm cubes
1½ tsp baking soda
¾ cup / 175ml water
3 Tbsp / 40g lard or
    vegetable oil
2 large onions, minced
2 tsp salt, plus more as needed
⅓ cup / 40g sweet paprika
2 Tbsp apple cider vinegar or
    white wine vinegar
3 Tbsp tomato paste
2 tsp dried marjoram
1 tsp ground caraway, optional
6 cups / 1.5L beef broth, plus
    more as needed
3 large waxy potatoes, peeled
    and cut into ½-inch / 1.3cm
    cubes
Freshly ground black pepper
2 Tbsp cornstarch, optional

Gulaschsuppe is a brothy, rust-colored soup dotted with cubes of beef and potato, not to be confused with thicker, stewier Gulasch (page 126). It's a classic canteen and outdoor market meal, always served with a crusty roll for dipping. This recipe is adapted from Ewald Plachutta's *Die Gute Küche*.

Treating the meat with a baking soda brine results in more tender beef. This step is by no means mandatory, but sometimes stew meat can be tough and the brine, which I learned from America's Test Kitchen, can help. Lard gives the soup a richer flavor but can be replaced with oil. Just before the end of the cooking time, you can decide whether you want to serve the soup as is, or if you want to thicken the broth with a simple cornstarch slurry.

1   First, tenderize the meat: Place the meat in a bowl. In a separate bowl, whisk together the baking soda with the water until the baking soda has dissolved. Pour this solution over the meat and mix well. Set the mixture aside for a minimum of 15 minutes and up to 45 minutes. Drain the meat, rinse briefly, and pat dry.

2   Place the lard in a large pot over medium heat and melt. Add the onions and salt and cook, stirring, for about 10 minutes, until the onions are glassy and fragrant and starting to take on some color.

3   Add the beef and stir well. Let cook for a minute or so, then stir again and let cook for another minute. Turn the heat to low and stir in the paprika, letting it cook for a minute, stirring constantly, then add the vinegar and stir well. Add the tomato paste, marjoram, and caraway, if using. Stir well and cook for a minute, then add the beef broth and turn up the heat. Bring to a boil, then lower the heat to a simmer and cover. Cook for 45 minutes.

4   Carefully add the potatoes, taking care not to splash yourself with the hot broth. Stir and cook until the potatoes are soft, about 15 minutes. Season with salt or pepper to taste. The soup can be served as is or, if you prefer a thicker broth, place the cornstarch in a small bowl and whisk in ¼ cup of the hot broth until the mixture is completely smooth, then whisk this into the simmering soup. Let it cook for about 3 more minutes, until slightly thickened, then serve.

KÄSESUPPE

Mountain Cheese Soup

SERVES 6 TO 8

2½ Tbsp unsalted butter, plus
    more for the croutons

2 medium onions, minced

½ tsp salt

Freshly ground black pepper

2½ Tbsp all-purpose flour

½ cup / 125ml white wine

2½ cups / 600ml vegetable
    broth

1 cup / 250ml heavy cream

7 oz / 200g Alpine mountain
    cheese, cubed or grated

25 scrapes of whole nutmeg

1 tsp caraway seeds, optional

1 tsp fennel seeds, optional

4 slices rye sourdough bread,
    cubed, optional

Käsesuppe, an Alpine specialty, is creamy, unctuous, and aromatic with wine, spices, and cheese. I think it is best served in little cups, as a deeply savory starter, especially in winter when we all need sustenance, indulgence, and a bit of molten cheese.

Build the flavors of Käsesuppe by caramelizing onions, then adding wine and broth and cream, making a thinned-out béchamel into which you melt cubes of fragrant Alpine cheese. Nutmeg adds flavor, as do toasted croutons rolled in caraway and fennel, which happen to have digestive properties as well as a wonderful rough crunch. This Käsesuppe has notes of mushroomy umami and renders everyone to whom I've ever served it slightly speechless. The best cheese for this soup is Bergkäse, or Alpine cheese, or Gruyère or Appenzeller, or a combination thereof. You can substitute a gluten-free flour blend for the flour.

1   For the soup: Place the butter in a large pot over medium heat to melt, then add the onions, salt, and pepper. Cook, stirring occasionally, regulating the heat so that the onions don't burn, for 8 to 10 minutes, until they start to caramelize.

2   Add the flour to the pot and stir well. Cook for about a minute, until the flour starts to toast. Pour in the wine and switch to a whisk. Whisk in the broth and cream. Over medium heat, bring the soup just to a simmer, then lower the heat, cover, and simmer for 10 minutes.

3   Remove the lid and add the cheese and nutmeg. Whisk over low heat until the cheese has fully melted. Remove from the heat and, using an immersion blender, blend the soup until completely smooth. If making croutons, set the soup back over very low heat and cover while you make the croutons. If not making croutons, serve the soup right away.

4   For the croutons: Melt a knob of butter in a sauté pan and add the spices, if using. Cook the spices for about 30 seconds, then add the cubed bread. Cook, tossing, until the bread is crisped and golden brown.

5   Divide the soup among small soup cups or bowls and scatter each portion with some croutons, if desired. Serve immediately.

RHEINISCHE ZWIEBELSUPPE

Onion and Sausage Soup

SERVES 4

3 Tbsp unsalted butter or
    vegetable oil
1.7 lb / 800g yellow onions,
    peeled, halved, and cut into
    thin half-moons
Salt and freshly ground
    black pepper
6 cups / 1.5L beef broth
3 large starchy potatoes, like
    Russet, peeled and cubed
4 smoked sausages, sliced
4 slices stale bread (ideally
    rye or sourdough), cut into
    small cubes
1 to 2 Tbsp apple cider vinegar
Handful of flat-leaf parsley,
    finely minced

I know that French onion soup gets all the attention with its jaunty cap of cheesy bread, but this simple onion soup, which is a regional specialty of North Rhine-Westphalia, encompassing cities from Bielefeld to Cologne, is my favorite. It's savory and comforting, incredibly simple to make, *and* it uses up stale bread, which we always seem to have around. The rounds of smoked sausages added toward the end guarantee that my children will eat it just as happily as I do, and we all like to scatter the homemade croutons across our portions.

What sets this onion soup apart from other regional onion soups is the sausage and the fact there is no need for a roux (Mehlschwitze in German) as the base of the soup—you just start with a big panful of sautéed onions. Smoked sausages pair well with the sweet onions and savory broth, but you could also use Bratwürste. Don't skip the vinegar, which lifts all the flavors up at the end and makes them sing.

1   Place 2 Tbsp of butter in a large pot over medium heat, then add the onions and 1 tsp of salt and pepper and stir well. Cook, stirring occasionally, until the onions have started to turn a very pale golden yellow, about 10 minutes.

2   Pour in the broth, add the potatoes, raise the heat and bring to a boil, then lower the heat and simmer, covered, for 15 minutes.

3   Add the sausages and cover the pot again for another 15 minutes over the lowest heat possible.

4   Melt the remaining 1 Tbsp of butter in a sauté pan over medium heat and add the bread. Cook, shaking the pan occasionally, until the bread cubes are crisp and golden brown.

5   Take the soup off the heat, stir in the vinegar to taste, and taste for seasoning, adding more salt or pepper if desired. Stir in the parsley.

6   Distribute the soup among the soup plates, then top each portion with a scattering of croutons.

KARTOFFELSUPPE

Potato-Sausage Soup

SERVES 4

2 Tbsp vegetable oil

Scant ⅔ cup / 2.7 oz / 75g
  minced lean Schinkenspeck
  or bacon

1 leek, root and dark green
  part trimmed, chopped

1 small onion, chopped

Pinch of salt

2 medium carrots, peeled and
  cut into small cubes

¼ celery root, peeled and
  cubed

2 tsp dried marjoram

1 bay leaf

Freshly ground black pepper

30 scrapes of whole nutmeg,
  optional

2.75 lb / 1.25kg starchy
  potatoes, like Russet,
  peeled and cubed

5 cups / 1.1L broth (vegetable,
  chicken, or beef)

4 Wiener sausages, sliced

Handful of flat-leaf parsley,
  minced

This simple potato soup is one of my favorite one-pot meals to make for my family. It is something that the whole family looks forward to, even if the kids regularly have it for lunch at their school cafeteria. The flavors of onions, bacon, marjoram, nutmeg, and bay are cozy alongside the soft chunks of potato and little rounds of Würstchen (Wiener sausages) bobbing here and there. It's also one of those meals that you can easily throw together on a weeknight with pantry ingredients. Serve it with some crusty rolls and you're all set for a delicious dinner. The bacon is completely optional; this soup is still full of flavor without it.

I prefer making Kartoffelsuppe with starchy potatoes that you crush toward the end of the cooking process, which makes for an appealingly stewy result. If you prefer a smoother soup, you could put it through a food mill. But do not puree the soup, as the starch in the potatoes will turn into a gluey mess. You can make this soup in advance, but don't freeze it; potatoes turn watery and awful in the freezer. If making ahead, keep the sausages out of the pot until just before serving.

For a variation on Kartoffelsuppe, add a quarter to a third of a head of Savoy cabbage, cored and chopped, between step 2 and step 3. Sauté the cabbage a bit before adding the potatoes and broth. You may need to add a bit more salt for seasoning. A good splash of apple cider vinegar at the end will be the finishing touch.

1 Place the oil in a large pot over medium heat and add the Schinkenspeck. Stir to coat and cook for 1 minute before adding the leek, onion, and salt. Cook, stirring occasionally, for about 5 minutes, until fragrant and the onions are translucent.

2 Add the carrots and celery root and stir well. Cook for another 5 to 7 minutes. Add the marjoram and stir to combine. Add the bay leaf, pepper, and nutmeg, if using.

3 Place the potatoes in the pot and stir to combine.

4 Pour in the broth, stir well, then raise the heat to high and bring just to a boil.

5 Lower the heat and cover. Simmer for about 30 minutes, until the potatoes are tender. Using a wooden spoon, crush about two-thirds of the potatoes against the side of the pot. The goal is to get a good mix of textures and to thicken the soup. Taste and adjust the seasoning. (If your broth wasn't very salty, you may need to add some salt here.)

6 Just before serving, place the sausages in the pot and stir well. Cover and let sit off the heat until the sausages are warmed through, about 5 minutes.

7 Divide among soup plates and sprinkle each portion with parsley.

LINSENSUPPE MIT PFLAUMEN

Lentil Soup with Sausage and Prunes

SERVES 4 TO 6

2 Tbsp vegetable oil

⅔ cup / 3.5 oz / 100g minced
   Schinkenspeck or bacon

1 leek, root and dark green
   part trimmed, or 2 small
   onions, finely diced

1 large carrot, peeled and
   finely diced

1 thick slice of celery root,
   peeled and finely diced

Salt

2 cups / 400g brown lentils

1 tsp dried marjoram

8 cups / 2L vegetable or
   beef broth

3 large waxy potatoes, peeled
   and cubed

4 Knacker sausages, sliced
   into ½-inch / 1.3cm rounds

½ cup / 100g prunes,
   quartered

Handful of flat-leaf parsley,
   minced

¼ cup / 60ml apple
   cider vinegar

Freshly ground black pepper,
   optional

My family's most consumed German food is probably lentil soup. I make it frequently for dinner, as it is such an easy and nutritious one-pot meal, and it is often served in the kids' school cafeteria and my husband's office canteen. Lentil soup in Germany is thick and stewy, studded with little bits of bacon or Schinkenspeck, cubed root vegetables, and meltingly tender brown lentils. And, of course, there are always rounds of sliced sausages. The final essential touch is a generous splash of vinegar that brings all the rich flavors together and lifts them up to the next level.

Lentil soup is made all over Germany with only minimal variations. In Swabia, they'll serve it with Spätzle and Saitenwürstchen, which are Wiener Würstchen elsewhere; in Berlin, it gets served with Knacker sausages, and old Berlin recipes include chopped prunes, too. I was skeptical about the prunes at first, but call me a convert now: Their dark, musky sweetness is a delicious foil to the rest of the stew. (You can leave them out if you prefer.)

1   Place the oil in a large pot over medium heat. Add the Schinkenspeck and cook for a minute or two, then add the leek, carrot, and celery root. Season with 1 tsp of salt and stir well. Let cook, stirring, for 5 to 8 minutes, until the onions are translucent and fragrant.

2   Add the lentils, marjoram, and broth. Stir well and bring to a boil over medium-high heat. Cover, lower the heat, and simmer for 15 minutes. Add the potatoes and cook for another 10 minutes.

3   Add the sausages and prunes and cover again. Cook for 10 minutes. The lentils and potatoes should be soft and tender.

4   Just before serving, stir in the parsley and vinegar. Taste for seasoning, adding more salt, pepper, or vinegar, if desired. Serve.

ERBSENEINTOPF

Thick Pea Stew

SERVES 4

3 Tbsp olive oil or vegetable oil
1 medium onion,
    finely chopped
⅓ cup / 50g minced Speck
    or lean bacon
1 leek, root and dark green
    part trimmed, chopped
1 medium carrot, peeled
    and diced
1-inch / 2.5cm thick slice of
    celery root, peeled and
    cut into small dice
2 tsp dried marjoram
1 tsp salt, plus more as needed
Freshly ground black pepper
1½ cups / 300g dried split
    green peas
5 to 6 cups / 1.1 to 1.4L
    vegetable or chicken broth
3 medium waxy potatoes,
    like Yukon Gold, peeled
    and diced
4 Wiener Würstchen or hot
    dogs, cut into bite-size
    rounds

This is my mother-in-law's Erbsensuppe recipe, a classic German Eintopf if you ever saw one. It's thick and satisfying; all you need with this is a crusty roll to clean the plate. While pea soups abound all over the world, in Germany they are usually associated with Berlin, historically a working-class city where thrifty but filling meals have always been essential. Aschinger's, an institution at Berlin's Zoo Station for decades, was famous for its cheap pea soup and free Brötchen.

Traditional Berlin pea soup used to be made with Eisbein (salted pork knuckle), but nowadays a bit of Schinkenspeck or even a thick slice of Kassler (cured, smoked pork loin, available at German butchers) will do (if you use Kassler, add it with the broth, then take it out at the end of cooking, shred it, and return it to the pot and mix well). In Germany, you use Suppengrün, that bundle of leek, carrots, and celery root sold at every grocery store, as the backbone of the soup. Marjoram is the classic herb to use; I think of it as the oregano of the north. It pairs beautifully with the rich porky flavor of the Schinkenspeck and the savory aromas of the Suppengrün.

If you happen to have some raw Sauerkraut on hand, try serving the pea soup with a forkful of it on top. The sour, crunchy cabbage is a great counterpoint to the creamy, hearty soup. Serve with crusty rolls.

1   Place the oil in a large pot over medium-high heat. Add the onion and Speck and cook, stirring occasionally, for about 5 minutes. Add the leek and stir well. Cook for another 5 minutes. Add the carrot and celery root and stir well. Cook for another 5 minutes. Add the marjoram, salt, and pepper.

2   Pour in the peas and the broth. Stir well and bring to a boil. Lower the heat to a simmer, cover, and cook for 20 minutes.

3   Add the potatoes and stir well. Cook for another 20 minutes. The peas and potatoes should be soft and tender. Taste for seasoning and adjust if necessary.

4   When the soup is ready, take it off the heat and stir in the Würstchen. Let sit for a few minutes, until the Würstchen are warmed through, then serve.

WESTFÄLISCHES BLINDHUHN

White Bean Stew with Bacon, Green Beans, Apples, and Pears

SERVES 4 TO 6

1¼ cups / 250g dried white
    beans (like navy beans) or
    2 (15-oz) cans, drained

5 cups / 1.25L water

8.5 oz / 250g slab bacon

3 large carrots, peeled
    and diced

2 large waxy potatoes,
    peeled and diced

2 apples, peeled, cored,
    and diced

2 very firm pears, peeled,
    cored, and diced

3 cups / 375g green beans, cut
    into 1½-inch / 4cm pieces

1 bay leaf

2 tsp dried summer savory
    or marjoram

1½ tsp salt, plus more
    as needed

Freshly ground black pepper

1¾ cups / 400ml beef
    or vegetable broth

Large handful of flat-leaf
    parsley, minced

One of the most classic dishes of northern Germany is called Birnen, Bohnen, und Speck—pears, beans, and bacon. It features small Kochbirnen, or cooking pears, which are difficult to source even in Germany, cooked with slab bacon and green beans. Cooking pears aren't meant to ever be eaten raw; uncooked, they stay green and hard. This classic white bean stew hails from Westphalia and shares the same flavors as Birnen, Bohnen, und Speck. Its name means "blind chicken," but there is no chicken to be found in the stew. A German expression—"even a blind chicken eventually finds a grain"—is the inspiration. This stew contains something for everyone. It is hearty and filling, with an interesting balance of savory and sweet.

The dish is traditionally made with dried white beans that you cook with slab bacon to get a flavorful broth. If you prefer to use canned white beans, I provide a different cooking method for the start of the stew in step 4. Speaking of convenience food, frozen cut green beans are a more than acceptable substitute for fresh ones. Try to use the hardest, greenest pears you can find. They will still probably be sweeter than German Kochbirnen, but their flavor will pair nicely with the rest of the stew. In this Eintopf, I like using apples that get soft and fluffy during cooking.

1   If using canned beans, skip to step 4. If using dried beans, place them in a large pot and add the water and bacon. Set over high heat and bring to a boil, then turn the heat down and cover. Simmer for about 1½ hours, until the beans are tender. (The length of time will depend on when you purchased the dried beans.) Add the carrots and simmer for 10 minutes.

2   Add the potatoes, apples, pears, green beans, bay leaf, summer savory, salt, and pepper to the beans. Pour in the broth. Over high heat, bring just to a boil, then lower the heat, cover, and simmer for 15 to 20 minutes, until the potatoes are soft. Remove the slab bacon and cut into bite-size pieces, discarding any excess fat and skin, then return to the pot.

3   Adjust the seasoning to taste, adding pepper and more salt if necessary, and stir in the parsley. Serve.

4   If using canned beans, first cut the slab bacon into small chunks and place the bacon in a large pot over medium-high heat. Let the bacon cook and render its fat for several minutes. Add the carrots, potatoes, apples, pears, and green beans and stir well. Let them cook for a minute or two, then add the drained beans and the seasonings. Stir well and add 5 to 6 cups / 1.2 to 1.4 liters of water or broth to the pot. Bring to a boil over high heat, lower the heat, cover, and simmer for 25 to 30 minutes. Serve sprinkled with parsley.

WIRSINGEINTOPF

Savoy Cabbage Stew

SERVES 6

1 Tbsp vegetable oil

3.5 oz / 100g smoked bacon, diced, or Kassler

1 leek, root and dark green part trimmed, cut in half vertically and sliced into half-moons

2 medium carrots, peeled and diced

1 tsp ground caraway, optional

Freshly ground black pepper

½ head of Savoy cabbage, cored, quartered, and thinly sliced

1 bay leaf

8 cups / 2L beef or vegetable broth

3 medium waxy potatoes, peeled and cubed

2 Tbsp apple cider vinegar

In fall and winter, green markets in Germany can be dispiriting places. The only local produce are potatoes, root vegetables, and cabbage. Savoy cabbage, with its ruffled, deep green leaves, is a rare glimpse of beauty on table after table of tubers. This classic Eintopf pairs the bittersweet flavor of cooked Savoy with bacon and caraway, along with a few potatoes thrown in to make this a full meal. The vinegar provides, like with many other German Eintöpfe, an essential finishing touch.

1   Place the oil in a large pot over medium heat and add the bacon. Cook, stirring, until the fat has rendered and the bacon is crisp, about 10 minutes. (If using Kassler, add with the broth.)

2   Add the leek and carrots to the bacon and stir well. Cook for about 10 minutes, stirring occasionally, until the leek has cooked down and is fragrant.

3   Add the caraway, if using, and pepper to taste, and cook for 1 minute.

4   Add the cabbage to the pot and stir well to combine. Let cook for 2 to 3 minutes, stirring occasionally. Add the bay leaf and broth and stir well. Raise the heat to high.

5   Add the potatoes. When the broth starts to bubble, lower the heat and cover.

6   Simmer for about 30 minutes, until the cabbage and potatoes are tender and the broth is sweet. If you used Kassler, take it out of the pot, shred it, and return the meat to the pot. Remove from the heat and stir in the vinegar, then serve.

GRAUPENSUPPE

Beef Barley Soup

SERVES 4

6 cups / 1.5L beef broth

12 oz / 350g bone-in beef
shank (1 thick slice)

2 Tbsp vegetable oil

1 large yellow onion, finely
diced

⅓ cup / 50g minced
Schinkenspeck or
lean bacon

1 leek, root and dark green
part trimmed, finely
chopped

⅓ celery root, peeled and
finely diced

½ parsley root, peeled and
finely diced, optional

½ tsp salt

Freshly ground black pepper

1 cup / 190g pearl barley

7 oz / 200g waxy potatoes,
peeled and diced

1 small bay leaf

2 Tbsp apple cider vinegar,
optional

Handful of flat-leaf parsley,
minced

A big pot of this soothing mix of barley, beef, vegetables, and potatoes is pure winter comfort food, the kind of soup most people in Germany associate with their grandmothers, who specialized in cooking economically with local ingredients and always with the goal of filling hungry bellies. The beef shank bone will have marrow in the middle that you can mix into the soup before serving.

1   Place the beef broth in a large pot and add the beef shank. Cover the pot and bring to a boil over medium heat, then lower the heat and simmer for 1 hour. Remove the shank from the pot and set aside to cool.

2   Place the oil in a separate soup pot over medium heat and add the onions and Schinkenspeck. Stir well and cook for 5 minutes, stirring occasionally.

3   Add the leek, celery root, parsley root, if using, and salt and stir well. Cook, stirring occasionally, for 8 to 10 minutes. Regulate the heat if necessary to keep the vegetables from burning. Season with pepper to taste.

4   Add the pearl barley and potatoes and stir well. Add the bay leaf and all of the beef broth and stir well. Raise the heat to bring the soup to a boil, then lower the heat and cover. Simmer for 30 minutes, stirring occasionally.

5   Meanwhile, remove all the connective tissue from the reserved piece of beef and cut the beef into small pieces. After the 30 minutes of simmering, add the beef to the soup pot, stir well, and simmer for another 10 minutes.

6   Remove the bay leaf. Stir in the vinegar, if using, and the parsley. Serve.

VEGETARIAN MAIN COURSES

Although Germany is famous for its meat dishes, the irony is that Germans have long had an intimate acquaintance with meatless or mostly meatless meals. Historically, due to the Church's strict dietary laws, more than half of the year was devoted to fasting, meaning that eating meat, eggs, and dairy was forbidden. Those days included not only the forty days before both Easter and Christmas, but also regular old Fridays and Saturdays and various other holy days. On the remaining days, the frequency of meat consumption was, of course, tied to prosperity. A lot of Germans ate meat only once a week, if that, saving the roast for Sunday. But for the poorest, even that was a rarity. In the nineteenth century, many poor Germans went years without even eating bread; their diet consisted mostly of potatoes, beans, and cabbage. In Ursula Heinzelmann's exhaustively researched culinary history of Germany, *Beyond Bratwurst,* she mentions a bleak report by Friedrich List, a nineteenth-century liberal revolutionary, of people passing around a herring tied on a string to rub onto their potatoes for some flavor (salt was taxed, making it a luxury good).

Depending on the region, people relied on vegetable and legume stews, sweet meals, and grain porridges to get their caloric needs met, and a resourcefulness with staple ingredients developed. Dumplings made of old bread or flour or potatoes, Sauerkraut and other preserved vegetables, and potatoes cooked in every way imaginable were just a few of the building blocks of everyday meals. The piquant flavors of paprika, marjoram, and nutmeg were threaded throughout, adding flavor and satisfaction to even the simplest meals.

In this chapter, mercifully, there is nothing remotely as bleak as a shared herring for seasoning. I have chosen regional recipes from north to south, some of which developed over centuries of tradition. There are meals rich with dairy, like fragrant melted Alpine cheese or verdant creamy herb sauces; meals for lean times that use up boiled potatoes and stale bread; twentieth-century meals such as celery root cutlets; and dishes that have been made for hundreds of years, like Swabian Spätzle (page 93). But throughout the book, not just in this chapter, you'll come across other meatless meals that Germans consider classics, like boiled potatoes with herbed Quark (page 33), Eintöpfe (just leave out the Speck or sausages), Maultaschen, but where spinach replaces all of the meat filling (page 155), and potato dumplings (page 216) that instead of being served with meat are topped with buttered, toasted bread crumbs, and chopped parsley.

EIER IN SENFSOßE

Eggs in Creamy Mustard Sauce

SERVES 4

8 eggs

2 Tbsp unsalted butter

2 Tbsp all-purpose flour

1 cup / 250ml whole milk

1 cup / 250ml vegetable broth

3 Tbsp yellow or whole-grain
   mustard, or a mix of both

1 Tbsp white wine vinegar

1 Tbsp sour cream

Salt and freshly ground
   black pepper

Chopped flat-leaf parsley,
   optional

Kartoffelpurée (page 210) or
   Salzkartoffeln (page 209)
   for serving

This vegetarian dish, a comforting classic in canteens, probably originated in northern Germany, though it has more than proved itself by remaining a favorite across the country for decades. Many people in Germany have fond memories of eating this as children. Boiled eggs, with just-set whites and jammy yolks, are cloaked in a creamy, mustard-flavored sauce. While the sprinkling of minced parsley on top is optional, the mashed potatoes (page 210) or Salzkartoffeln (page 209) to mop up the copious amounts of sauce are not. I consider this dish a prime example of German Armeleuteessen—aka "poor man's food"—because it's hearty and filling and requires very little in terms of cost and time to get it on the table. Adding more potatoes to the pot easily stretches the meal to feed more bellies.

The traditional flavoring for the Senfsoße is German mittelscharfer Senf, which is the standard yellow mustard usually served with Bratwurst or other sausages. I've made this with whole-grain mustard as well, which is delicious and visually quite appealing. (Even my very German husband, who grew up eating this dish, prefers the whole-grain mustard version.) You can also mix the two. Traditionally, the sauce was further enriched with egg yolks or whipping cream, but I like to whisk in a spoonful of sour cream to round out the flavor instead.

1 Bring a medium pot of water to a boil. Lower the eggs into the pot and cook for 7 minutes. Drain and plunge them into a bowl of cold water and let them sit for a minute. Set aside.

2 Place the butter in a medium saucepan over medium-high heat and melt. Whisk in the flour and cook, continuing to whisk for a few minutes, until the mixture turns a light golden color.

3 Whisk in the milk and cook, whisking constantly, until the mixture is thick and smooth. Then whisk in the broth. When the mixture is creamy and smooth, whisk in the mustard, vinegar, and sour cream. Taste and adjust the seasoning with salt and pepper, if necessary.

4 Peel the boiled eggs. You can cut them in half lengthwise for serving, if you like. Put the eggs in a serving dish. Pour the mustard sauce over the eggs. Sprinkle with chopped parsley, if desired.

5 Serve immediately with mashed potatoes or Salzkartoffeln.

KÄSESPÄTZLE

Swabian Noodles with Mountain Cheese and Caramelized Onions

SERVES 4

2½ cups / 400g all-purpose
    flour
3 tsp salt
4 eggs
About 1 cup / 250ml club soda
2 Tbsp unsalted butter, plus
    more for the serving dish
2 medium yellow onions, cut
    into thin half-moons
2.6 oz / 75g Alpine cheese,
    grated

Spätzle are Germany's most famous noodles. Swabia, a region in Germany's prosperous southwest, has long laid claim to them, though they are made widely throughout southern Germany and neighboring Austria and Switzerland. In fact, there are paintings dating to the Middle Ages that depict people holding the board traditionally used to make Spätzle, though their provenance beyond that point is unknown.

Spätzle show up in a variety of different ways on German tables. They are a frequent side dish to Germany's many roasts, often swimming in a pool of rich brown gravy. One beloved Swabian dish pairs Spätzle with lentil stew and boiled sausages; another has them float in a savory beef broth with cubed potatoes and shreds of soup meat (Gaisburger Marsch). They can be made verdant with the addition of boiled, pureed spinach or chopped fresh herbs to the batter. Spätzle can even show up as dessert or nursery food, lightly sweetened and served with confectioners' sugar and ground poppyseeds or applesauce. But, arguably, their most beloved role is as the anchor of this popular dish in which freshly boiled Spätzle are layered with redolent heaps of grated mountain cheese, then topped with a panful of caramelized onions. Chewy, cheesy, savory, and endlessly comforting, Käsespätzle are Germany's version of mac and cheese.

Spätzle batter is simple, made of just flour, eggs and milk or water, plain or sparkling, which is supposed to help achieve a light and chewy texture of the noodles.

Then the batter, which is quite sticky, is either smeared on a board and scraped into boiling water with a knife or bench scraper or poured or pressed through a special Spätzle press or sieve. Spätzle were traditionally made with spelt flour, but today many use wheat flour. They're quite robust and can be cooked in advance (if making in advance, rinse the just-cooked noodles with water, cool completely, then store in the refrigerator for a few days). This recipe serves four but is easily scaled up or down. The rule of thumb when making Spätzle is to calculate about ½ cup plus 2 Tbsp / 100g of flour and one egg per person.

In German-speaking countries, the traditional cheese for Käsespätzle is Bergkäse, or mountain cheese, meaning it is either made in the Alps or from milk from Alpine cows. You can use Gruyère, Appenzeller, and Emmentaler, either on their own or mixed. If you have access to a good-quality cheese shop, you may be able to find Allgäuer Bergkäse, a raw milk mountain cheese from the Allgäu region.

CONTINUED

1   First, make the Spätzle batter: Place the flour and 2 tsp of salt in a large bowl. Crack in the eggs and beat briefly with a wooden spoon, then pour in half of the club soda. Stir vigorously, then add the remaining club soda a bit at a time, until the batter is smooth and falls off the spoon in sheets. Cover the bowl and set aside for 30 minutes.

2   Meanwhile, make the onions: Melt the butter in a medium sauté pan. Place the onions in the pan and sprinkle with the remaining 1 tsp of salt. Cook over medium-low heat, stirring frequently, until the onions are well-browned and fragrant, about 20 minutes. (Depending on your stove, this may take a little longer, up to 35 minutes.) Set aside.

3   Bring a large pot of salted water to a boil. Butter the bottom of a serving dish or bowl and set aside.

4   Scrape a ladleful of batter onto a small wooden cutting board without a lip. Hold the cutting board at a slight angle over the pot of boiling water and, using a sharp bench scraper or a knife dipped in water, shave off very thin ribbons (about ⅛ inch / 3mm thick) of batter directly over the pot so that the noodles fall into the water. When they rise to the surface, which will only take a moment, scoop them out with a spider, letting the excess water drain off, and place them in the buttered dish. Top with a sprinkling of cheese. Repeat with the remaining batter and cheese, working in batches.

5   When the Spätzle are finished and topped with a final layer of cheese, add the browned onions to the Spätzle and toss until well-combined. Serve immediately.

SCHUPFNUDELN MIT APFEL-SAUERKRAUT

Potato Noodles with Apple Sauerkraut

SERVES 4, WITH
LEFTOVERS

FOR THE NOODLES

2.2 lb / 1kg starchy potatoes,
　like Russet, peeled and
　cut into large chunks

1 Tbsp coarse salt

2 eggs

1 tsp salt

1¾ cups plus 2 Tbsp / 300g
　all-purpose flour, plus more
　for kneading

Butter for the pan

FOR THE SAUERKRAUT

2 Tbsp unsalted butter, lard,
　or vegetable oil

2.6 oz / 75g Schinkenspeck
　or lean smoked bacon,
　minced, optional

1 large onion, minced

1 large cooking apple, peeled,
　cored, quartered, and
　thinly sliced

1 lb / 500g Sauerkraut, drained

1 cup / 250ml vegetable or
　chicken broth

1 bay leaf

½ tsp salt

½ tsp sugar

Freshly ground black pepper

Consider these hand-shaped, pan-fried potato noodles southern Germany's riposte to Italian gnocchi. Though opinions differ on the most traditional way to make Schupfnudeln, most contemporary recipes have you boil them briefly first, then fry them in a pan until golden brown. It's a bit of a production to make the noodles: first you make the dough, then you shape them, boil them, drain them, and fry them (repeating in batches)—so maybe keep this recipe for a weekend rather than a weekday meal. But the upside is that there is no real skill involved in shaping the noodles; you simply roll them into pointy little sausages. Children are good helpers here.

Schupfnudeln are quite plain, unadorned with any spice beyond salt, which make them ideal paired with something deeply flavorful, like a rich, meaty gravy or, as below, a pungent tangle of braised Sauerkraut. To balance out its aggressive sourness, I particularly like Sauerkraut that has been cooked with sliced apples for natural sweetness. Choose a cooking apple that gets fluffy and soft in cooking. The Schinkenspeck is completely optional, though very tasty. You can also take Schupfnudeln in an entirely different direction by sprinkling them with ground poppyseeds and confectioners' sugar (Mohnnudeln) or serving them with cinnamon-sugar as a snack or sweet meal.

1　Place the potatoes in a large pot and cover with cold water by an inch. Add the coarse salt. Bring to a boil over high heat, then lower the heat. Cover and simmer until just tender, about 20 minutes, depending on the size of the potatoes.

2　While the potatoes are cooking, prepare the apple Sauerkraut: Place the butter in a medium pot over medium-high heat. When the butter has melted, add the Schinkenspeck, if using, and let cook for a few minutes. Add the onions and apples and cook over medium heat for about 5 minutes, stirring occasionally, until fragrant and softening.

3　Add the Sauerkraut, loosening it with a fork, and mix well. Raise the heat to high and cook for a minute or two, then pour in the broth and add the bay leaf, salt, sugar, and pepper. Mix well. As soon as it starts to bubble, turn the heat down to low and cover the pan. Braise for 30 minutes. Taste for seasoning, adding more salt or sugar if necessary, then set aside until ready to serve.

CONTINUED

SCHUPFNUDELN MIT APFEL-SAUERKRAUT
continued

4   The potatoes will be done while the Sauerkraut is cooking. Drain them very well, return them to the pot, and mash them until smooth with a potato masher.

5   Add the eggs and salt to the potatoes and mash to combine. Stir in the flour with a wooden spoon and as soon as a dough starts to take shape, scrape it out onto a lightly floured surface and knead until a cohesive dough emerges, adding more flour only if absolutely necessary. You want the dough to be soft but not sticky.

6   Using a bench scraper, cut the dough into four equal pieces. Working with one piece of dough at a time, roll it into log 1 inch / 2.5 cm thick. The other pieces should rest on the floured counter. Cut the log into 1-inch / 2.5cm sections. Take each section of dough and roll it between your palms until an oval noodle with tapered ends takes shape. Set aside on the floured work surface and continue with the remaining 1-inch / 2.5cm sections of dough and then with the three remaining chunks of dough, repeating the process until you have a work surface covered with noodles.

7   Bring a large pot of salted water to a boil. You will cook the noodles in batches. Drop a quarter of the noodles gently into the boiling water and stir once carefully. When the noodles bob at the surface, remove them with a spider and let them drain briefly over the pot.

8   Place the next round of noodles in the boiling water and repeat. Repeat with all the remaining noodles.

9   While the noodles cook, melt a knob of butter in a sauté pan over medium-high heat. As soon as the first batch of noodles have drained, place them in the sauté pan and cook, shaking the pan occasionally, until the noodles have browned on all sides. Shake the noodles into a serving bowl and repeat with more butter for the next batch. Proceed until all the noodles have been used.

10 Serve the noodles together with the Sauerkraut. Leftover Sauerkraut can be refrigerated for several days and reheated with a splash of water in a pot. Leftover noodles can be refrigerated for a few days and revived by sautéeing them in some melted butter.

KARTOFFELN MIT FRANKFURTER GRÜNE SOβE

Potatoes with Creamy Green Herb Sauce

SERVES 3 TO 4

3 eggs

2 cups / 500g low-fat yogurt

2 Tbsp Dijon or
    yellow mustard

2 Tbsp olive oil

2 Tbsp white wine vinegar

1 tsp salt

1 tsp sugar

Juice of ½ lemon

7 oz / 200g mixed herbs
    (if possible, they should be
    borage, watercress, sorrel,
    chervil, chives, parsley,
    and burnet)

Boiled potatoes for serving

Boiled eggs for serving,
    optional

Legend has it that this dish of boiled potatoes served in a deep puddle of dairy-rich, herbaceous sauce was the favorite meal of Johann Wolfgang von Goethe, a native son of Frankfurt. The sauce must be made with a mix of seven specific herbs: borage, watercress, sorrel, chervil, chives, parsley, and salad or garden burnet (which tastes remarkably like cucumber, giving it the alternative nickname of Gurkenkraut, or "cucumber weed"). White paper-wrapped bundles of these specific herbs are sold at markets every spring with varying ratios of herbs depending on the weekly harvest. It's traditional to serve this dish, and other green ones such as Hessian Grüner Kuchen—a recipe for which is in my previous book, *Classic German Baking*—on Maundy Thursday, which is called Gründonnerstag, or Green Thursday, in Germany.

The most traditional recipes for Grüne Soße call for sour cream, or even sour cream mixed with mayonnaise, for the base of the sauce, but I fell for this version from my friend Lena Schimmelbusch, who is a native Hessian. Lena uses low-fat yogurt as its base, arguing that the lean yogurt adds an additional fresh and sour flavor to the sauce. And I must say that after making it Lena's way, I'm a convert. The yogurt lets the flavors of the herbs shine through and also allows you to really pile the sauce on your plate, because it's not too heavy or rich.

But if there's one thing I've learned in writing this book, it's that German cooking is far more flexible and Germans are far less doctrinaire about their recipes than their Italian or French neighbors. If you prefer a richer base, use whole milk yogurt or even sour cream. You can leave the eggs out of the sauce or, instead of chopping them up, serve them whole with the boiled potatoes, covered with the sauce. Finally, yes, if you can't find every single one of the seven classic herbs required for this dish, you can come up with your own combination.

This recipe is easily doubled or even tripled. While it is most famously paired with boiled potatoes as a meal, you can also serve Grüne Soße with thin slices of Tafelspitz (page 147) or fried fish.

1   First, bring a small pot of water to a boil and cook the eggs until hard-boiled, about 9 minutes. Drain and plunge into a bowl of cold water. Set aside.

2   Place the yogurt in a large bowl. Whisk in the mustard, oil, vinegar, salt, sugar, and lemon juice. Taste and adjust the seasoning if you want it sharper or saltier.

3   Wash and dry the herbs and stem them. Pulse them in a food processor until finely minced. (You can also do this by hand.)

4   Peel and chop the eggs, then mix them into the yogurt.

5   Fold in the herbs. Adjust the seasoning. The sauce can be refrigerated for up to 8 hours or served right away with boiled potatoes and boiled eggs, if desired.

ERDÄPFELGULASCH

Austrian Potato Paprika Stew

SERVES 4

1 Tbsp unsalted butter

1 Tbsp vegetable oil

2 medium onions, minced

1 tsp salt

2 garlic cloves, peeled and
    crushed

1 Tbsp sweet paprika

3 Tbsp tomato paste

1 tsp dried marjoram

1 tsp caraway seeds, optional

2 cups / 500ml vegetable broth

2.2 lb / 1kg waxy potatoes, like
    Yukon Gold, peeled and cut
    into bite-size pieces

1 Tbsp white wine vinegar

Freshly ground black pepper

2 Tbsp sour cream

4 Wiener sausages or an
    equivalent amount of
    kielbasa, sliced into 1-inch
    / 2.5cm pieces, optional

My German husband, true to form, has never met a potato dish he hasn't liked, and this rich and hearty Austrian potato Gulasch, which can be made vegetarian by withholding the sliced sausages at the end, may be his favorite. (Just don't tell the potato strudel from my previous cookbook, *Classic German Baking.*) Ground paprika and tomato paste give the stew its gorgeous rusty color, and marjoram, caraway, and onions layer flavor upon flavor. Vinegar and sour cream both brighten and smooth out the gravy. This is the perfect meal for cold, gray days.

It's quite important to make sure you use waxy potatoes, not starchy ones, so that the potato chunks keep their shape and integrity during the cooking. Starchy potatoes will fall apart and soak up too much of the delicious cooking broth, which you want to be able to spoon up from a deep soup plate.

Paprika turns bitter if it burns, so take care when adding it to the stew, letting it cook only briefly in the fat before adding the tomato paste. If necessary, lower the heat while doing so. Once you add the broth, you're in the clear. You can keep this vegetarian, if you like, or add sausages at the end.

1   Place the butter and oil in a large pot over medium heat. When the butter has melted, add the onions and salt, stir well, and cook for 5 to 7 minutes. Don't let the onions brown. Add the garlic. Stir and cook for another 2 minutes.

2   Add the paprika and stir well, letting it bloom briefly in the cooking fat, then add the tomato paste and stir well. Cook for 2 minutes, stirring constantly. Add the marjoram and caraway, if using, and mix well. Add the broth and stir to combine. As soon as the mixture starts bubbling, add the potatoes. Lower the heat, cover, and simmer for about 25 minutes, until the potatoes are completely tender but not falling apart.

3   Add the vinegar and the pepper to taste, then simmer for 5 minutes more. Remove from the heat and stir in the sour cream. If using the sausage, stir in and let sit for 5 minutes to heat through before serving.

KARTOFFELPUFFER

Potato Pancakes

MAKES 13 (3½-INCH /
9CM) PANCAKES

2.2 lb / 1kg waxy potatoes,
    like Yukon Gold, peeled
1 large onion (about 100g),
    peeled
1½ Tbsp salt
Freshly ground black pepper
30 scrapes freshly grated
    nutmeg
3 Tbsp all-purpose flour
2 eggs
Vegetable oil for frying
Applesauce for serving
Kräuterquark (page 33)
    for serving
Smoked salmon for serving
    (optional)

Is there any dish more German than the potato pancake? There seem to be as many recipes for potato pancakes out there as there are German home cooks. Depending on the region, potato pancakes can be called everything from Kartoffelpuffer to Reibekuchen or Rievkooche or Reiberdatschi, from Baggers to Bambes, Krumberkiechelcher to Klitscher (among others). The general agreement, no matter what part of Germany you're from, is that you're meant to use grated raw potatoes as the base of the potato pancake and that the most popular accompaniment to them is applesauce. (They're also very good with smoked salmon, herbed Quark [page 33], a tangle of braised Sauerkraut, or tangy lingonberry preserves.)

This recipe creates potato pancakes so crisp, savory, and delicious that every German I've served them to has said they're better than their grandmother's. I'm not sure there is higher praise to be had! They're irresistible still hot from the pan, eaten standing up at the counter. But I've also served them at room temperature at picnics and garnered ravishing praise for them. I use a food processor to grate my potatoes, so I can get them grated in seconds. There are those who insist on grating them by hand; to me, it doesn't end up making enough of a difference in the final product. So, food processor it is. If you don't have one, never fear! Just use the largest holes on a box grater, and try to work quickly so the potatoes don't have too much time to oxidize. I think including an onion is nonnegotiable for the delicate savory flavor it adds, securing these pancakes firmly in the realm of main course or snack. I also believe grated nutmeg makes for superior potato pancakes, because the flavors of nutmeg and potatoes were made for each other.

Most importantly, we should discuss squeezing out the grated potatoes. There are those who say that the grated potatoes must be squeezed out before proceeding with the rest of the recipe, because otherwise the water they cast out as they sit will ruin the pancakes. I tried many recipes and kept finding this process overly onerous, eventually coming to the following conclusion: If you work quickly and skip squeezing out the potatoes at the beginning, yes, your batter will become watery as you shape and cook the first few batches of pancakes. But all you have to do is gently squeeze out the water as you form your patties before slipping them into the hot pan. It's less work and, perhaps more importantly, is less of a barrier to making these delightful pancakes in the first place.

You can substitute a gluten-free flour blend for the flour.

1   Place a cooling rack over a sheet pan and set this next to the stove.

2   Using a food processor fitted with a shredder attachment with small holes, shred all the potatoes. Dump them in a large bowl. Holding a box grater over the potatoes, grate in the onion so as not to lose a drop of juice or onion. Add the salt, pepper, nutmeg, flour, and eggs. Using your hands, mix everything together until well-combined.

3   Place a well-seasoned cast-iron or nonstick skillet over medium-high heat and add enough oil to come up about ⅛ inch / 3mm on the sides of the pan. When the pan is hot, scoop out three or four equal portions (about a handful each) of the potato mixture and place them in the pan, patting them down so that they are about even in thickness. Lower the heat to medium.

4   Cook for 3 to 4 minutes on one side, then flip and press down gently. Cook them for another 4 minutes, then flip again. Continue to cook and flip until both sides are an even, deep golden brown, about 12 minutes total (6 minutes per side). Regulate the heat as you go so that the pancakes don't brown too quickly, which could leave the center raw, or cook too slowly and inadvertently absorb too much oil. Remove the pancakes and place them on the cooling rack.

5   If necessary, add a bit more oil to the pan and repeat with the next three or four portions of potato mixture. As the pancakes cook, liquid will start to accumulate in the bowl of raw potatoes. Just gently squeeze out the excess liquid of the portions as you go, so that when you place the portions in the pan, they always have about the same level of moisture. (Discard the excess liquid at the end of the cooking process.) Continue to cook, adding more oil if necessary, until all of the pancakes have been fried.

6   Serve the pancakes with applesauce, Kräuterquark, and/or smoked salmon.

SAUERKRAUTPUFFER MIT KRÄUTERSCHMAND

Sauerkraut-Potato Pancakes with Herbed Sour Cream

MAKES 12 PANCAKES

1.3 lb / 600g (about 4 large) starchy potatoes, like Russet, peeled

10.5 oz / 300g Sauerkraut, drained if in liquid

2 eggs

2 Tbsp unseasoned bread crumbs

2 Tbsp potato starch

2 tsp salt, plus a pinch for the sour cream

Freshly ground black pepper

½ tsp ground caraway

¼ tsp sugar

Clarified butter for frying

Minced chives for serving

Sour cream for serving

I'd never eaten these Sauerkraut-potato pancakes before working on this cookbook, but once I came across them, I was smitten. The Sauerkraut gives the pancakes a deeper, more complex flavor, as well as a wonderfully chewy texture. I like serving them as an unexpected appetizer (try to get your guests to guess the secret ingredient) with a bowl of chive-flecked sour cream to dip them into.

Since this recipe calls for just four large potatoes, you can skip the food processor here in favor of grating them by hand. If your Sauerkraut comes packed in liquid, drain it before adding the Sauerkraut to the grated potatoes. Some people even rinse the Sauerkraut to lessen the acidic bite. But to me, that's what Sauerkraut is all about, so I never rinse it. To give these pancakes a little bit of ballast, potato starch and bread crumbs are added, plus a bit of ground caraway, which is marvelous combined with both potatoes and cabbage.

I like to fry the patties in clarified butter, which has a higher smoke point than regular butter, and adds richness and flavor. If you can't find clarified butter, use vegetable oil.

1 Grate the potatoes on the largest holes of a box grater placed over a mixing bowl. Squeeze out the potatoes as best you can with your hands, then pour off the liquid.

2 Using a fork, loosen the Sauerkraut and mix it into the grated potatoes. Mix in 1 egg at a time. Add the bread crumbs and potato starch and mix thoroughly.

3 Mix in the salt, pepper, caraway, and sugar.

4 Heat two spoonfuls of clarified butter in a well-seasoned cast-iron or nonstick pan over medium-high heat. Scoop out four portions of batter into the pan and press down firmly on each one. Cook for about 5 minutes on one side, until golden brown, regulating the heat so that they don't burn, then flip and cook the other side for 4 to 5 minutes, pressing down once again. If necessary, add a bit more clarified butter to the pan as you cook.

5 Place on a serving platter and repeat with more clarified butter and the remaining batter.

KASPRESSKNÖDEL

Pan-Fried Cheesy Bread Dumplings

MAKES 13 DUMPLINGS

6 stale Kaiser or hard white
    rolls (about 13 oz / 380g
    total)
2 Tbsp unsalted butter
2 medium onions,
    finely minced
1 tsp salt
Medium handful of flat-leaf
    parsley, finely minced,
    optional
Freshly ground black pepper
25 scrapes of whole nutmeg
1 cup / 250ml whole milk
3 eggs
7 oz / 200g Alpine cheese,
    grated
Clarified butter or vegetable
    oil for frying
Beef or vegetable broth for
    serving, optional
Minced chives for serving

My husband comes from a family of athletes who spend their free time moving their bodies outdoors in a variety of different ways. I come from a family of readers who spend their free time prone with a book. He indulges my family's ways each summer on the beach in Italy; I indulge his by agreeing to go skiing with him in Austria for a week each winter. Marriage is all about compromise, isn't it?

While I came to skiing later in life and do not, in fact, consider it the pinnacle of outdoor movement, there are worse things than spending a week in Austria each year in the depths of winter, which happens to be the perfect time to indulge in the best of Austrian comfort food. We each have our favorite Austrian dishes that we look forward to ordering after a morning of exertion on the slopes: my husband loves a piping hot plate of Tiroler Gröstl, which are like Bratkartoffeln (page 211) topped with fried eggs; my older son adores golden bowls of aromatic Frittatensuppe (page 69); my younger son would eat Wiener Schnitzel (page 142) every day if he could. As for me, my ideal Austrian lunch is one perfect cheesy-toasty Kaspressknödel floating in a pool of amber beef broth flecked with chives.

A Kaspressknödel is a patty made of cubed bread and grated aromatic cheese, bound together with a mix of sautéed onions, eggs, and minced parsley, then fried in a pan until crusty and melting at the same time. The flavors are reminiscent of a grilled cheese that died and went to heaven. While most dumplings are poached in liquid first, Kaspressknödel are first shaped and fried, and *then* slipped into broth (or eaten with a salad and no broth). Kas is Austrian dialect for cheese and a Pressknödel is a squashed and fried dumpling rather than a round, poached one.

On the Austrian government's website for the national ministry of farming and forestry, regions and water management (that just rolls off the tongue, doesn't it?), I learned that Kaspressknödel are typical for the entire Alpine region of Austria; the only thing that differs from province to province is the type of cheese used. It may not be easy for you to find Salzburgian Bierkäse or Tyrolean Bergkäse, though if you can, you should use them here. Acceptable substitutes are Swiss Gruyère or Emmentaler and French Cantal or Comté.

In Austria, every baker and grocery store sells enormous bags of Knödelbrot, or cubed dried bread specifically for dumplings. Since we can't get that here, I use stale Kaiser or white rolls instead.

CONTINUED

1   First, cut the rolls into ½-inch / 1.3cm cubes. Place the cubed rolls in a large bowl.

2   Next, melt the butter in a small sauté pan over medium heat and add the onions and salt. Cook, stirring occasionally, for 5 to 8 minutes, until the onions are glassy and fragrant but not browning. Remove from the heat, add the parsley, and stir well. Scrape the onions into the bowl with the bread. Season to taste with pepper and add the nutmeg.

3   Place the milk in a bowl and whisk in the eggs until completely smooth. Pour this mixture evenly over the bread and, using your hands, toss lightly until all of the cubes are evenly moistened and the ingredients are well-distributed.

4   Add the cheese to the bowl, mixing lightly to evenly distribute the cheese. Now gently pack down the mixture and set aside for 5 to 10 minutes.

5   Place a well-seasoned cast-iron or nonstick pan over medium heat and melt a knob of clarified butter or use a couple of spoonfuls of vegetable oil.

6   Using your hands, shape four dumplings out of the mixture, 3 inches / 7.5cm across and about 1 to 1½ inches / 2.5 to 4cm thick. Smooth the sides of the dumplings, then place them in the hot pan, pressing down gently. Cook for 3 to 4 minutes on one side, then flip and cook for another 3 to 4 minutes on the other side. Flip again and cook for another minute or two. The dumplings should be a deep golden brown and slightly crisp on the outside and soft and gooey on the inside.

7   Place the dumplings on a serving platter and repeat with the next batch, adding more butter or oil to the pan. If you plan to serve these in broth, heat it up now. Serve two dumplings per person in a ladleful or two of broth and a sprinkle of chives on top.

SELLERIESCHNITZEL MIT REMOULADENSOßE

Celery Root Cutlets with Remoulade

SERVES 4

FOR THE REMOULADE

½ cup plus 2 Tbsp / 150g sour
    cream
1 tsp yellow or Dijon mustard
2 Tbsp capers, chopped
1 dill pickle, chopped
2 handfuls of flat-leaf parsley,
    minced
Juice of ½ lemon
Salt and freshly ground
    black pepper
2 hard-boiled eggs, minced

FOR THE CUTLETS

1 large celery root
1 cup / 125g all-purpose flour,
    plus more as needed
1 egg
2 Tbsp milk
1 cup / 110g unseasoned
    bread crumbs, plus
    more as needed
1 tsp salt
Vegetable oil for frying

Celery root cutlets sound so hopelessly 1970s, don't they? When I think about them, I envision musty health food stores stocked with bendy carrots and bulk bins of buckwheat groats. It doesn't help that they often show up as the mirthless vegetarian option at canteens and cafeterias. But I gained a new appreciation of them after eating them at my friend Joanie's house; she made them for lunch for me and her husband, Dietrich, and they were crisp, brightly seasoned with a generous squeeze of lemon, and so tasty when dragged through a sharply flavored remoulade on the side.

In Germany, celery root is as common as celery stalks are in the United States. It has a unique flavor—delicate, yet also both herbal and meaty—and, when cooked, it has a surprisingly creamy texture. In this preparation, thick rounds of celery root are blanched, then breaded and fried, creating a crunchy coating. They're enlivened with a squeeze of lemon juice and served with a dollop of creamy remoulade sauce. (If you like remoulade, earmark this recipe to serve with Tafelspitz [page 147], cold slices of Schweinebraten [page 137], or fried fish.)

1   First, make the remoulade: Place the sour cream in a medium bowl and add the mustard, capers, pickle, parsley, lemon juice, ½ tsp of salt, and the pepper. Add the eggs to the bowl. Stir everything together until well-combined. Set aside.

2   Make the cutlets: Peel the celery root with a knife and slice crosswise into ½-inch / 1 cm slices. Select the eight nicest slices and set aside. Cube the remaining celery root and set aside or freeze for another use.

3   Bring a large pot of salted water to a boil. Place the celery rounds in the pot and bring it back to a boil. Cook for 5 minutes, until just tender, then drain and set aside.

4   Set out three soup plates or shallow bowls. Place the flour in the first, whisk together the egg and milk in the second, and place the bread crumbs and salt in the third, stirring carefully to mix.

5   Working with one piece of celery root at a time, dredge it in the flour first, being sure to tap or brush off the excess—you want just a very thin coating on the celery root—then turn it in the egg wash, then place it in the bread crumbs, making sure the bread crumbs coat the entire slice. Set aside. Repeat with the remaining pieces.

6   Set a well-seasoned cast-iron skillet or nonstick pan over medium heat and add 2 Tbsp of oil. When the oil is hot, carefully slip in as many celery root cutlets as will fit. Cook until golden brown on both sides, about 5 minutes per side. Remove from the pan and repeat with more oil and the remaining cutlets. Serve immediately with the remoulade sauce.

SERVIETTENKNÖDEL MIT PILZGULASCH

Bread Dumplings with Mushroom Goulash

SERVES 8

FOR THE KNÖDEL

10.5 oz / 300g stale white
    bread, Kaiser rolls,
    or Brötchen
¾ cup / 200ml whole milk
2 tsp salt
40 scrapes of whole nutmeg
3 eggs
4½ Tbsp / 70ml heavy cream
3 Tbsp unsalted butter
1 medium onion, finely minced
Handful of flat-leaf parsley,
    minced
Freshly ground black pepper

FOR THE GOULASH

3 Tbsp unsalted butter
3 Tbsp vegetable oil
2 medium onions, minced
1½ tsp salt, plus more
    as needed
3 Tbsp sweet paprika
¼ cup / 60ml apple
    cider vinegar
¼ cup / 60ml vegetable broth
    or water
3.5 lb / 1.6kg mushrooms,
    washed and cut into bite-
    size pieces
Freshly ground black pepper
¾ cup plus 1 Tbsp / 200g sour
    cream

This dish is festive and absolutely dinner party–worthy. The goulash can be made with whatever mushrooms are currently available to you, though chanterelles are probably the most elegant ones you could use. Chanterelles are called Pfifferlinge (FIFF-er-ling-uh) in German, just one of many words that prove how lovely the German language can be. Austrians call them Eierschwammerl. Chanterelle season in Germany is a little like white asparagus season; the mushrooms appear between June and October (approximately) in grocery stores and green markets, on special chanterelle-themed menus at restaurants, and even in boxes outside of people's houses in the countryside where they've foraged for them to sell to passersby. If you have a good source for fresh chanterelles, you can make this stew exclusively with them. But at a dinner party I recently threw for a group of girlfriends, I used a mix of button, oyster, king oyster, and portobello mushrooms and the combination of textures, sizes, and flavors was delightful, too.

It is traditional to serve bread dumplings with this rust-colored, creamy mushroom stew. The two dumpling options are Semmelknödel or Serviettenknödel. Their ingredients are the same, but Semmelknödel (page 222) are shaped into round dumplings and then poached directly in salted water, while Serviettenknödel are shaped into a log, wrapped in a kitchen towel, poached, then unwrapped, sliced, and served. During the research for this book, however, I stumbled upon an oven-baked version that intrigued me because it swapped out the poaching steps for a simple bake in the oven. The oven version makes slightly more compact dumpling slices, while poaching them leaves them a bit airier and moister. Since you're using the Knödel to soak up the delicious gravy, I think a slightly more compact dumpling slice is delicious. But if you'd like, try both and see what you prefer!

No matter what kind of dumpling you make, you need to know what to do with leftover bread dumplings: Knödelgröstl! (The adorable contraction of geröstete Knödel, or fried dumplings.) To start, let any leftover dumplings cool to room temperature, then cover them and refrigerate. The next day, slice them into ½ inch / 1cm slices. Melt some butter in a sauté pan and fry the sliced dumplings until golden brown on each side. You could stop here, or, while the dumplings are browning, add minced onions and minced Speck to the pan for a bit more flavor. Then add a few beaten eggs to the pan, letting them set a bit before flipping and frying until the eggs are cooked and the dumpling pieces are golden brown. Shower with some minced parsley and chives and serve.

CONTINUED

VEGETARIAN MAIN COURSES   *111*

1   Preheat the oven to 400°F / 200°C. Cut the bread into slices as thinly as possible or cut into ¼ inch / 6mm cubes and place in a very large bowl.

2   Either on the stove or in a microwave, heat the milk with the salt and nutmeg until it just starts to boil. Pour over the bread and toss briefly. Let sit for 10 minutes.

3   In a small bowl, whisk together the eggs and cream.

4   In a small sauté pan over medium heat, melt the butter and add the onion. Cook, stirring occasionally, until the onion is glassy and fragrant, about 5 minutes. It shouldn't brown too much. Add the parsley and the pepper to taste to the pan and stir well.

5   Pour the egg mixture into the bowl with the bread and scrape in the cooked onions and drippings.

6   Stir the bread mixture to combine, but do not press or squeeze the bread. You want the bread to be evenly moistened and the ingredients to be well-distributed.

7   Place two large squares of parchment paper on a work surface. Divide the bread mixture evenly between the two pieces. Shape the bread into even rolls that are 3 inches / 7.5cm thick and 10 inches / 25cm long. Roll them tightly in the parchment paper, then wrap each roll in an additional layer of aluminum foil so that it can't unroll.

8   Place the rolls on a rack in the middle of the oven and bake for 30 minutes, then turn off the oven and let the rolls sit in the oven for an additional 10 minutes.

9   While the Knödel are baking, make the goulash: Place the butter and oil in a large pot over medium heat. When hot, add the onions and ½ tsp of salt. Cook, stirring occasionally, until glassy and fragrant, about 5 minutes.

10   Add the paprika and stir well to moisten completely, then immediately pour in the vinegar. Stir well, then add the broth. As soon as it's bubbling, add the mushrooms and the remaining 1 tsp of salt and the pepper to taste. Stir, cover, and lower the heat. Simmer for 10 minutes, stirring occasionally. Taste and adjust the seasoning if necessary.

11   Remove from the heat and stir in the sour cream.

12   Unwrap the Knödel rolls and slice into 1-inch / 2.5cm slices. Serve immediately with the mushroom goulash.

SPARGEL MIT KRATZETE UND HOLLANDAISE

White Asparagus with Herbed Pancakes and Hollandaise Sauce

SERVES 4

FOR THE KRATZETE

4 eggs

1½ cups plus 1 Tbsp / 375ml
 whole milk

Scant 1⅔ cups / 200g
 all-purpose flour

¾ tsp salt

Small handful of flat-leaf
 parsley, finely minced

Small bunch of chives, finely
 minced

Butter for cooking

Club soda

4.4 lb / 2kg white asparagus

Salt

FOR THE HOLLANDAISE

2 egg yolks

1 Tbsp plain whole milk yogurt
 or sour cream

½ tsp salt

Juice of ½ lemon

11½ Tbsps / 160g unsalted
 butter

White asparagus season, colloquially known as Spargelzeit in Germany, is a brief window of time each spring when German white asparagus is harvested and eaten by the kilo. The season usually begins in mid-April, though the exact start date is determined by the length of the winter, but it always ends on Saint John the Baptist's birthday, June 24. During that time, white asparagus appears in markets, on special menus at restaurants, and in people's homes, then vanishes entirely once the season is over. Germans insist on peeling white asparagus, which makes the cooked spears silky. But the peeling is onerous if you're used to simply snapping the ends off green asparagus and tossing them in the oven to roast. Still, for a few brief weeks a year, Germans are more than happy to pay top Euro for bags of the plump stalks and to stand over a countertop peeling them.

The most classic way of cooking white asparagus is to boil them in salted water and plate them with a few boiled new potatoes and a creamy dollop of hollandaise sauce. Depending on your taste or hunger, you can add a few thin slices of cured ham, cooked ham—my preference, since the texture pairs better with the asparagus—or a crisp Schnitzel to the plate. (Ham was also traditionally a spring treat after being cured all winter, appearing around the same time the first asparagus was harvested.) In some regions, the hollandaise is eschewed for a simpler accompaniment: melted or browned butter.

In Baden, white asparagus is most traditionally served with Kratzete, a simple pancake batter that is mixed and fried on one side, then torn into pieces in the pan and browned and crisped all over. I like this slightly elevated version with chopped herbs for a brighter flavor. Whatever side you end up making, I hope you will try the hollandaise made with an immersion blender; it is a swift and simple way to make this classic emulsified sauce, which pairs so beautifully with everything on the plate, no matter the configuration.

1   To make the Kratzete: In a large bowl, whisk together the eggs, then whisk in the milk, flour, and salt. Whisk the herbs into the batter. Set aside at room temperature, covered, for 30 minutes.

2   While the batter is resting, cook the asparagus. Bring a large pot of salted water to a boil over high heat. Cut off the woody ends of the asparagus, then place the peeler on the just-cut end of the asparagus and peel upward. Repeat with the remaining asparagus.

3   When the water is boiling, place the peeled asparagus in the water and cover the pot. Lower the heat and let the asparagus cook, just simmering, for 10 to 12 minutes. The asparagus should be tender and silky. Drain carefully and place the asparagus on a serving platter.

4   While the asparagus is cooking, prepare the hollandaise: Put the egg yolks and yogurt in a medium bowl and use an immersion blender to blend them together (you can also use a stand blender). Add the salt and lemon juice. Blend again.

5   In a small pan or in the microwave, melt the butter. Pour the butter into a measuring cup with a spout. With the immersion blender running, very slowly drizzle the melted butter into the egg yolk mixture. Continue blending until the butter is completely incorporated and the mixture is thick and creamy. Taste and adjust the seasoning, if necessary. Set aside, but use within the next 30 minutes.

6   When ready to cook, melt a small knob of butter in a 10-inch / 25cm nonstick skillet over medium heat. Pour a splash of club soda into the batter just to aerate it, mix briefly, then immediately pour one-third of the batter into the hot pan. Cook for about 2 minutes, until the pancake is set, then flip it. Don't worry if the pancake breaks. Cook on the other side for another minute, then, using two wooden spoons, tear the pancake into 2- to 3-inch / 5 to 7.5cm pieces. Add a bit more butter to the pan, if necessary, and let the pancake shreds crisp up for another minute or so. Scrape them onto a serving plate, wipe out the pan, and repeat with the remaining batter two more times.

7   Serve the torn pancake with the boiled asparagus and hollandaise sauce.

MEAT & FISH

What sets this chapter apart from the others in this book is its length; there is no getting around the fact that traditional German cuisine features a lot of meat. But what a paradox, when one considers the fact that for hundreds of years, for a wide section of the German populace, meat was largely out of reach. From the start of the twentieth century to now, the availability of meat as an integral part of the diet waxed and waned with the political fortunes of the country. Two World Wars, the economic troubles of the 1920s, and the utter devastation of Germany at the end of the Third Reich meant that, for the first half of the twentieth century, meat was scarce, and hunger lurked constantly. Once the Second World War and the first few terrible postwar years were over, West Germany, aided greatly by the United States, transformed itself into an economic powerhouse, and with that success came food.

The recipes in this chapter are a collection of twentieth-century favorites, the kinds of meals that were cooked by housewives who were thrifty and careful home economists (and who had direct memories of begging for food, eating a rare stolen or gifted potato, and gathering stinging nettles for sustenance after the war), as well as older traditional meals that had been a part of the culinary canon for the bourgeoisie, aristocrats, and even royalty in earlier times. Many of the recipes are examples of what Germans call Hausmannskost, sturdy home-cooked fare that the average German family ate on weekends (as weekday lunches were often consumed in canteens or cafeterias, and dinner was usually Abendbrot), and there is quite a bit of Austro-Hungarian influence, from Schnitzel (page 142) to stuffed peppers (page 123), cabbage rolls (page 139) to Tafelspitz (page 147).

Some of you will note that there is a dearth of sausage recipes in this chapter. It isn't always easy to find good-quality German sausages outside of Germany, especially regional specialties. But I also wanted to show that German cooking is a lot more than just sausages and Sauerkraut, as it is so often depicted. In fact, besides the odd Wiener Würstchen that my children insist I include in lentil and potato soups, we rarely eat sausages at home. We, like many families in Germany, are far more likely to consume Thüringer Bratwürste grilled and stuffed into a crusty bun at an outdoor market, or Berlin Currywurst cloaked in curry-flavored ketchup and eaten at an Imbiss (snack stand), or Bavarian Weißwürste with sweet mustard and soft pretzels for breakfast while visiting Munich.

In this chapter, you will find meals for weeknights as well as special occasions, regional specialties as well as dishes that most Germans would consider a national dish. There is something here for every skill level. The recipes that follow best illustrate the influences that German cuisine has absorbed over the centuries, from the west, the east, the north, and the south, but also show you the influence that German and Austrian cuisine has had elsewhere. Here are meals for both comfort and celebration.

BULETTEN

Savory Meat Patties

MAKES 16 PATTIES

½ cup / 60g unseasoned bread
  crumbs
¼ cup / 60ml whole milk
2 small shallots or small
  onions, grated or very
  finely minced
2 eggs
1 lb / 500g ground beef
1 lb / 500g ground pork
2 tsp salt
2 tsp Dijon or yellow mustard
2 tsp dried marjoram
2 tsp sweet paprika
Freshly ground black pepper
Vegetable oil for frying

The French name (originally "boulette") of these seasoned meat patties betrays their provenance, though there is some dispute over whether they were introduced to German tables from French Huguenot refugees who sought asylum in Prussia after the Edict of Nantes was revoked in 1685 or from the occupation of Berlin by Napoleon's troops some two hundred years later. Either way, the Bulette or Boulette swiftly became one of Berlin's most treasured recipes. It has numerous other names depending on what region of Germany you're in: Fleischpflanzerl in Bavaria, Frikadelle in the north, and Fleischküchle in Swabia. But since I'm a Berliner, they'll always be Buletten to me.

Traditionally Buletten are made with a mix of beef and pork and aggressively seasoned with sautéed onions, mustard, and marjoram. I think paprika adds a nice warmth. They can be eaten hot or cold, large or small; they make good leftovers; and they are crowd-pleasers. When my neighbors make Buletten, they often ring our doorbell to share a little plate of them with us. Buletten are usually served with mustard and a soft little bun or a Brötchen.

1 Mix the bread crumbs and milk together in a large bowl. Set aside for 5 minutes.

2 Add the shallots, eggs, both meats, and seasonings to the bread crumbs. With your hands, mix well until all the ingredients are evenly distributed and the mixture is smooth and combined.

3 Shape the mixture into sixteen patties, 3 to 4 inches / 7.5 to 10cm in diameter. You can also make smaller patties for finger food (subtract a few minutes from the cooking time).

4 Heat 2 Tbsp of oil in a 10-inch / 25cm skillet over medium-high heat and, working in batches, fry the patties. Do not crowd the pan. Sear on one side for 2 to 3 minutes, until brown, then flip and sear an additional 2 to 3 minutes, until brown. Then lower the heat and cook for 8 to 10 minutes more, flipping once in between, until cooked through.

5 Place the cooked patties on a serving plate and repeat with the remaining meat, adding more oil if necessary, and wiping out the pan in between if necessary.

KÖNIGSBERGER KLOPSE

Meatballs in Lemon-Caper Sauce

SERVES 4 TO 6

FOR THE MEATBALLS

2 stale white rolls or 100g
   white bread
1.1 lb / 500g ground beef
1.1 lb / 500g ground pork
6 anchovy fillets, minced
2 small onions, finely minced
2 eggs
Grated zest of 1 lemon
1½ tsp salt
Freshly ground white pepper

FOR THE BROTH

6 cups / 1.5L water
1 Tbsp salt
2 bay leaves
1 small onion, halved
10 whole black peppercorns

FOR THE SAUCE

4 Tbsp / 60g unsalted butter
½ cup / 60g all-purpose flour
½ cup / 60g drained capers
   in brine
Juice of 1 lemon
1 tsp Dijon mustard
2 egg yolks
Pinch of sugar
Salt
Freshly ground white pepper
Salzkartoffeln (page 209) or
   mashed potatoes (page 210)
   and Red Beet Salad
   (page 48) for serving

Conduct an informal poll in Berlin about people's favorite dishes and Königsberger Klopse are guaranteed to be in everyone's top five. This dish of delicate meatballs blanketed in a creamy lemon-caper sauce originated in what used to be East Prussia (its capital, Königsberg, is now Kaliningrad and belongs to Russia) and is evergreen on restaurant and canteen menus in Berlin and the surrounding region. Klopse, a Prussian term for "little meatballs," were even immortalized in a 1925 song in Berlin dialect written by Kurt Weill.

I was lucky enough to be given this recipe by two family friends, Tina and Christoph Müller-Stüler, both excellent home cooks. Shortly after moving to Berlin, I was invited over to their cozy 1920s house near Krumme Lanke to make Königsberger Klopse together. We looked through their appealingly stained and dog-eared cookbook collection until we found the Klops recipe they've been using for years, amended with a ballpoint pen each time they got a little closer to perfecting the recipe.

Tina and Christoph's tricks for delicious Königsberger Klopse include using softened bread instead of bread crumbs for a nice fluffy texture, adding grated lemon zest to the meat mixture to lighten it, and doubling the number of capers in the sauce, since they make every bite more savory and delectable. Their recipe results in brighter, more fully flavored Klopse while still retaining its traditional soul. Königsberger Klopse are best served with mashed potatoes (page 210) and beet salad (page 48), to soak up every drop of sauce and chase each stray caper.

While we cooked together, Christoph told me about his childhood in Berlin. He had been a very little boy when the war ended and, like so many others, had suffered from terrible hunger in the first postwar years. During that time, he was sent to live with his aunts in the countryside, the hope being that more food would be available there than in the destroyed city. Each day, Christoph and his aunts made the rounds of neighboring houses and fields looking for scraps of food, like an egg or a stray potato, relying entirely on the charity of the farmers and their meager harvest. He told these harrowing stories in his gentle voice as he stood over the stove, elbow deep in raw meat, aromatic Klops broth steaming up the windows.

Now, whenever I make Königsberger Klopse, I do so with conscious gratitude for the kindness and friendship of people such as Tina and Christoph and with a heartfelt prayer for peace.

CONTINUED

KÖNIGSBERGER KLOPSE
continued

1　Make the meatballs: Cut off the crisp outer skin of the rolls or the crusts of the bread. Soak the bread in cold water to cover for 10 minutes. Drain, then squeeze the bread as best you can and pluck the crumb into small pieces. Place in a large bowl with the meat. Add the anchovies, onion, eggs, and zest. Season with the salt and white pepper and mix well with your hands until everything is well-combined. Set aside.

2　Make the broth: Place the water in a large pot. Add the salt, bay leaves, onion, and peppercorns. Bring to a boil, then turn down the heat to a simmer.

3　While the water is coming to a boil, shape the meat mixture into 1½ inch / 4cm balls and set aside. When the water is at a simmer, gently place the meatballs in the water. Cover and let the meatballs cook very gently in the barely simmering water for about 20 minutes.

4　When finished cooking, take the meatballs out of the water with a slotted spoon and place in a covered dish to keep warm. Strain the broth into a separate pot or container. Measure out 3 cups.

5　Make the sauce: First, melt the butter in a medium saucepan. Whisk in the flour and cook, stirring, for about 3 minutes, until pale golden. Whisk the 3 cups of reserved broth into the roux until smooth. Add the capers, lemon juice, and mustard. Let simmer for about 5 minutes, whisking frequently.

6　Beat the egg yolks in a small bowl, then, off the heat, add to the sauce, whisking. Add the pinch of sugar and the salt and white pepper to taste. Adjust the seasoning as desired. The sauce should be smooth and silky.

7　Pour the sauce over the meatballs and serve immediately with Salzkartoffeln or mashed potatoes and red beet salad.

GEFÜLLTE PAPRIKA

Stuffed Peppers

MAKES 8 PEPPERS

1 stale Kaiser or dinner roll

6 Tbsp olive oil, plus more
    for drizzling

4 yellow onions, minced

1 Tbsp salt, plus more
    for seasoning

3 Tbsp tomato paste

1 (24 oz / 690g) bottle tomato
    passata or 2 (14-oz)
    cans pureed tomatoes

1 tsp sugar

1 Tbsp red wine vinegar

1 large bay leaf

8 large bell peppers (ideally,
    a mix of red and yellow)

2 cups / 300g cooked white
    rice (if cooking from
    scratch, use ½ cup / 100g
    raw and you'll have a
    bit left over)

1 lb / 500g ground beef

1 lb / 500g ground pork

Handful of flat-leaf parsley,
    finely chopped

2 tsp dried marjoram

2 tsp sweet paprika

40 scrapes of whole nutmeg

Freshly ground black pepper

At my elementary school in Boston, lunch was something mostly to be endured—gloppy tuna fish salad on hot dog buns, pasty squares of pizza on Fridays, a lunch counter worker who said "hubba hubba" to all the little girls in line. When I got to my public school in Berlin, the lunch was an entirely different ball game. We were served traditional German food, like Kohlrouladen (page 139) with boiled potatoes and Milchreis (page 170) with cherry compote. The food was fresh, hot, and quite good. I was privately chagrined when, in tenth grade, my friends started leaving campus to buy sandwiches instead; I would have been happy to eat the cafeteria lunch every day. For some reason, the stuffed peppers made a particular impression on me.

The truth is, I have never met a stuffed pepper I didn't like. Many cultures have a stuffed pepper tradition, and from rice to bread crumb fillings, flavored with mint or cilantro, I love them all. This one has Austro-Hungarian roots, with paprika and marjoram for flavoring, and has been warmly welcomed into the German food canon for many years. My high school cafeteria's version only ever used green bell peppers, which I normally avoid. I tested this recipe with both green peppers and red and yellow ones and found that, while the green ones delivered on nostalgia, they were blander and less sweet than red and yellow ones. I had such fun developing this recipe and was so gratified to finally produce something that delivered a perfect time machine back to my high school lunches.

The peppers are baked nestled in a punchy tomato sauce, which provides brightness and acidity to the rich, meaty peppers.

1   Shave off the outer crust of the roll, then pour cold water over it and set aside for 10 minutes.

2   In a small sauté pan, heat 2 Tbsp of olive oil over medium-high heat and cook half of the onions with a pinch of salt, stirring occasionally, for about 5 minutes, until glossy and fragrant. Set aside to cool.

3   Next, make the sauce: Place the remaining 4 Tbsp of olive oil in a saucepan over medium-high heat and add the remaining half of the onions with a pinch of salt. Cook, stirring, until glossy and fragrant, about 5 minutes.

CONTINUED

GEFÜLLTE PAPRIKA
continued

4   Add the tomato paste to the pot and cook, stirring, until it loosens, then pour in the tomato passata. Bring to a simmer, then add another pinch of salt, the sugar, vinegar, and bay leaf. Lower the heat, cover, and simmer for about 15 minutes. Set aside.

5   Preheat the oven to 400°F / 200°C.

6   Prepare the peppers: Cut the tops off and reserve, then discard the seeds and ribs inside. Insert the tip of the knife into the bottom of each pepper to make a small slit (this helps the pepper release its liquid into the sauce as it cooks). Set aside.

7   In a large bowl, combine the rice, the cooled, reserved onions, the meat, parsley, marjoram, paprika, nutmeg, 1 Tbsp of salt, and black pepper to taste.

8   Squeeze out the roll as best you can, then pluck into pieces and add to the rice mixture. Using your hands, mix everything together until well-combined. If you like, pluck off a small piece to fry up in the same pan you sautéed the onions in to see if you like the seasoning.

9   Divide the filling evenly among the prepared peppers, then top with their lids. Pour the tomato sauce into a roasting pan large enough to fit all the peppers. Place the peppers on top of the sauce. Drizzle with a bit of olive oil, then cover the pan tightly with aluminum foil.

10   Bake the peppers for 45 minutes, then remove the aluminum foil and continue baking for another 15 minutes or so, until the peppers are blistered and tender. Remove from the oven and let cool for 15 minutes before serving. Make sure to serve each pepper with some of the sauce.

WIENER SAFTGULASCH

Austrian Beef Stew

SERVES 6

1 Tbsp baking soda

1½ cups / 350ml water

2.2 lb / 1kg beef stew meat, cut
    into 1-inch / 2.5cm pieces

¼ cup / 60ml vegetable oil
    or lard

2.2 lb / 1kg onions, diced

1½ tsp salt, plus more
    as needed

3 garlic cloves, crushed

3 Tbsp sweet paprika

2 Tbsp tomato paste

1 tsp ground caraway

2 tsp dried marjoram

1¾ cups / 400ml beef broth

1 Tbsp cornstarch

1 to 2 Tbsp apple cider vinegar
    or red wine vinegar,
    optional

Semmelknödel (page 222),
    Spätzle (page 93), or boiled
    egg noodles for serving

Gulasch, while clearly of Hungarian origin, has become one of the great classics of Austrian cuisine. What defines Austrian Gulasch are the equal amounts, by weight, of onions and meat and the main flavoring of ground paprika, with marjoram and ground caraway playing supporting, yet essential, roles. Its official name in Austria is Wiener Saftgulasch or Rindsgulasch, to set it apart from the many other types of Gulasch that abound, but Gulasch is how it's known in Germany. Despite its Austro-Hungarian pedigree, it features in the top ten favorite dishes of many Germans. It's a rich and savory meal, especially when paired with plump Semmelknödel (page 222) to soak up the copious amounts of delicious gravy. Though even plain boiled egg noodles are a good accompaniment; in my friend Maja Welker's family, those noodles are dusted with butter-toasted bread crumbs before serving. (A fat slice of Böhmische Knödel, page 224, would also be divine with Gulasch.)

Classic Austrian recipes recommend making Gulasch with beef shank for optimum flavor and texture. If you can find beef shank at a butcher's, they may cut the meat off the bone for you, saving you some tedious work, though you should save the bones to make Rinderbrühe (page 66). Beef shank can be hard to find, though, so you can substitute stew meat. I recommend treating the stew meat to a baking soda brine to tenderize it before cooking. I learned this tip from America's Test Kitchen.

Gulasch's flavor, like all good stews, improves with an overnight rest. If possible, make this a day ahead of serving. Leftovers can be frozen.

1   Dissolve the baking soda in the water. Place the meat in a large bowl and pour the baking soda solution over the meat. Stir well and set aside for 15 to 45 minutes to tenderize.

2   Place the oil in a large pot over medium-high heat and, when hot, add the onions. Cook for 5 minutes, stirring occasionally, then add the salt and garlic and cook for another 5 minutes, stirring frequently. The onions will have cooked down considerably but will not have taken on any color.

3   Turn the heat down to low and add the paprika. Stir well and cook for about 30 seconds. Add the tomato paste and stir well. Cook for about 30 seconds. Add the caraway and marjoram and stir well.

CONTINUED

4   Drain the beef, rinse briefly, then pat dry. Add the beef to the onion mixture and stir well. Pour in the beef broth, stir well, and raise the heat to high.

5   When the mixture comes to a boil, lower the heat, cover, and simmer for about 2 hours, stirring occasionally. If necessary, during the last 20 minutes of cooking, remove the lid to let some of the liquid reduce. You want there to be a generous amount of gravy, but it shouldn't be too loose.

6   When the Gulasch has finished cooking, taste for seasoning, adding more salt if necessary. To thicken the gravy, place the cornstarch in a small bowl and add 3 Tbsp of the gravy. Whisk until completely smooth, then whisk the slurry back into the pot of Gulasch. Let cook for a few minutes until just thickened, then remove from the heat.

7   If you'd like to add a touch of acidity, stir in the vinegar. Serve with Semmelknödel, Spätzle, or boiled egg noodles.

SZEGEDINER GULASCH

Pork and Sauerkraut Stew

SERVES 8

¼ cup / 60ml vegetable oil

3.3 lb / 1.5kg pork shoulder,
    trimmed and cut into
    1-inch / 2.5cm pieces

5 or 6 onions, diced

1 tsp salt

Freshly ground black pepper

¼ cup / 60g tomato paste

4 cups / 1L vegetable broth

2 small bay leaves or 1 large
    one

1 lb / 500g Sauerkraut

1 Tbsp dried marjoram

1 Tbsp caraway seeds

2 tsp sweet paprika

1 tsp hot paprika

1⅔ cups / 400g sour cream

Salzkartoffeln (page 209)
    for serving

You would be forgiven for thinking that Szegediner Gulasch originated in the Hungarian city of Szeged, but in fact it has little to do with Szeged. It is likely that the stew, a lusty, rib-sticking combination of pork and Sauerkraut stewed with onions and paprika, comes from the area of Siebenbürgen (part of Romania today), which is the ancestral home of the Székely people. No matter its origins, this stew is cooked throughout Germany and is an excellent dish to serve at a winter buffet party as it can more than handle being kept over low heat for a long time. It keeps well, freezes well, and warms the bones. Be sure to include both sweet and hot paprika, as the hot paprika gives the dish a most welcome, faintly spicy kick.

1   Place the vegetable oil in a very large pot over medium-high heat. Working in batches, sear the pork pieces on one side until golden brown, 3 to 5 minutes, then flip and brown the other side. Don't crowd the pot. Depending on your pot size, this should be done in three or four batches. Remove with a slotted spoon and set aside in a bowl, then repeat with the remaining pork.

2   When all the pork has browned, scrape the onions into the pan and season with the salt and pepper. Cook, stirring occasionally, until the onions have softened and taken on color, 5 to 8 minutes. Add the tomato paste and cook for a few minutes, stirring, until the paste has loosened and combined with the onions.

3   Return the meat and all its juices to the pot and stir well, then pour in the broth. Add the bay leaves to the pot. When the liquid starts to boil, turn down the heat and cover the pot. Simmer for 1½ hours.

4   After 1½ hours, stir in the Sauerkraut, marjoram, caraway, and both paprikas. Raise the heat until it just starts to simmer again, then lower the heat and cover the pot. Simmer for about 15 minutes. Adjust the seasoning if desired.

5   Remove the bay leaves and, off heat, stir in the sour cream. Serve with Salzkartoffeln.

ZÜRCHER GESCHNETZELTES

Swiss Veal Strips and Mushrooms in Cream Sauce

SERVES 4

1 to 2 Tbsp clarified butter
    or 1 Tbsp unsalted butter
    and 1 Tbsp vegetable oil,
    plus more if necessary
1½ lb / 700g veal sirloin,
    thinly sliced, then cut into
    strips against the grain
1 Tbsp all-purpose flour
Salt and freshly ground
    black pepper
1 yellow onion, finely minced
10.5 oz / 300g button
    mushrooms, thinly sliced
6½ Tbsp / 100ml white wine
1 cup / 250ml heavy cream
6½ Tbsp / 100ml beef broth
1 Tbsp cornstarch
Handful of flat-leaf parsley,
    minced

The German word "schnetzeln" means to cut something into thin, even strips. Geschnetzeltes, therefore, refers to a dish featuring thin strips of meat. One of Switzerland's most famous dishes is Zürcher Geschnetzeltes, a panful of fried veal strips in a delectable mushroom cream sauce. If you can't get yourself to Zürich's Kronenhalle, where I have it on good authority that the world's best Zürcher Geschnetzelte are served, you will be pleased to know that this simple dish is easily executed at home.

In Germany, Geschnetzeltes is one of a handful of everyday dishes that most cooks have in their back pocket. While veal may be the most classic form, Geschnetzeltes can be made with most meats, like chicken, beef, or pork.

Essential to the recipe's success is the prep; it helps immensely to have all the ingredients ready before starting to cook. Like all stir-fries, this one comes together in minutes, and you do not want to be frantically slicing mushrooms while the frying onions threaten to burn. If you are on good terms with your butcher, ask them to procure for you veal bottom sirloin, which will be the most tender, but if you can only find veal sirloin, so be it. If your butcher will slice the veal thinly for you, then cut it against the grain into strips, reward them with your loyal business and gratitude as they've just done the hardest part of this dish for you.

I very much like the ratio of meat to mushrooms here, as well as the amount of sauce they are served in, but you can absolutely increase both the amount of mushrooms and of meat, by about 3.5 oz / 100g each. Don't skip the parsley; it gives the dish a boost both visually and flavorwise.

The traditional accompaniment to Zürcher Geschnetzeltes is a gorgeous golden brown Rösti (page 214). But steamed rice or buttered noodles would be very nice, too.

You can substitute a gluten-free flour blend for the flour.

1   Preheat the oven to 140°F / 60°C. Keep a large, rimmed plate warm in the oven. (If you plan on serving the dish from a serving platter or bowl, keep one warm in the oven as well.)

2   Place the clarified butter in a large sauté pan over high heat. When the butter is bubbling, distribute half of the veal strips in the pan and cook, flipping once or twice, for about 3 minutes total, until the meat has barely

CONTINUED

lost its pink. Sprinkle half of the flour evenly over the meat and scrape into the warming plate, then season well with salt and pepper and put back in the oven. Repeat with the remaining veal and flour, season well with salt and pepper, and place back in the oven.

3   If necessary, add a bit more butter to the pan, then add the onion. Cook over medium heat for a few minutes, then add the mushrooms. Cook, stirring occasionally, for about 5 minutes, until fragrant and tender.

4   Pour in the wine and raise the heat. Stir well and let the wine bubble away until almost entirely evaporated.

5   In the meantime, whisk the cream, broth, and cornstarch in a small bowl until no lumps remain. When the wine has almost fully evaporated, pour in the cream mixture. Cook for about 3 minutes, until thickened and bubbling. Remove the meat from the oven.

6   Scrape the meat into the cream sauce along with half of the parsley and mix well. Heat through just until ready to serve (do not let this boil).

7   Sprinkle with the remaining parsley just before serving either directly from the pan or scraped into a heated serving bowl or platter.

PAPRIKA GESCHNETZELTES

Sliced Chicken with Peppers and Paprika

SERVES 4

1 lb / 500g chicken or turkey
   breast

1 tsp salt, plus more as
   necessary

Freshly ground black pepper

3 Tbsp vegetable oil, plus more
   as necessary

3 or 4 bell peppers (a mix of
   red and yellow), cut into
   ½-inch / 1cm strips

1 medium onion, diced

2 Tbsp tomato paste

1 Tbsp sweet paprika

½ cup / 125ml white wine

1 cup / 250ml chicken or
   vegetable broth or water

⅓ cup plus 1 Tbsp / 100g sour
   cream

Buttered egg noodles, Spätzle
   (page 93), or cooked rice
   for serving

This variation on Zürcher Geschnetzeltes (page 130) is probably the most contemporary recipe in the book. It's made with either turkey or chicken breast and a mix of sliced peppers that simmer together in a rust-colored gravy consisting of wine, broth, paprika, and a good dollop of sour cream. It comes together very quickly, making it perfect for weeknight dinners, and is likely to please big and small eaters at your table, if my children are any indication. (Being the child of a food writer doesn't make you particularly adventurous; my children would be thrilled to just eat spaghetti with tomato sauce every night. But this dish makes them both rapturous with praise.) Make sure to serve this with a side that will soak up every drop of the delicious gravy.

1   Slice the poultry into strips that are about ½-inch / 1cm thick and 3 inches / 7.5cm long. Season with ½ tsp of salt and black pepper to taste.

2   Place 1 Tbsp of oil in a large sauté pan over high heat. As soon as it's hot, add half of the poultry strips and cook, stirring occasionally, until just barely cooked through, about 5 minutes. Scrape onto a plate and repeat with another tablespoon of oil and the remaining poultry. Set aside.

3   If there is any liquid in the pan, pour it out, then add the last tablespoon of oil to the pan and set over medium-high heat. When hot, add the peppers and onion. Cook, stirring occasionally, for about 5 minutes, until the vegetables have softened and the onion is fragrant. Add the tomato paste and stir to loosen. Turn the heat down to low and add the paprika. (If the pan seems too dry, add just a small glug of oil so that the paprika won't burn.) Stir well and cook for 30 to 60 seconds, stirring frequently.

4   Pour in the wine and stir to loosen any stuck bits on the pan. Let bubble for a minute or two, then add the broth. Raise the heat to bring the mixture to a simmer, then cover, lower the heat to medium-low, and cook for 10 minutes. Remove the lid, raise the heat just a little bit, and cook for another 10 minutes. The sauce should be thickening and somewhat reduced.

5   Return the poultry strips to the pan and stir well to combine. Turn the heat up until the mixture starts to bubble. Put the lid on and cook for just another minute or two. Remove from the heat and stir in the sour cream. Adjust the seasoning and serve immediately with buttered egg noodles.

GÄNSEBRATEN

Roast Goose

SERVES 6

FOR POACHING THE GOOSE

1 (10 lb / 4.5kg) goose

1 large onion, halved

2 celery stalks

2 large carrots

2 large sprigs of
    flat-leaf parsley

1 leek, root and dark green
    parts trimmed, halved
    lengthwise

2 big garlic cloves

½ lemon

1 bay leaf

10 whole black peppercorns

1 large bunch of mugwort
    or thyme

2 (11 oz / 330ml) bottles dark
    Bavarian beer

FOR ROASTING THE GOOSE

Salt and freshly ground
    black pepper

1 medium sweet, juicy apple,
    quartered

2 small yellow onions,
    quartered

1 cup / 250ml good-quality
    red wine

FOR THE GRAVY

3 Tbsp unsalted butter

3 Tbsp all-purpose flour

Salt and freshly ground
    black pepper

¼ to ½ cup / 60 to 125ml heavy
    cream, optional

Saint Martin's Day, November 11, commemorates the Roman soldier Martin, later the bishop of Tours, who gave his cloak to a beggar on a cold winter's night and then dreamed that the beggar was Jesus in disguise. In Germany and Austria, the feast of Saint Martin is celebrated by young children who go on processions with lanterns in the dark November evening and by eating roast goose, or Martinsgans. Traditionally, Saint Martin's Day was the end of the farming year, when wages were paid and taxes (in the form of geese and other goods) and debts were settled. It was also the last day before the beginning of a forty-day fast before Christmas, plenty enough reasons to eat a goose and avoid having to continue feeding it during the colder months. Roast goose became synonymous with a festive meal.

Over the centuries, Germans developed different culinary traditions for one of the most festive meals: Christmas. While some ate roast goose, Schweinebraten (page 137) was traditional for others; a whole poached carp was essential for some regions, while others ate sausages. German Christmas festivities begin with Heiligabend (Holy Evening), which is Christmas Eve, the evening of December 24. Traditionally, this is the evening the tree is decorated, and requires a simple meal that can be made in advance, like potato salad with boiled sausages. Christmas Day is "der erste Weihnachtstag," or the first day of Christmas. And December 26 is "der zweite Weihnachtstag," or the second day of Christmas. December 25 and 26 are federal holidays.

If your family eats potato salad and sausages on Christmas Eve, then you are most likely serving a holiday roast on Christmas Day (and eating leftovers on December 26). But my mother and I spent many years celebrating Heiligabend with our next-door neighbors and dear friends. Christa, who is from Hamburg, had grown up eating roast goose on the twenty-fourth, so that is what I grew up with, too. Christa served her crisp-skinned goose with braised red cabbage (Rotkohl, page 202) and pillowy potato dumplings (Kartoffelklöße, page 216), all bound together on the plate with a rich gravy.

In Germany and Austria, fresh local goose is only available between November and December; the rest of the year you can buy it frozen, either whole or in pieces, usually from Poland and Hungary. When I first moved to Berlin in 2010, a 10-pound goose from a local farm cost me $105. (Industrially raised or imported geese aren't quite as expensive.) For some, this will put it out of reach. For others, one festive yearly meal is reason enough to spend the money. To make the choice a little easier: If you do choose to make the goose, you will be investing not only in one spectacular meal, but also in a delicious pot of goose stock that you can make with the goose carcass and, perhaps more importantly, in a supply of snowy-white goose fat that will last you for months. Incidentally, goose fat, I learned from Gabrielle Rossmer Gropman and Sonya Gropman's wonderful *German-Jewish Cookbook* is similar in nutritional value to olive oil. Goose fat is kosher, of course, and was the preferred cooking fat of German Jews. ("Schmalz" is the German word for animal-derived cooking fat, no matter which animal it comes from.) Goose fat has incredible flavor and will improve anything you add it to— Rotkohl, roasted potatoes, Eintöpfe, or even just as a spread on a fresh piece of dark German bread.

Geese are very fatty animals. The two-day method of preparing roast goose below has you first poach the bird in a broth of aromatics, beer, and water to coax much of the fat out of it. You roast the bird only once that step has been completed. This method results in less greasy meat and in a pristine layer of fat that you can easily separate and set aside. It also gives you an aromatic base for the succulent gravy. You can substitute gluten-free flour for the flour in the gravy.

1   Remove the giblets and the neck from the cavity of the goose and wash and dry the bird. Place it breast-side up in a roasting pan (that can be used on the stovetop) or pot that is large enough to hold the bird and the vegetables. Add the onion halves, celery, carrots, parsley, leek, garlic, lemon, bay leaf, peppercorns, and half of the mugwort to the pan or pot. Pour in the beer and add enough water to fill the pan or pot halfway. Tightly cover the pan with aluminum foil or the pot with its lid and set it on the stove over high heat. When the liquid has come to a boil, lower the heat, and let it simmer for 1½ hours.

2   Remove the bird from the pan and place it on a large platter. Remove all the solids from the broth with a spider or slotted spoon. When the bird has cooled somewhat, refrigerate it overnight. Also refrigerate the pan or pot of liquid.

CONTINUED

3 The next day, a thick layer of white goose fat will have formed on the surface of the broth. Carefully remove it and put it in a glass jar or other container. This can be used for Rotkohl (page 202), for roasting potatoes, or for any other preparation calling for lard or goose fat. Refrigerated, the goose fat will keep for at least a few months. Pour the jellied broth into a smaller pot and save for the gravy in step 7.

4 A few hours before roasting, remove the bird from the refrigerator.

5 Preheat the oven to 400°F / 200°C. Cut the wing tips off the goose and season with salt and black pepper all around the outside and inside the cavity. Stuff the goose with the remaining mugwort and the quartered apple and onions. Place the stuffed, seasoned bird breast-side down in a roasting pan and put it in the oven.

6 After 20 minutes, pour half of the wine over the bird. After another 20 minutes, turn the goose breast-side up and pour the remaining wine over it. Thereafter, every 20 minutes, take some of the liquid in the pan and baste the goose with it until the goose is crisp-skinned and a rich brown. In total, it will have roasted for 1½ to 2 hours. If the bird seems to be getting too dark before it's done cooking, tent some aluminum foil over it.

7 While the bird roasts, make the gravy. Heat the broth (you might not use all of it, but it's easier to just heat it all). Melt the butter in a saucepan and add the flour, stirring for a few minutes to let the flour cook in the butter. Add small ladlefuls of hot goose broth, whisking constantly, until you have a smooth and silky gravy. Season to taste with salt and black pepper and keep warm until serving time. To enrich the gravy further, whisk in heavy cream to taste just before serving.

8 When the goose has finished roasting, remove it from the oven and let it sit for 10 minutes before carefully transferring it to a cutting board. Carve, then plate the goose on a serving platter. At the table, pass the gravy with the roasted goose. (Save the carcass and bones to make goose stock later.)

SCHWEINEBRATEN

Herbed Pork Roast

SERVES 6 TO 8

4 large garlic cloves, peeled

2 tsp salt

1 tsp ground caraway

4.4 lb / 2kg pork shoulder roast

Freshly ground black pepper

2 medium onions, peeled and
  sliced into thin half-moons

2 medium carrots, peeled and
  sliced thickly

2-inch / 5cm thick slice of
  celery root, peeled and
  cubed

1 cup / 250ml dark Bavarian
  beer

A classic German pork roast always comes with the thick layer of fat still attached. You crosshatch it before roasting, resulting in a deliciously crusty crackling. When you serve the pork, you always make sure that each slice of pork gets a little bit of the crust. If you're lucky enough to live in a country where you can find a pork roast with the rind still attached, make the recipe below with that. (Crosshatch the fat layer before you begin cooking it or have your butcher do it for you.) In the United States, it's nearly impossible to find pork roast with the rind still attached. Luckily, pork roast is delicious without the crackling, too, though perhaps not quite as visually impressive when brought to the table.

In Germany, this pork roast is widely identified as being Bavarian. During the roasting, you pour dark Bavarian beer over it, which adds flavor and sweetness both to the roast and to the gravy later. Schweinebraten is traditionally served with dumplings, either made with bread (page 222) or potatoes (page 216), and either braised red cabbage (page 202), Sauerkraut (page 206), or Krautsalat (page 52). It is a special occasion meal or, at the very least, only cooked for Sunday lunch. I've kept the recipe as simple as possible, with just the classic flavorings of caraway and garlic, though you could add a teaspoon of dried marjoram to the rub as well, if you like. For the gravy, all you do is puree the roasted vegetables and the roast drippings into a creamy, rust-colored sauce. This roast is delicious served warm, right away, but can also be served at room temperature. Despite it being classic winter food, I once brought it to a summer picnic where we ate it in cold, thin slices and it was very well received.

Schweinebraten is traditionally served with gravy made from its own cooking juices. But while leftover Schweinebraten is delicious, leftover gravy is less so. So instead, you can pair cold slices of Schweinebraten with creamy Remoulade (page 108) or tangy Cumberland Sauce (recipe follows).

1   Preheat the oven to 400°F / 200°C.

2   Crush the garlic to a paste and mix with the salt and caraway. Rub this mixture all over the top and sides of the pork. Season with pepper to taste. Set aside.

CONTINUED

3   Place the vegetables in a roasting pan and toss together, then push to the sides to make room for the roast. Place the roast in the middle of the pan.

4   Roast for 45 minutes, then pour half of the beer evenly over the roast. Roast for another 30 minutes, then pour the remaining beer evenly over the roast. Roast for a final 35 minutes. Remove from the oven and let sit for 15 to 20 minutes. Do not touch the roast as it rests.

5   Place the roast on a cutting board. Scrape all the vegetables and drippings into a food processor and blend until smooth. If desired, adjust the seasoning.

6   Slice the roast (thinly if without the rind/fat, slightly thicker slices if with) and serve with the gravy and Cumberland sauce.

CUMBERLAND SAUCE

MAKES ABOUT ¾ CUP / 200ML

½ cup / 150g red currant jelly or jam
¼ cup / 60ml port
Zest and juice of 1 lemon
Zest and juice of 1 orange
1 Tbsp Dijon mustard
Salt and freshly ground black pepper

Place the red currant jelly, port, zest and juice, mustard, and salt and pepper in a small saucepan over medium-high heat and stir. Bring to a boil and let simmer at medium heat, uncovered, for 5 to 8 minutes. Pour into a serving bowl and let cool completely. Serve with cold sliced meat. The sauce will keep for 1 week, refrigerated. It is easily doubled.

KOHLROULADEN

Stuffed Cabbage Rolls

SERVES 4

3 Tbsp vegetable oil

2 onions, minced

1 tsp salt, plus more as needed

2 stale white rolls, very thinly
    sliced, or equivalent
    amount of stale sandwich
    bread, cut into ¼-inch /
    6mm cubes

½ cup / 125ml whole milk

1 head of Savoy or green
    cabbage

½ lb / 250g ground beef

½ lb / 250g ground pork

1 egg

1 tsp dried marjoram

Freshly ground black pepper

Small bunch of flat-leaf
    parsley, minced

⅓ cup / 1.7 oz / 50g minced
    Speck or bacon

2 Tbsp tomato paste

½ cup / 120ml red wine

1 cup / 250ml beef broth

1 tsp cornstarch, optional

Petersilienkartoffeln
    (page 210), Kartoffelpurée
    (page 210), or
    Kartoffelklöße (page 216)
    for serving

Stuffed cabbage will always remind me of the wholesome lunches I was fed at the cafeteria in my public school in Berlin. From stuffed cabbage to Milchreis (page 170) to chicken fricassee (page 144), school lunch was a meal my classmates and I ate with gusto. Freshly prepared by grumpy ladies in white hats, dolloped out onto trays with pudding and fruit, and costing a little less than five Deutschmark per child, it was good, honest food. Sure, the older we got, the more we thought the kebabs down the street were a way better use of our lunch money, and by the time twelfth grade rolled around, eating in the lunchroom with seventh graders was, like, *totally* out of the question, but while it lasted, I sure loved those lunches.

Even with my rose-colored memory glasses on, though, I can assure you that this recipe will be even better than any cafeteria fare, especially if you use Savoy cabbage, which must be the most beautiful cabbage far and wide. Despite being blanched and browned and braised here, it manages to retain its structure and some of its color at the end. For Germans, the flavorful sauce is almost as important as the stuffed cabbage itself. In my memory, the cabbage and its sauce was always served with mashed potatoes (page 210), but Petersilienkartoffeln (page 210) would also be good here.

1   Place 1 Tbsp of oil in a small sauté pan and cook half of the onions with ½ tsp of salt over medium heat until translucent and fragrant, about 8 minutes. Set aside.

2   Place the bread in a large bowl. Heat the milk and pour over the rolls. Toss well, then set aside while you prepare the cabbage.

3   Bring a large pot of salted water to a boil. Place a large bowl of cold water on your work surface. Carefully loosen about 10 outer leaves from the head of cabbage without tearing them (set torn ones aside to use elsewhere). Cut out the thick rib. Blanch the leaves in the boiling water for 5 minutes, then place them in the bowl of cold water to stop the cooking process. Set them on a kitchen towel and pat dry.

CONTINUED

4 The bread should have completely absorbed all the milk by this point. To the bowl with the bread, add the remaining ½ tsp of salt, the sautéed onion, both meats, the egg, marjoram, pepper to taste, and the parsley. Mix very well until you get a homogenous mixture.

5 Fill the cabbage leaves: Start by spreading one cabbage leaf out in front of you. You have enough filling to make between 8 and 10 cabbage rolls. Place around 3 oz / 85 to 90g (scant ½ cup) of filling on the cabbage leaf, centering it. Fold the side edges over the filling, then roll up the cabbage leaf from the bottom. No filling should emerge or be visible. Tie with kitchen twine and set aside. Repeat with the remaining leaves and filling.

6 Place the remaining 2 Tbsp of oil in a large pan over medium-high heat. Sear the cabbage rolls until golden brown on both sides, 5 to 8 minutes total. Do this in batches, if necessary. Don't crowd the rolls. Remove the rolls from the pan and set aside on a plate.

7 Add the remaining half of the onions to the pan along with the Speck. Cook, stirring, for 5 to 8 minutes, until the fat has started to render and the onion is translucent and fragrant. Add the tomato paste and stir well to loosen and distribute. Continue to cook for another 3 minutes. Pour in the wine and bring to a boil, then pour in the beef broth. As soon as the sauce comes to a boil, carefully place the cabbage rolls into the sauce. Cover, turn down the heat, and simmer for about 45 minutes.

8 When the cabbage rolls have finished cooking, take them out of the pan and set aside. Snip off the kitchen twine. Taste the sauce and adjust the seasoning if necessary. If you want a slightly thickened sauce, take 3 Tbsp of sauce out of the pan and whisk with the cornstarch in a small bowl until no lumps remain, then whisk this slurry back into the sauce. Let the sauce simmer, stirring, for another few minutes until it starts to thicken just ever so slightly. Turn off the heat. Place the cabbage rolls back in the sauce and serve with Petersilienkartoffeln, Kartoffelpurée, or Kartoffelklöße.

WIENER SCHNITZEL

Breaded Veal Cutlets

SERVES 4 TO 6

4 to 6 veal cutlets (4 to 5 oz / 120 to 150g each)

4 eggs

4 tsp vegetable oil, plus 2 to 3 cups for frying

1 Tbsp water

2 cups / 250g all-purpose flour, plus more as needed

2 to 3 cups / 220 to 330g unseasoned bread crumbs, plus more as needed

Salt

Quartered lemons for serving

Wiener Schnitzel is one of Vienna's most famous delicacies. Imagine a thinly pounded, delicately breaded veal cutlet whose breading puffs and ripples in hot oil and that is crisp on the outside, tender on the inside. There is a beautiful word for this rippling—"soufflieren"—which tells you something about the French influence on Austria's refined cuisine. The bread crumb coating should, like a soufflé, puff and lift as it cooks. Schnitzel is beloved all over the world, though perhaps nowhere more than in German-speaking countries. In Germany and Austria, Wiener Schnitzel can only ever be made with veal; if you use other meat, like pork cutlets, you must call the breaded cutlets "Wiener Art," or Vienna-style.

Wiener Schnitzel, despite their pedigree, are relatively straightforward to prepare, cooking in mere minutes. There are just a few important things to note. To start, you must make sure to buy boneless veal, ideally slices from the top round. You must pound these until each cutlet is even and quite thin. This allows the cutlets to cook in just a few minutes, which keeps them buttery and tender. Next, you must do the triple coating of flour, then eggs, then bread crumbs; otherwise the breading will not be correct. Last, you must use much more oil than you might feel comfortable with. The goal is for each cutlet to be nearly submerged in oil as it cooks. Don't worry—if the oil temperature is correct, the cutlets will not soak up much oil. Only by submerging them will your Wiener Schnitzel develop that signature wavy, rippled crust.

Some experts think that it is important to have some kind of butter flavor in the oil, so you can, if you want, use a combination of vegetable oil and clarified butter to fry, or add some clarified butter to the pan just before the cutlet finishes frying. But I find that the butter flavor isn't essential—if you've bought good-quality veal, and done the breading as described, the Schnitzel will be just as delectable when fried in vegetable oil alone.

As easy as Wiener Schnitzel is to prepare, for my family it remains a special occasion meal as we don't like to consume veal frequently.

It is common to serve Wiener Schnitzel with vinegary potato salad (page 62), even better if you fold in some very thinly sliced peeled cucumber with the potatoes before marinating. It is essential to serve Wiener Schnitzel with lemon wedges to squeeze over each piece—the acidity is the perfect foil to the crisp, buttery cutlets.

1　First, pound each veal cutlet with the smooth side of a meat mallet until each piece is completely even and between ⅛ and ¼ inch / 5mm thick. Set aside.

2　Place the eggs in a wide, shallow bowl or soup plate and whisk until well-combined, then whisk in the 4 tsp of oil and the water. Set aside.

3　Place the flour in a second wide, shallow bowl or soup plate. Place the bread crumbs in a third wide, shallow bowl or soup plate. Set aside.

4　Lightly salt each side of every cutlet. Dredge the first cutlet in the flour, shaking off any excess. Next drag it through the beaten eggs so that the entire piece of veal is completely coated with egg. Finally, dredge the cutlet in bread crumbs, gently tossing the bread crumbs on top so that it is completely coated. Do not press the meat into the bread crumbs. Gently place the breaded veal cutlet on a clean cutting board. Repeat with the second piece of veal.

5　Pour 2 to 3 cups of oil into a 10- to 12-inch / 25 to 30cm skillet with high sides. The oil should come up about an inch in the pan. Place the skillet over medium-high heat. When the oil is hot, slip the first two prepared cutlets into the pan. They should be completely covered with boiling oil. As it cooks, the coating will puff gently in the pan. Do not touch the cutlets for 1½ to 2 minutes. Using tongs, pick each one up and flip so that the second side can cook. After another minute or so, remove the cutlets with the tongs, letting the excess oil drip into the pan, and plate them.

6　While the first cutlets are cooking, prepare the next two cutlets. As soon as the first cutlets are out of the pan, slip the next two in. Continue with the remaining meat and coatings. The oil in the pan should always remain the same level, so for the last batch of cutlets, you may need to add a bit more oil to the pan; otherwise the last cutlets may stick to the bottom of the pan.

7　Distribute lemon quarters on each of the plates and serve immediately.

HÜHNERFRIKASSEE

Chicken Fricassee

SERVES 4 TO 6

1 (2 lb / 1kg) chicken

8 cups / 2L water

1 Tbsp salt, plus more
 as needed

1 medium onion, peeled

1 large carrot, peeled and
 cut into thirds

1 celery stalk, cut into thirds

10 whole black peppercorns

3 Tbsp unsalted butter

3 Tbsp all-purpose flour

1 cup / 140g frozen or fresh
 peas

6 medium white or brown
 button mushrooms,
 trimmed and sliced into
 ¼-inch / 6mm slices

2 egg yolks

3 Tbsp heavy cream

Juice of ½ lemon, plus more
 as needed

Freshly ground black pepper

Chopped flat-leaf parsley for
 serving, optional

How much do I love chicken fricassee? This may be one of my favorite recipes in this book. Tender chicken, silky slices of mushrooms, and little pops of peas swathed in a velvety, savory sauce that is best soaked up with rice. You can either cook the chicken from scratch (and garner yourself some homemade chicken broth in the process) or you can use this recipe to repurpose leftover chicken (or Thanksgiving turkey!). And you don't need to necessarily cook a whole chicken—you can also make the recipe with equal amounts of chicken parts. Carrots and peas are the traditional vegetables, but when asparagus is in season, I highly recommend using them here (cut off the tips and slice the stalks in ¼-inch rounds and add in step 4). If you use asparagus, I'd probably leave out the carrots, but not the peas or mushrooms.

To add flavor, in step 3, you can replace some of the broth with ½ cup / 125ml of white wine. This gives the sauce a bit more complexity, but rest assured that it is plenty delicious without the wine. The old-fashioned culinary trick of whisking egg yolks into the sauce at the end makes for an impossibly velvety sauce. Don't skip it!

I usually serve this with rice, but a German woman that I know who grew up eating fricassee on Christmas Eve was scandalized by the thought; at their house, fricassee was always served with buttered toast.

1 Place the chicken in a large pot and cover with the water. Add the salt, whole onion, carrots, celery, and peppercorns. Bring to a boil, uncovered, over high heat, skimming any scum from the surface. When it comes to a boil, lower the heat and cover. Simmer for 1½ hours. Remove from the heat, then remove the chicken from the broth and place in a large bowl. Set aside to cool.

2 When the chicken has cooled enough to handle, peel off the skin and pull the meat from the bones. Discard the bones, any cartilage, and the skin. Cut or shred the chicken into bite-size pieces. Set aside. Pour the broth through a fine-mesh sieve. Set aside the carrot pieces and discard the celery, onion, and peppercorns. Measure out 1¾ cups / 400ml of the broth and set aside. Save the rest of the broth to use in the future.

CONTINUED

HÜHNERFRIKASSEE

continued

3   In a large saucepan or frying pan with high sides, melt the butter over medium heat. Sprinkle in the flour and whisk together until no clumps remain. Cook for a few minutes, stirring occasionally. When the mixture starts to turn a pale golden color, slowly whisk in the reserved broth. Whisk until no clumps remain. Cook, whisking occasionally, for about 7 minutes. The sauce should be thickening. Taste for seasoning, adding more salt if necessary.

4   Add the peas and mushrooms to the sauce and stir well. Raise the heat a bit and cook for 5 to 7 minutes, until tender, stirring occasionally. If the sauce thickens too much, thin with a spoonful or two of additional broth.

5   Place the egg yolks in a small bowl and whisk in the cream, then whisk in 2 Tbsp of the simmering sauce (taking care not to add any peas).

6   Turn the heat off under the fricassee and whisk in the yolk mixture until completely combined. Stir in the lemon juice and fold in the reserved chicken. Slice the carrot and fold gently into the stew. Taste for seasoning and add more salt, black pepper, or lemon juice as desired.

7   Sprinkle with chopped parsley, if desired, and serve immediately.

TAFELSPITZ

Austrian Boiled Beef with Horseradish Sauce

SERVES 4

1 Tbsp vegetable oil

1 large onion, unpeeled and
    halved through the root end

1 carrot, peeled and cut into
    quarters

1 leek, root and dark green
    part trimmed, cut into
    quarters

¼ celery root, peeled and
    cut into chunks

1 parsley root, peeled and
    cut into chunks, or a small
    bunch of curly parsley,
    optional

6 cups / 1.5L water

1 bay leaf

1 tsp whole black peppercorns

About 1.1 lb / 500g top round,
    rinsed

2 tsp salt, plus more as needed

Horseradish Applesauce
    (recipe follows) and
    Creamy Chive Sauce (recipe
    follows) for serving

Tafelspitz is the Austrian name for a dish of sliced boiled beef. The cut comes from the very end of the beef rump; the closest American cut is the top round. Although similar dishes are eaten throughout southern Germany, Tafelspitz has become one of Vienna's most iconic main dishes. In Viennese restaurants, Tafelspitz is traditionally served with horseradish-spiked applesauce and a creamy chive mayonnaise, and the ritual presentation is often quite special, with the various sides and sauces coming to the table in their own pots and jugs. Rahmspinat (page 198) and Bratkartoffeln (page 211) are typical sides (leave out the Speck). Tafelspitz is very much considered a special occasion meal.

Tafelspitz is the gift that keeps on giving: preparing it leaves you with delicious beef broth and any leftover Tafelspitz can be repurposed in future meals by being thinly sliced and marinated in a marvelous little salad with beans and herbs (page 66).

1   Place the oil in a large pot over high heat. As soon as the oil is hot, place the onion cut-side down into the pan and let it sear for 2 to 3 minutes, until well-browned.

2   Add the remaining vegetables. Stir well, then pour in the water and add the bay leaf and peppercorns. Bring to a boil, then turn down the heat to a simmer. Slip in the piece of beef.

3   Simmer the beef on low heat, covered, for 1½ hours. If necessary, skim the broth and discard the scum.

4   Add the salt to the broth and simmer for another 30 minutes. Test the meat by inserting a skewer into the thickest part. If it slides easily off the skewer, it is finished. If not, let it simmer for another 30 minutes or so.

5   Remove the meat from the pot and set aside. Pour the broth through a fine-mesh sieve. Do not press down on the vegetables. Discard the vegetables and adjust the seasoning of the broth, if necessary. Set aside to serve as a first course or for another day.

6   Slice the meat thinly against the grain and serve with horseradish applesauce and creamy chive sauce.

CONTINUED

APFELKREN
Horseradish Applesauce

SERVES 4 TO 6

 4 cooking apples, peeled, cored, and chopped
 1 to 1½ Tbsp sugar, plus more as needed
 ⅛ tsp salt, plus more as needed
 Juice of 1 lemon
 2 Tbsp grated horseradish, plus more as needed
 1 to 2 tsp apple cider vinegar, optional

1 Place the apples in a small pot with 1 Tbsp of sugar, the salt, and lemon juice. Bring to a boil over medium-high heat, then lower the heat to a simmer and cook, covered, until the apples are completely soft. Stir the apples until they have turned into sauce.

2 Remove from the heat and stir in the horseradish. Taste for seasoning. If desired, add more horseradish, sugar, or salt. Add the vinegar, if desired. Let cool completely. Serve at room temperature with the sliced Tafelspitz.

SCHNITTLAUCHSOßE
Creamy Chive Sauce

SERVES 4 TO 6

 2 slices white sandwich bread
 ½ cup / 125ml whole milk
 1 hard-boiled egg yolk
 1 raw egg yolk
 1 Tbsp Dijon mustard, plus more as needed
 1 Tbsp apple cider vinegar
 ½ tsp salt, plus more as needed
 ¼ tsp white pepper, plus more as needed
 1⅔ cups / 150ml vegetable oil
 1 bunch of chives, minced

1 Place the bread in a small bowl and cover with the milk. Let soak for 10 minutes, turning periodically.

2 Place the boiled and raw egg yolks in a medium bowl or narrow container. Add the mustard, vinegar, salt, and pepper. Pour off the milk from the bread, only gently squeezing out the bread slices, and add them to the eggs. Using an immersion blender, blend everything together until smooth.

3 Then, with the motor running, slowly drizzle in the oil until the mixture is thick and creamy. Taste and adjust the seasoning by adding more salt, pepper, or mustard, if desired. Just before serving, stir in the chives.

RINDERROULADEN

Braised Beef Rolls with Mustard and Pickles

SERVES 8

8 slices of top round beef
    about 4 by 6 inches / 10 by
    15cm in size and ¼ inch /
    6mm thick

Salt and freshly ground
    black pepper

Dijon or yellow mustard

16 slices of bacon

4 shallots or small onions,
    thinly sliced

Cornichons or German spiced
    pickles, sliced lengthwise
    into 3 or 4 slices

3 Tbsp vegetable oil

1 medium carrot, peeled
    and diced

1 parsley root, peeled
    and diced

1-inch / 2.5cm thick slice of
    celery root, peeled and
    diced

1 leek, dark green parts
    trimmed, diced

¼ cup / 60g tomato paste

½ cup / 120ml red wine

1¾ cups / 400ml beef broth

Boiled potatoes or dumplings
    for serving

In polls conducted around the country of Germans' favorite meals, Rinderrouladen consistently take the top spot. Rouladen, as they are colloquially known, are very thin slices of beef layered with mustard, bacon, pickles, and onions, then rolled up and braised in a rich gravy until tender. Making them is a bit of a time commitment, which is why most people save this dish for special occasions like a loved one's birthday. The recipe probably originated in what was once Bohemia. Germans feel quite strongly that their sweet, spiced pickles (Gewürzgurken, found in German markets or online) are the best pickles for the filling, but regular pickles or even cornichons are also good here. Because pickle sizes vary so much, quantities will vary, which is why I haven't given a specific number. You should use about 3 slices of pickle per roll.

To keep their shape during cooking, you must tie Rouladen before cooking them. Traditionalists will use a "Rouladennadel" or thick needle or skewer to bind them together, but I don't think it's necessary. You do need kitchen twine. If the beef has been pounded thinly enough, the roll will keep its shape while you tie it up. You just need to wrap the twine around it as if you were tying up a present: place the twine horizontally across the roll, bring it under the roll, cross the twine, flip the roll, and tie up the twine at the top in a knot or bow. Just before serving, you snip off the twine with kitchen shears so that you can serve the rolls without the twine getting in the way.

The classic accompaniments to Rouladen are Kartoffelklöße (page 216) and Rotkohl (page 202).

1   Take one slice of top round and pound it with a meat mallet until it is slightly larger than its original size and just under ¼ inch thick. Take care not to tear the meat. Repeat with the remaining pieces.

2   Working with one piece of meat at a time, season it lightly with salt and pepper, then spread a thin layer of mustard all over the meat. Place 2 slices of bacon over the mustard. Distribute an eighth of the shallots over the bacon and place 3 slices of pickle on top. Fold in the sides of the meat a bit, then roll up the meat tightly and place seam-side down on a plate.

3   Repeat with the remaining meat and ingredients. When all the meat rolls have been assembled, tie them with kitchen twine (like a birthday present; see headnote).

CONTINUED

RINDERROULADEN

continued

4 Place 2 Tbsp of oil in a large pot over medium-high heat. Sear the beef rolls for a few minutes on each side, until well-browned. Transfer the beef rolls to the plate and proceed with the rest of the recipe.

5 Heat the remaining 1 Tbsp of oil in the pot, then add the carrot, parsley root, celery root, and leek to the pot and cook, stirring to loosen the browned bits. Season with a pinch of salt and continue to cook until the vegetables have softened and taken on some color, about 8 minutes.

6 Add the tomato paste to the pot and stir well to distribute. Cook, stirring, for another minute or two.

7 Pour the wine into the pot and stir well. The mixture will thicken and bubble. Cook for 2 minutes.

8 Pour in the broth and stir well to combine. As soon as the mixture starts bubbling, place the beef rolls back in the pot and cover. Let simmer for 1½ to 2 hours, turning the rolls occasionally, until fork-tender.

9 Remove the beef rolls from the pot and set aside. Using an immersion blender, puree the sauce until creamy and smooth. Place the rolls back in the sauce. Serve with boiled potatoes or dumplings.

SAUERBRATEN

Spiced Braised Beef

SERVES 4 TO 6

1 cup / 250ml red wine vinegar

3 cups / 750ml water

1 large carrot, peeled and cut
   into 1-inch / 2.5cm chunks

2 onions, peeled and cut into
   1-inch / 2.5cm chunks

1-inch / 2.5cm thick slice of
   celery root, diced

1 Tbsp plus 1 tsp sugar

1½ tsp salt

1 tsp mustard seeds

1 tsp cloves

1 tsp juniper berries

1 tsp whole black peppercorns

1 tsp allspice berries

2 large bay leaves

2.2 lb / 1kg beef rump roast,
   eye of round, or bottom
   round

Salt and freshly ground
   black pepper

2 Tbsp clarified butter
   or vegetable oil

2 Tbsp tomato paste

1 Tbsp molasses or sugar beet
   syrup

2 to 3 Soßenlebkuchen,
   crumbled, optional

2 or 3 slices German
   pumpernickel, crumbled,
   optional

2 to 3 Tbsp lingonberry jam,
   optional

Scant ½ cup / 60g raisins,
   optional

1 Tbsp cornstarch, optional

Sauerbraten is one of Germany's most famous dishes. A relatively lean piece of raw beef roast (though horsemeat, tough and lean, used to be traditional for Sauerbraten) is placed in an aggressively spiced vinegar marinade and refrigerated for days. A minimum of three days, I was told sternly by various home cooks, and up to five days, though plenty of older cookbooks say up to seven days. The roast is seared, then braised in the marinade until tender. The cooking liquid is reduced and thickened until ready to serve with the sliced roast.

Sauerbraten is prepared all over Germany with regional variations. Rhenish Sauerbraten veers sweet, with sugar beet syrup and raisins in the sauce, while Franconian Sauerbraten eschews raisins but includes Lebkuchen (gingerbread) and sometimes cream in the sauce. Westphalian Sauerbraten uses pumpernickel crumbs for thickening the sauce instead of Lebkuchen. Swabian Sauerbraten doesn't use any thickener besides the vegetables that have been cooked with the beef. And Saxonian Sauerbraten is larded with thick batons of pork fat, which is also the way Sauerbraten in Nashville (where it is called Rinderbraten) was traditionally prepared, thanks to immigrants from Saxony who emigrated in the nineteenth century. Sauerbraten's classic accompaniments are potato dumplings (page 216) or Spätzle (page 93) and Rotkohl (page 202).

The Lebkuchen traditionally used to thicken and flavor the Sauerbraten sauce are called Soßenlebkuchen or Soßenkuchen. In some areas, they're even called Fischlebkuchen, because they were used in a traditional sauce for carp. Outside of Germany, they can be difficult to track down, though online stores have them. They are less sweet than regular Lebkuchen and are only used for thickening gravy. If you can't find them, you can substitute German pumpernickel, which is very dark and somewhat sweet (this, too, can be sourced online or in German or import markets). If worse comes to worst and you can't find any of those thickeners, just call your Sauerbraten Swabian and thicken it with the pureed vegetables and a bit of cornstarch. It will still be delicious. Lingonberry jam can be used to finish the gravy as well.

The recipe below is an amalgam of one from my friend Lena Häusler's aunt's Franconian grandmother Babette and several traditional recipes from other regions. Depending on how you'd like to serve your Sauerbraten at the end, I've given a few different variations in step 9.

1   Place the vinegar and water in a heavy-bottomed pot large enough to contain the roast and marinade. Place all the vegetables in the pot. Add 1 Tbsp of the sugar, the salt, and all of the spices.

2   Bring the marinade to a boil over high heat, then lower the heat, cover, and simmer for 15 minutes. Remove from the heat, uncover, and let the marinade cool completely.

3   Place the beef in the marinade. Cover and refrigerate for 4 to 5 days, turning the meat once a day.

4   On the day you plan to cook, remove the meat from the marinade and pat it dry with paper towels. Season with salt and black pepper. Pour the marinade through a fine-mesh sieve into a separate bowl or liquid measuring cup and set aside. Reserve the vegetables from the marinade.

5   Place the butter or oil in a pot large enough for the roast and set over high heat. When the butter has melted or the oil is shimmering, place the roast in the pot and sear for about 3 minutes on each side, until crusty and brown all over.

6   Remove the roast from the pot and place on a plate. Set aside. Lower the heat to medium and put the vegetables from the marinade into the pot and stir well. Cook for a few minutes, stirring, to loosen the browned bits on the bottom of the pot. Add the remaining 1 tsp of sugar, the tomato paste, and the molasses and stir well, then continue to cook for a few minutes.

7   When the paste has loosened the browned bits on the bottom of the pot and they have been incorporated into the vegetable mixture, place the beef roast on top of the vegetables and pour in the reserved marinade. It should come up about halfway the sides of the roast. Raise the heat, bring the marinade just to a boil, then lower the heat, cover, and simmer for 1 hour.

CONTINUED

8 After 1 hour, flip the roast, add the Soßenlebkuchen or pumpernickel, if using, and simmer for another hour. At this point, the roast should be very tender. Remove the roast from the pot, put on a plate, and cover with aluminum foil.

9 To finish the sauce, you have a few different possibilities:

a. Pour the sauce through a fine-mesh sieve into a small pot and discard the vegetables. Boil the sauce until the liquid has reduced by half. Taste for seasoning, adding more salt, pepper, or sugar, or lingonberry jam, if using. Add the raisins to the sauce, if using, and simmer for about 5 minutes. Slice the roast against the grain and serve with the sauce.

b. Pour the sauce through a fine-mesh sieve into a small pot and press the vegetables through the sieve. (Discard what remains.) Boil the sauce until the liquid has reduced by half. Taste for seasoning, adding salt, pepper, and/or lingonberry jam, if using. Place the cornstarch in a small bowl and add 2 to 3 Tbsp of the sauce to the bowl, then whisk until smooth. Pour the slurry back into the pot with the sauce and simmer for another minute or so, stirring, until thickened. Slice the roast and serve with the sauce.

c. Pour the sauce through a fine-mesh sieve into a small pot. Carefully pick out all the spices from the vegetables in the sieve and discard. Scrape the cooked vegetables back into the pot. Using an immersion blender, puree everything until completely smooth. Depending on the consistency of the sauce, you may want to reduce it a bit—bring to a boil and cook, uncovered, until it has the consistency you'd like. Taste for seasoning, then slice the roast and serve with the sauce.

MAULTASCHEN

Swabian Meat and Spinach Dumplings

MAKES 24 DUMPLINGS

FOR THE DOUGH

2¾ cups / 350g all-purpose
    flour, plus more for the
    surface
1 tsp salt
3 eggs
3 Tbsp vegetable oil
3 Tbsp water

FOR THE FILLING

1 lb / 500g frozen spinach
3 oz / 85g stale white rolls (2)
    or equivalent amount of
    stale white sandwich bread,
    roughly cubed
2 Tbsp unsalted butter
1 medium onion, finely minced
2 tsp salt
½ bunch of flat-leaf parsley,
    minced
½ lb / 450g ground beef
½ lb / 450g ground pork
2 eggs
Freshly ground black pepper
1 tsp dried marjoram
30 scrapes of whole nutmeg
2 Tbsp unseasoned bread
    crumbs
8½ cups / 2L beef broth
    (page 66)
Minced chives for serving
Caramelized onions (recipe
    follows) for serving,
    optional

There may be no more revered Swabian dish than Maultaschen, plump dumplings of noodle dough stuffed with a hearty mixture of meat and minced spinach and shaped into little square pillows. Maultaschen are traditionally served in a savory beef broth or pan-fried with caramelized onions or scrambled eggs or both. Swabian potato salad (page 62) is also a typical accompaniment.

The legend behind Maultaschen, whose nickname in local dialect is Herrgottsbscheißerle, which translates approximately to "fooling the lord God," is that although they were originally conceived as a vegetarian dish to be eaten during the fasting days when eating meat was strictly forbidden by the Church, an enterprising monk started adding a little bit of ground meat to the spinach filling, figuring that even God wouldn't be able to detect the meat hidden within those delicious little dumplings. (Incidentally, you can make these Maultaschen vegetarian by using vegetable broth; just make sure to also increase the other filling ingredients, especially the seasoning.)

My Korean American friend Jane Joo Park, who spent many years in Stuttgart raising a family, learned how to make Maultaschen from her Swabian next-door neighbor and adoptive grandmother. Jane generously shared this recipe with me, and I have adapted it, incorporating some Maultaschen wisdom from a famous Michelin-starred Swabian chef named Vincent Klink. I call for frozen spinach, because I find it easier to deal with than fresh, though you can, of course, use fresh spinach in its place.

Each Swabian home cook has a slightly different way of rolling and shaping their Maultaschen. I've given instructions that I think are easiest for novices to follow. If you go to my Instagram account @wednesdaychef, I've saved the process of shaping Maultaschen as a highlighted Story on my profile.

One final note: You'll notice that I've only written the yield on this recipe and not how many it serves. The reason is that it varies widely from eater to eater! One of my testers and her husband finished the entire batch on their own. Another tester fed her family of four. You will have to decide for yourself whether you want to serve two per person, or four or more.

CONTINUED

7   8   9

10   11   12

1   First, make the dough: Mix the flour and salt in a bowl and make a well in the middle. Crack the eggs into the well, then pour the oil into the well. Using a fork, break the eggs and mix them with some of the flour. Continue to mix as you add the water. As soon as you get a shaggy dough, turn it out onto a lightly floured surface and knead until smooth, about 5 minutes. When the dough is smooth and elastic, place it back in the bowl and cover with a towel or plastic wrap. Set aside for 30 minutes.

2   While the dough rests, make the filling. First, cook the frozen spinach according to the package directions and set aside to drain well.

3   Place the rolls in a bowl with water to cover. Set aside.

4   Melt the butter in a 10-inch / 25cm skillet over medium heat and add the onion and 1 tsp of salt. Cook, stirring occasionally, until faintly golden and fragrant, 5 to 8 minutes.

5   In the meantime, press out as much water from the spinach as possible, then transfer the spinach to a cutting board and mince finely. Add the spinach to the onions and cook, stirring, for about 5 minutes, until the excess liquid evaporates. Stir in the parsley, turn off the heat, and set aside.

6   In a large bowl, mix the beef, pork, eggs, the remaining 1 tsp of salt, the pepper, marjoram, and nutmeg.

7   Drain the soaking bread and squeeze out as much water as possible. Add to the bowl with the meat and scrape in the somewhat cooled spinach mixture and the bread crumbs.

8   Using your hands, mix everything together, pressing and squeezing as you go to distribute the ingredients evenly and to create a homogenous, smooth mixture. It should be quite moist but still hold its shape somewhat. Set aside.

9   Divide the dough in half, covering one-half with a towel. Using a rolling pin, roll out the first piece of dough to a long rectangle about 28 inches / 70cm long and 7 inches / 18cm wide. The dough should be nearly translucent.

If, by the end, it's too elastic to hold its shape as you roll, you can set aside the rolling pin and gently pull on the dough to make it even thinner.

10 Spread half of the filling all over the dough evenly with your hands or an offset spatula, leaving about 1 inch / 2.5cm of a border on one long end and about ½ inch / 1.3cm border on the other three sides. Fold in the shorter sides of the dough over the filling a little and pull one of the longer sides (the one with the smaller border) gently over the filling, then roll up the dough. Moisten the inch-wide border with a bit of cold water just before you finish rolling. The seam should be on the bottom now. Using your hands, gently flatten the dough roll.

11 Using the round handle of a wooden spoon, mark the roll into 12 equal pieces (I start by marking the middle, then work my way outward). Then, using a bench scraper or sharp knife, cut the roll into 12 pieces. Set aside. Just before cooking, gently plump each square with your thumb and index finger as if plumping a pillow.

12 Repeat with the second piece of dough and the remaining filling.

13 Bring a large pot with the beef broth just to a simmer. When the broth is simmering, gently place about 10 Maultaschen in the hot broth and immediately cover the pot. Let the Maultaschen cook for about 10 minutes on the lowest heat possible (some Swabians turn off the heat entirely). Place two Maultaschen per person in soup plates along with a ladleful or two of hot broth. Sprinkle some snipped chives over each serving. Repeat with the remaining Maultaschen and hot broth.

14 Alternatively, you can cook the Maultaschen in simmering salted water, as above, then drain and serve them boiled with caramelized onions (recipe follows). Any leftover boiled Maultaschen can be pan-fried in vegetable oil or butter for a few minutes on each side the next day. It's traditional to scramble an egg in the pan with the fried Maultaschen. Once the Maultaschen are boiled and cooled, you can freeze them for up to 3 months.

CONTINUED

GESCHMELZTE ZWIEBELN
Caramelized Onions

The recipe can be scaled up or down as needed. Any leftovers can
be refrigerated for up to 5 days.

MAKES 1 CUP / 200G

3 Tbsp / 42g unsalted butter
6 to 8 medium onions, peeled and cut into thin half-moons
1 tsp salt
1 tsp sugar
Freshly ground black pepper
¼ cup / 60ml water

1   Melt the butter in a sauté pan over medium to medium-high heat. Add
the onions, salt, sugar, and pepper. Cook, stirring occasionally, for 15 to
20 minutes, regulating the heat so that the onions take on good color but
don't burn. When the pan starts to get dry and the onions seem like they're
on the edge of getting too brown, add the water to the pan.

2   Stir well and let simmer for about 5 minutes, until most of the liquid has
evaporated. Taste and adjust the seasoning, then serve with the Maultaschen
(if serving without broth).

MATJES HAUSFRAUEN ART

Herring in Cream Sauce with Apples and Onions

SERVES 4

8 matjes herring filets
    (1.3 lb / 600g)

¾ cup plus 1 Tbsp / 200g sour
    cream

3 Tbsp heavy cream

2 Tbsp apple cider vinegar

1 tsp sugar

2 small crisp, juicy apples,
    peeled, cored, cut into
    quarters, and then into
    thin slices

2 small onions, peeled, halved,
    and cut into thin half-moons

1 dill pickle, thinly sliced
    crosswise

Bratkartoffeln (page 211) or
    Pellkartoffeln (page 209)
    for serving

During the writing of this book, I was ruthless about only including recipes from Germany's enormous recipe canon that I personally loved. This one is really the only exception, but I included it because its fans are legion. My own father, in fact, eats matjes herring two or three times a week when he's in Germany. Outdoor markets almost always have a vendor selling Fischbrötchen, which are crusty white rolls filled with cold-smoked salmon and onion rings, pickled herring, or Matjes herring and sliced onions and pickles, and he can never resist them. In his honor, I'm including this dish, which features matjes herring in a cream sauce with apples and onions and is a stalwart on traditional German restaurant menus and at canteens and deli counters, usually served with boiled potatoes or fried potatoes (page 211). My father was the excellent and willing recipe tester for this recipe, so all credit goes to him.

Matjes herring is a young herring that is salted and preserved in brine and usually a bit of neutral oil. For this recipe, avoid herring that has already been pickled or marinated with onions, vinegar, and/or sugar. In the United States, you can find this kind of matjes, usually packed in a plastic container, at almost any Eastern European grocery store.

Sour cream in Germany is looser than American sour cream, so in this recipe, I ask you to thin it with heavy cream. You can also use light cream or half-and-half in place of the heavy cream if you prefer.

1   Soak the matjes in water for 30 minutes. Drain and, if you'd like, cut into bite-size pieces.

2   In a serving bowl, whisk together the sour cream and heavy cream until smooth, then whisk in the vinegar and sugar.

3   Fold the apples, onions, and pickle slices into the cream sauce.

4   Fold the matjes into the cream sauce. Marinate for at least 1 hour before serving. The dish keeps well in the refrigerator for up to 3 days.

5   Serve with Bratkartoffeln or Pellkartoffeln.

HECHTKLÖßCHEN

Pike Dumplings in Cream Sauce

SERVES 3 TO 4

FOR THE SPINACH

1 Tbsp unsalted butter

1 lb / 500g frozen spinach or
an equivalent amount of
fresh spinach, washed,
cooked, and drained

15 scrapes of whole nutmeg

Salt and freshly ground
black pepper

FOR THE DUMPLINGS

1 stale white roll or Kaiser
roll, cut into ¼ inch / 6mm
cubes

¼ cup / 60ml whole milk

1 lb / 450g fresh or frozen
pike, cod, or pollock,
thawed

1 lemon, halved

1 tsp salt

¼ tsp white pepper

1 egg

FOR THE SAUCE

1 Tbsp unsalted butter

½ onion, finely minced

Salt

1 Tbsp all-purpose flour

1 cup / 250ml heavy cream

White pepper

15 scrapes of whole nutmeg

Handful of flat-leaf parsley,
finely minced

Juice of ½ lemon

The resemblance of these tender little poached dumplings of minced fish mixed with delicate seasonings to gefilte fish is no coincidence, though German Jews stopped eating gefilte fish for Sabbath in the nineteenth century, which I learned in *The German-Jewish Cookbook* by Gabrielle Rossmer Gropman and Sonya Gropman. Hechtklößchen, as their name indicates, were traditionally made with pike (Hecht in German), though pollock or cod also works very well here. Mixing the fish with bread and milk would have been one way to make a bit of fish go further in times when fish would have been scarce or economically out of reach for regular preparation.

Today, I think of them as a lighter alternative to fish cakes, and I usually make them with cod, which is easier to source in Berlin than pike. To make them, you use your hands to shape the fish mixture into oval quenelles (also known as Nocken in Austrian), then poach them in simmering water. They're covered in a delicate cream sauce and served with spinach.

1 Cook the spinach: Melt the butter in a sauté pan over medium heat. Add the well-drained spinach to the pan, as well as the nutmeg. Add salt and black pepper to taste. Toss until well-combined and heated through. Scrape onto a serving platter.

2 For the dumplings: Place the bread in a small bowl. Add the milk and toss a few times. Set aside for 5 minutes.

3 Cut the fish into chunks and place in a food processor fitted with the blade attachment. Add the juice of half of the lemon, the salt, and white pepper. Squeeze out the soaked bread cubes and add to the food processor (discard the milk, if there is any). Finally, crack in the egg. Run the food processor until the mixture is smooth and creamy. Set aside.

4 Fill a wide, lidded pan with water and bring to a boil. Season with salt and the juice of half of the lemon. While the water is coming to a boil, use your hands to shape the fish mixture into oval quenelles that are about 2½ inches / 6cm long and about 1 inch / 2.5cm wide; you should have about 15 dumplings.

CONTINUED

5   When the water is boiling, turn the heat down and slip the dumplings into the water. Cover and poach on the lowest heat for 10 to 12 minutes.

6   While the dumplings are cooking, make the sauce: Place the butter in a saucepan over medium heat and when it has melted, add the onions and a pinch of salt. Cook, stirring, for 4 to 5 minutes, until the onions are starting to turn translucent and fragrant. Sprinkle in the flour and stir well to help the flour cook in the onions and butter. Cook for 1 to 2 minutes, lowering the heat if necessary, until the flour has lost its raw flavor. Slowly pour in the cream, whisking constantly.

7   When all the cream has been poured into the pan, continue to whisk and season with salt, white pepper, and the nutmeg. Cook for a few more minutes, until the sauce has a creamy and thickened but still pourable consistency. Remove from the heat and stir in the parsley and lemon juice. Whisk until completely combined.

8   Using a spider, remove the dumplings from the poaching water and let drain very well, then place them on the bed of spinach. Pour the cream sauce all over the dumplings and serve immediately.

HAMBURGER PANNFISCH

Pan-Fried Cod and Potatoes in Mustard Sauce

SERVES 4

3 Tbsp vegetable oil

⅓ cup / 1.7 oz / 50g minced
Speck or bacon

1 medium onion, minced

1½ lb / 700g waxy potatoes,
boiled, peeled, and sliced
¼-inch / 6mm thick

Salt and freshly ground
black pepper

1 lb / 500g cod, cut into four
pieces

All-purpose or gluten-free
flour for dusting

½ cup / 120ml white wine

3 Tbsp Dijon mustard

Generous ¾ cup / 200ml
heavy cream

Small bunch of flat-leaf
parsley, minced

This hearty dish of fish and fried potatoes in a mustard cream sauce originated in the nineteenth century in Hamburg, which is Germany's most important port city. It was developed as a nourishing way to use up leftover potatoes and fish, two plentiful foodstuffs that were always available to even the poorest in Hamburg. The original concept was a panful of Bratkartoffeln with onions and Speck (like on page 211) into which you would flake leftover cooked fish. And that is still one way to make it today. But it's even more delicious with freshly cooked fish. Cod, with its big, silky flakes, is ideal here. The light dusting of flour gives the fish a bit of structure as it fries, but also leaves behind delicious crusty bits in the pan that get incorporated into a sumptuous pan sauce with cream and lashings of mustard.

Some traditional recipes for Hamburger Pannfisch include sliced pickles in the finished dish, but I prefer it without them. If you'd like to include them, try to source German Gewürzgurken, which are sweeter and more spiced than regular pickles. Slice a handful of them into coins, then fold them into the potatoes once they finish cooking, or stir them into the pan sauce before topping with the potatoes.

1   Place 1 Tbsp of oil in a cast-iron or nonstick pan over medium heat and add the Speck and onion. Cook, stirring occasionally, for about 8 minutes, until the onions are golden brown. Scrape out into a small bowl and set aside.

2   Add another tablespoon of oil to the pan, set it back over medium-high heat, and add the potatoes. Cook without stirring or touching the pan for about 5 minutes, then shake the pan to move the potatoes around. You can flip them with a spatula, too. Season with salt and pepper. Cook for another 10 minutes, periodically flipping the potatoes until they are golden brown and crisp.

3   While the potatoes are cooking, lightly salt and pepper the cod, then dust each side of the fish lightly with flour. Place the remaining oil in a separate skillet over medium-high heat and slip the fish pieces into the pan. Cook for a few minutes on each side, until the fish is just barely cooked through, then transfer to a plate.

CONTINUED

4   Pour the wine into the pan and use a spatula to scrape up the bits on the bottom of the pan. Let simmer for 1 minute, then whisk in the mustard and cream. When the sauce is smooth and creamy, slip the pieces of fish back into the pan and cover the pan. Turn the heat down and let the fish absorb the flavors of the sauce for 5 minutes. Turn off the heat.

5   Just before the potatoes are finished, scrape the Speck and onions back into the pan. Add the parsley to the potatoes and stir well to incorporate. Adjust the seasoning to taste, then turn off the heat.

6   Scoop the potatoes out of the cast-iron pan and arrange them around the edge of the fish pan, directly in the sauce. Serve from the pan, scooping out some fish, sauce, and potatoes onto each plate.

SWEET MAIN COURSES

Sweet main courses are one of the more idiosyncratic traditions of German food culture. It is not unusual for German families to sit down to a meal of warm rice pudding topped with cinnamon-sugar or a plate of thin, eggy pancakes filled with jam. From Austria come more complex dishes such as fruit-filled dumplings rolled in toasted, buttered bread crumbs or a grand frying pan full of Kaiserschmarrn, a sweet main course meant for an emperor. The tradition partly emerged from the influence of the Catholic Church's strict adherence to fasting days, meaning that meals on those days had to be meatless. Things like dumplings, pancakes, grain puddings, and casseroles made with old bread could be prepared very cheaply, and were hot and filling, all three important factors for the average German eater for centuries. Long ago, these dishes weren't necessarily sweetened. But over time, and influenced both by the Habsburg monarchy and, later, the Austrian royal court, regional specialties like the sweet yeasted buns of Bohemia and thin pancakes from Hungary brought a sweeter profile to many of these traditional dishes.

In contemporary times, several of the recipes in this chapter are considered nursery food, typically made for young children as a quick, pleasing meal. I can always tell what my downstairs neighbors are making for their daughter for dinner when the kitchen windows are open and the scent of butter browning in a pan and sweet, eggy pancake batter curling up at the edges comes wafting up to our apartment. Milchreis—hot rice pudding—is a standard at school cafeterias. These dishes are considered treats of a sort, but still quite sensible. Desserts in Germany are more likely to be puddings, creams, or compotes, far less dough- or batter-focused; cakes and cookies are typically eaten in the afternoon for Kaffeezeit and not as dessert after a meal.

But, just to complicate things, there are a few dishes in this chapter that absolutely can be served as dessert, in particular the spectacularly convivial Kaiserschmarrn, which can be brought to the table under a cloak of confectioners' sugar and which absolutely no one will refuse even after a full meal.

To incorporate these dishes into your weekly life, and to balance your blood sugar, especially at midday, when many of us still have hours of work ahead of us, I suggest serving them either before or after a small cup of savory soup or a sharply dressed salad.

MILCHREIS MIT KIRSCHKOMPOTT

Warm Rice Pudding with Sour Cherry Compote

SERVES 4 ADULTS OR
6 CHILDREN

FOR THE RICE
4 cups / 1L milk
1¼ cups / 250g short-grain rice
2 Tbsp sugar
½ tsp salt
1 tsp vanilla extract
1 Tbsp unsalted butter

FOR THE SOUR CHERRY
  COMPOTE
1 (24 oz / 680g) jar or can
  pitted sour cherries in
  sugar water
2 Tbsp cornstarch
Cinnamon-sugar (page 16)
  for serving

The longest lines at my school cafeteria in Berlin were on Milchreis days. It seemed like almost everyone wanted in on the big white bowls filled with hot, creamy rice topped with a scarlet jumble of cherry compote. In Germany, both Milchreis and Grießbrei (page 175) are archetypal nursery foods and are often given as a main meal to children. They're easy to prepare, crowd-pleasing, and cheap. Many Germans of my generation associate them with mealtimes at their grandmothers' houses. Unlike rice pudding, Milchreis is always served hot, fresh from the pot. A bit of cold fruit compote dolloped on top provides a welcome pairing in texture, flavor, and temperature to the creamy, milky rice, or you can keep it simple with just a sprinkling of cinnamon-sugar. The cherry compote, below, is a classic pairing, but plum compote (page 186), apricot compote, or even just plain applesauce are wonderful with Milchreis, too.

1   For the rice: Place the milk in a medium pot. Add the rice, sugar, and salt. Stir well and set over medium heat. Bring to a boil, watching the pot to prevent the milk from boiling over. As soon as it begins to boil, lower the heat as far as it will go and cover. Cook for about 25 minutes, stirring occasionally, until the rice is cooked and creamy.

2   Turn off the heat and stir in the vanilla and butter until well-combined. Cover again and let sit for another 5 minutes before serving.

3   For the cherry compote: Drain the cherries over a small pot to catch all the canning liquid. Set the cherries aside. Place 2 Tbsp of the cherry liquid in a small bowl and whisk in the cornstarch.

4   Place the pot over medium heat and bring to a boil. As soon as the water is boiling, whisk in the cornstarch slurry until completely combined. The liquid should start to thicken. Let bubble for 30 seconds to 1 minute, then remove from the heat and whisk until completely smooth. Stir in the reserved cherries.

5   Serve the hot Milchreis in soup plates, passing the cinnamon-sugar and cherry compote to top the rice.

GRIEßSCHNITTEN MIT ZIMT-ZUCKER

Pan-Fried Custardy Farina Squares with Cinnamon-Sugar

SERVES 4 TO 6

Vegetable oil

4 cups / 1L whole milk

¼ cup / 50g sugar

Pinch of salt

1 cup plus 2 Tbsp / 200g wheat
  farina (Cream of Wheat)

1 egg

Grated zest of 1 lemon,
  optional

1 tsp vanilla extract, optional

Clarified butter for frying

Cinnamon-sugar (page 16)
  for serving

Applesauce for serving

I was absolutely delighted to discover these delicious farina treats during the research for this book. You cook up a thicker batch of farina pudding and immediately spread it out in a quarter sheet pan to cool. Once cooled, the pudding solidifies into a sliceable mass, like polenta. You cut it into squares and pan-fry them in clarified butter until golden brown on each side. The Schnitten have a lovely balance of textures between the crisp outside and the custardy inside. Cinnamon-sugar and a dollop of cool applesauce are essential accompaniments.

Some recipes will have you coat the Schnitten in beaten egg and bread crumbs before frying them for a crisper coating; I wanted to see if one could skip this step, which is often messy, and fell in love with this far simpler way of frying the Schnitten. But if you would like a crunchier result, absolutely try breading the Schnitten before frying them. Either way, the squares will be delicious.

1   Line a quarter sheet pan with plastic wrap and spread a thin layer of oil all over the plastic with your hands. Set aside.

2   Place the milk in a medium pot and add the sugar and salt. Place over medium-high heat and bring just to a boil.

3   Pour the wheat farina into the milk in a thin stream, whisking constantly. Lower the heat slightly and cook, whisking constantly, for another minute or two, until the mixture is thick and creamy.

4   Remove from the heat and swiftly and thoroughly whisk in the egg. If using zest or vanilla, whisk those in now.

5   Scrape the mixture evenly into the prepared pan and, using a flexible spatula, smooth the top evenly and make sure the mixture is pushed into all the corners. Cover with a second piece of plastic wrap that you place directly on top of the pudding. Set aside to cool to room temperature, then refrigerate for at least 1 hour and up to 8 hours.

CONTINUED

6   When ready to cook, remove the plastic wrap from the top and invert the pudding onto a cutting board. Remove the second piece of plastic wrap.

7   Using a sharp knife, cut the pudding into 3-inch / 7.5cm squares, dipping the knife into water as needed to prevent sticking. Alternatively, you can cut it into diamonds or triangles.

8   Place 1 to 2 Tbsp of butter in a nonstick or well-seasoned cast-iron pan over medium-high heat. When the butter is hot, place as many squares as will fit without crowding into the pan. Cook until golden brown on one side, 3 to 5 minutes, then flip and cook the other side until golden brown, another 3 to 5 minutes.

9   Repeat with the remaining squares, adding more butter to the pan if necessary. Serve with cinnamon-sugar and applesauce.

GRIEẞBREI

Warm Farina Pudding

SERVES 4

4 cups / 1L whole milk

2 Tbsp sugar

¼ tsp salt

½ cup plus 1 Tbsp / 100g
    wheat farina (Cream of
    Wheat)

1 egg, at room temperature,
    separated

1 tsp vanilla extract, optional

Grated zest of ½ lemon,
    optional

Applesauce for serving,
    optional

Sour Cherry Compote
    (page 170) for serving,
    optional

Cinnamon-sugar (page 16)
    for serving, optional

German Grießbrei is sweetened wheat farina, a spoonable pudding, served fresh from the stove, still piping hot. It is classic nursery food, given to young children as part of their first diet of solid foods, frequently on the menu at daycare centers and school cafeterias. But it is also a staple simple meal for Germans of all ages. *Brei* is the German word for "porridge" or "pap" and *Grieß* is the word for both "wheat farina" and "semolina."

At its simplest, Grießbrei is simply wheat farina cooked in boiling milk with a bit of sugar. Adding vanilla or lemon zest takes it up a notch in flavor, and an egg enriches it and adds texture. The yolk gets whisked into the hot pudding off the heat (whisk swiftly and steadily so the yolk doesn't scramble), while the egg white is whipped and then folded in to give the pudding a delicate wobble. Don't worry about consuming raw egg white; the temperature of the hot pudding will heat it enough to not be a problem. Grießbrei is served warm and is spoonable, like the Milchreis on page 170, and best served with applesauce or fruit compote or even just cinnamon-sugar to sprinkle on top.

1   Place the milk, sugar, and salt in a large pot over high heat. (Watch carefully; it will boil over if you get distracted.) When it just comes to a boil, turn the heat down to medium and whisk in the wheat farina. Regulate the heat so that the mixture simmers and cook for 2 minutes, whisking. (No lumps desired!) When it is thick and creamy, cover the pot, remove from the heat, and let rest for 5 minutes.

2   Meanwhile, place the egg white in a medium bowl. Whip with electric beaters or a whisk until stiff peaks form. Set aside.

3   After 5 minutes, take the lid off the pot and whisk in the egg yolk very quickly, then whisk in the vanilla and/or zest, if using, until well-combined.

4   Fold in the beaten egg white very thoroughly until no streaks of white remain.

5   Serve with either applesauce or cherry compote or simply sprinkled with cinnamon-sugar.

KIRSCHENMICHEL

Sour Cherry Bread Pudding

SERVES 4 TO 6

9½ Tbsp / 130g unsalted
    butter, at room
    temperature, plus more for
    the pan

10.5 oz / 300g stale white
    sandwich bread or rolls
    (about 7), sliced

1¾ cups / 400ml whole milk

4 eggs

Salt

½ cup plus 2 Tbsp / 125g sugar

½ tsp ground cinnamon

Grated zest of 1 lemon

1 tsp baking powder

10.5 oz / 300g pitted sour
    cherries (frozen or fresh,
    or canned and drained)

Scant 1 cup / 100g slivered
    almonds

Brötchen, which also go by the names of Weck, Semmel, and Schrippe, depending on your location in Germany, are plain white bread rolls typically eaten at breakfast or second breakfast. When spread with butter and jam or topped with cheese or ham, they're best the day they're made, but once they become stale, their usefulness increases. They soak up milk and flavorings well and are easily turned into dumplings or used as bolstering for meat fillings. They can also be used to make cozy bread puddings, like this one featuring sour cherries. If you don't have access to stale white bread rolls, this recipe is just as good made with stale sliced sandwich bread or even stale challah or other enriched breads (like the Rosinenzopf in my cookbook *Classic German Baking*).

The stale bread is sliced and oven-crisped with some butter to add both texture and flavor, then mixed with both beaten egg whites and a little batter made with the yolks. Sour cherries are the classic fruit to use here, though you can also use sweet cherries. Most German home cooks would use sour cherries that come in jars (they're sweetened, but canned in water or juice, not syrup). If you have a German or Eastern European grocery store near you, that may be the best source to find them. Otherwise, if you use fresh or frozen sour cherries, you may want to increase the sugar in the bread pudding just a touch.

Kirschenmichel (or Kirschenplotzer as it is also known, depending on the region) is best eaten hot from the oven, and if you're eating it as a main course, served as is (though a little bowl of soup for everyone beforehand rounds out the meal nicely). However, you can also easily turn this into dessert by making a jug of Vanillesoße (page 238) to serve alongside. The cool, silky sauce is a lovely pairing with the crusty, creamy, sweet-sour "pudding."

1   Preheat the oven to 350°F / 180°C. Butter the bottom and sides of a 9-inch / 23cm baking pan and set aside.

2   Place the slices of bread on a baking sheet in one layer and dot with 3½ Tbsp / 50 grams of the butter, cut into small pieces. Place in the oven and bake for 10 to 15 minutes, until fragrant and starting to crisp.

3   Place the hot bread in a large bowl and pour over the milk. Tear the bread into pieces as you mix it with the milk so that the pieces are evenly moistened. Set aside.

4   Separate the eggs, putting the egg whites in a clean bowl and the egg yolks in a separate mixing bowl. Using electric beaters, whip the egg whites with a generous pinch of salt. Beat until the egg whites hold firm peaks.

5   Using the same beaters, beat the sugar into the egg yolks, immediately followed by the remaining 6 Tbsp of butter. Beat until the mixture is creamy and well-combined, about 2 minutes. Beat in the cinnamon, zest, and baking powder.

6   Using a large spatula, fold the butter mixture into the soaked bread until well-combined. Fold in the sour cherries until well-distributed, then fold in the egg whites.

7   Scrape the mixture into the prepared baking pan. Scatter the almonds on top.

8   Bake for about 40 minutes, until toasty brown. Remove from the oven and let cool for a minute or two. Serve hot.

SCHEITERHAUFEN

Apple Bread Pudding

SERVES 4

5 small or 3 large tart, juicy
    apples, cored, peeled,
    quartered, and thinly sliced
¼ cup plus 2 Tbsp / 75g sugar
Unsalted butter, at room
    temperature, for the pan
4 eggs
2 cups / 500ml whole milk
1 tsp ground cinnamon
1 tsp vanilla extract
Pinch of salt
1 small stale challah loaf or
    brioche (about 10.5 oz /
    300g), or an equal amount
    of stale white sandwich
    bread or rolls (about 7),
    thinly sliced
½ cup / 50g sliced almonds

Scheiterhaufen is a bread pudding made with thinly sliced enriched bread, like challah or brioche, and apples, layered together and poured over with sweetened eggs and milk. The apples give it moisture and sweetness, which you can dial up with raisins if you like, and the almonds on top give it texture and crunch. Alternatively to the almonds, make a simple meringue by beating together 2 egg whites and 6 Tbsp / 50g of confectioners' sugar until glossy and stiff, then spread this evenly over the top of the casserole after 40 minutes of baking. Raise the oven temperature to 400°F / 200°C and return the meringue-topped casserole to the oven for the last 5 minutes of baking, until the meringue is a toasty golden brown.

If you don't have challah or brioche, you can substitute an equal amount of stale sandwich bread or sliced white rolls. I really like using sweet-tart apples here that hold their shape a little bit when sliced and baked. Use any apple that doesn't turn to mush when cooked and ideally one that has a bit of acidity.

As always, serving this with Vanillesoße (page 238) will take it to dessert, but it can also be served after a simple soup at lunch, or in place of cake or cookies at Kaffeezeit in the afternoon.

1   Preheat the oven to 350°F / 180°C. Place the apples in a bowl and sprinkle with 2 Tbsp of sugar. Toss well and set aside.

2   Butter a 9 by 13-inch / 23 by 33cm baking pan liberally with butter.

3   In a large bowl, whisk together the eggs, then whisk in the milk, the remaining ¼ cup / 50g of sugar, the cinnamon, vanilla, and salt.

4   Line the bottom of the prepared pan with a third of the challah slices, then cover with half of the apples. Cover the apples with a third of the bread, then repeat with the remaining apples. Top the apples with a final layer of bread and pour the milk mixture evenly over everything. Set aside for 5 to 10 minutes.

5   Before baking, scatter the almonds evenly over the top. Cover with aluminum foil and bake for 20 minutes, then remove the foil and bake for another 20 to 25 minutes, until the top is golden brown and the custard has set.

6   Remove from the oven and let cool for 10 to 15 minutes before serving.

QUARKAUFLAUF

Oven-Baked Quark Soufflé with Fruit

SERVES 4

Butter for the baking pan

3 eggs, separated

½ cup / 100g sugar

2 cups / 500g Quark (page 30)

Grated zest of 1 lemon

½ tsp baking powder

½ tsp ground cinnamon

¼ cup / 40g wheat farina
    (Cream of Wheat)

2 cups peeled and sliced tart,
    juicy apples or drained sour
    cherries from a jar

¼ tsp salt

Cinnamon-sugar (page 16) for
    serving, optional

Auflauf is the German word for casserole and can encompass everything from sweet bread puddings to savory bakes. My very favorite Auflauf is this lightly sweet one made with a pound of Quark (page 30) that is lightened with beaten eggs and thickened with wheat farina (Cream of Wheat). Fruit, like drained sour cherries or sliced apples, gets folded in, and then the entire creamy mixture is scraped into a baking pan and baked until puffed and golden brown. You spoon out big quivering portions of it and eat it warm from the oven. My friend Joanie used to make this for me when I was a little girl at her kitchen table and still sometimes makes it when my boys and I come over for lunch. If you like, you can pass cinnamon-sugar around to sprinkle over each portion—this topping isn't just for kids; it adds a nice crunch and flavor. Other fruits you can use in place of the apples or cherries are sliced pears, canned peaches or apricots, or even slices of sugared rhubarb.

1　Preheat the oven to 375°F / 190°C. Butter an 8 by 11-inch / 20 by 28cm baking pan that is at least 2½ inches / 6.5cm deep. Set aside.

2　In a large bowl, use electric beaters to beat the egg yolks and sugar together until pale yellow and frothy, 1 to 2 minutes. Beat in the Quark, zest, baking powder, cinnamon, and wheat farina until smooth and creamy. With a spatula, fold in the apples or cherries.

3　In a clean bowl, use an electric mixer to beat the egg whites until frothy, then whip in the salt and continue whipping until the whites hold medium peaks. With a spatula, fold in half of the egg whites into the farina mixture to lighten it, then fold in the remaining egg whites until no white streaks remain.

4　Scrape the mixture into the prepared pan and bake for about 30 minutes, until the Auflauf has set and is starting to brown. There might be a crack or two in the top.

5　Remove from the oven and serve hot or warm, sprinkled with cinnamon-sugar if desired.

PFANNKUCHEN / EIERKUCHEN

Thin Pancakes

SERVES 3 TO 4 AS A
LIGHT MEAL OR SNACK

2 eggs
2 cups / 500ml whole milk
¾ tsp salt
1 Tbsp vegetable oil
2 cups / 250g all-purpose flour
4½ Tbsp / 70ml boiling water
Cinnamon-sugar (page 16)
    for serving, optional
Applesauce for serving,
    optional

These delicate pancakes go by a couple of different names in Germany. Eierkuchen, which translated literally means "egg cake," are also known as Pfannkuchen, but not in Berlin, where Pfannkuchen are what Berliners call jelly doughnuts, which are known as Berliner elsewhere—are you confused yet? Pancakes are a beloved afternoon snack for German children, or even a light meal. Usually, they're served with cinnamon-sugar and/or applesauce or a thin layer of jam (or Nutella) as a filling, then rolled up and gobbled out of hand. In some regions, these pancakes are served during asparagus season, laid out with a thin layer of cooked ham and some boiled white asparagus, then rolled up and eaten with a knife and fork (a variation of this can be found on page 114).

I made my way through several different recipes to cobble together a recipe that produced my platonic ideal of an Eierkuchen, thin yet soft and slightly spongy. Many swore by a 30-minute resting time for the batter, or a splash of sparkling water to lighten the batter. But ultimately, I found Ukrainian food writer Olia Hercules's method (published in her wonderful book *Summer Kitchens*) to be best: She adds a splash of boiling water to the batter, which lightly pre-cooks the flour and allows you to use the batter straight away with no resting time. The recipe below, which is adapted from hers, is easily doubled.

1   Crack the eggs into a mixing bowl and whisk briefly. Whisk in the milk, salt, and oil, then whisk in the flour until smooth. Pour in the boiling water and whisk quickly until completely incorporated.

2   Heat a 10- to 12-inch / 25 to 30cm cast-iron or nonstick skillet over medium heat. (You can oil the pan if you like, but it probably won't be necessary.) Pour in a small ladleful of the batter and tilt and shake the pan to help the batter spread evenly. Cook until small bubbles form on the surface of the pancake, about 1 minute.

3   Flip the pancake and cook for another 30 to 60 seconds. The pancakes should be lightly golden brown on one side and speckled light brown on the other. Place on a serving plate and repeat with the remaining batter.

4   Serve immediately, sprinkled with cinnamon-sugar and/or applesauce and rolled up.

APFELPFANNKUCHEN

Apple Pancakes

MAKES 4 PANCAKES

2 eggs, separated

½ tsp salt

¼ cup / 50g granulated sugar

¾ cup / 200ml whole milk

¾ cup / 100g all-purpose flour

1 medium sweet, tart apple

Lemon juice

3 to 4 Tbsp clarified butter
    or vegetable oil

Cinnamon-sugar (page 16)
    or confectioners' sugar
    for serving

In my hazy memory I was still a child when I first heard about pancakes with thick apple slices fried into them. Were Hansel and Gretel fed apple pancakes by the witch to entice them to stay with her? I certainly would have been bewitched by anyone who served me a fluffy pancake with tart apple slices caramelized at the edges. This is German nursery food at its best—simple, cozy, and nutritious. My boys' eyes light up when I make these for dinner.

We prefer the crunch of cinnamon-sugar on the finished pancakes, but confectioners' sugar is also nice. The beaten egg whites stirred into the batter make each pancake fluffy and light and provide the grip that keeps the apple slices in place. In many German families, apple pancakes or apple fritters (page 35) are traditionally served before or after vegetable Eintopf. Choose apples that will hold their shape during cooking.

1 Place the egg whites in a clean bowl and begin to whip. As soon as they start to foam, add the salt and continue to whip until the egg whites hold stiff peaks. Set aside.

2 Place the egg yolks and granulated sugar in a mixing bowl and whip together until very pale and creamy, about 1 minute. Whip the yolks and sugar together until very pale and creamy, about 1 minute. Add the milk and flour and beat until smooth.

3 Stir the egg whites into the batter until smooth and no white streaks remain. Set aside for 15 minutes.

4 Peel, core, and quarter the apple, then cut each quarter into four or five slices. You will be using a quarter of an apple for each pancake. Sprinkle the apples with lemon juice and toss briefly.

5 Place 1 Tbsp of butter in a pan over medium-high heat. When the pan is hot, add a quarter of the batter and shake the pan a little to spread the batter a bit. Arrange four or five apple slices on top of the pancake. Cook for about 2 minutes, until bubbles start appearing on the surface. Flip and cook for another 2 minutes, until golden brown. Remove from the pan and repeat with the remaining batter and apples until you have four pancakes, adding more butter to the pan if necessary.

KAISERSCHMARRN MIT ZWETSCHGENRÖSTER

Torn Souffléd Pancake with Plum Compote

SERVES 4

¼ cup / 40g raisins, optional

2 Tbsp rum, optional

1¼ cups / 300ml whole milk

4 eggs, separated

1 tsp vanilla extract

½ tsp plus ⅛ tsp salt

1¾ cups / 220g all-purpose
flour

¼ cup / 50g granulated sugar

3 to 4 Tbsp unsalted butter

¼ cup / 30g slivered or sliced
almonds, toasted, optional

Confectioners' sugar
for serving

Plum Compote (page 186) and/
or applesauce for serving

Kaiserschmarrn, an airy souffléd pancake torn into fluffy shreds, is one of Austria's most famous dishes. When brought to the table, Kaiserschmarrn are showered with confectioners' sugar and served with a little dish of stewed plums or applesauce for dragging the fluffy pancake through. The acidic and cooling bite of the fruit compote is a wonderful contrast to the hot, sweet pancake. It's no surprise that they are on virtually all mountaintop restaurant menus in the Tyrolean Alps; there may be no better restorative lunch than a platter of white-capped Kaiserschmarrn eaten after a strenuous morning of skiing.

There are a handful of explanations for the name (which means "emperor's nonsense"), but it seems to be widely accepted that the dish was a favorite of Emperor Franz Joseph I of Austria (1830–1916) and his wife, Elisabeth, more widely known as Sissi. Kaiserschmarrn are usually categorized as a dessert, and they are indeed a very lovely dessert, especially when served on a large platter with many forks for many eaters. But Kaiserschmarrn are also often eaten as a sweet main course in Austria.

There are many variations on Kaiserschmarrn. Some recipes include rum-soaked raisins. Some caramelize the pancake shreds in the pan with additional sugar. Some just cover them with a thick cloak of powdered sugar. Some add sliced almonds to the pan, some use chopped almonds. Some cook the Schmarrn only on the stove, others use a combination of stove and oven.

After many, many tests, the recipe below is the one I like the best. You make a simple batter lightened with a glossy mass of egg whites, then cook it on the stove in a well-seasoned cast-iron pan to set the bottom before transferring it to the oven, where it puffs up and cooks to completion. At the end, tear up the pancake with two knives in the pan and then toast the pieces a few more times with a little extra butter to crisp up any soft edges. (If you'd like to add sliced or slivered toasted almonds to the pan, this would be the moment to add them.)

1 Preheat the oven to 350°F / 180°C. If desired, place the raisins in a small bowl and pour in the rum (alternatively, use just enough hot water to cover). Set aside to plump.

2 In a mixing bowl, whisk the milk into the egg yolks until well-combined, then whisk in the vanilla and ½ tsp of salt. Whisking constantly, slowly add the flour. Whisk until smooth.

CONTINUED

3   If using the rum raisins, drain the plumped raisins and stir them into the batter. Set aside.

4   In a separate clean bowl, use electric beaters to beat the egg whites. As soon as they begin to froth, add the remaining ⅛ tsp of salt. As soon as large bubbles form, slowly pour in the granulated sugar. Continue beating until the whites hold stiff, glossy peaks.

5   Stir a quarter of the egg whites into the flour and yolk mixture to lighten it, then stir the remaining egg whites into the lightened batter until no white streaks remain and the batter is creamy and airy.

6   Melt 2 Tbsp of butter in a well-seasoned cast-iron skillet (10 to 12 inches / 25 to 30cm) over medium heat. When the butter starts to foam, pour the batter into the pan and smooth the top. Cook for about 5 minutes, always at medium heat, until the pancake bottom is just set (you can test this by delicately running a very thin knife or spatula around the edges of the pan to see if the pancake holds its shape).

7   Immediately place the pan in the oven and bake for about 12 minutes if using a 12-inch / 30cm pan and about 15 minutes if using a 10-inch / 25cm pan. The pancake will have puffed up and the top should be a pale golden color.

8   Remove the pan from the oven and, using two dinner knives, slice the pancake crosswise four or five times, then rotate the pan and slice again four or five times. Add the remaining 1 or 2 Tbsp of butter to the pan with the torn pancake pieces and set the pan over medium heat. (If adding the toasted almonds, now is the moment.) Using a spatula, toss and continue to cut the pancake pieces for just another minute or so, creating bite-size and smaller pieces and letting them brown a bit more in the pan.

9   Place the pan on the table (on a trivet!) and, if serving for dessert, sift a generous amount of confectioners' sugar over the top. If serving for lunch, you can skip the confectioners' sugar if you like. Pass plum compote and/or applesauce to be eaten with each portion of Kaiserschmarrn.

ZWETSCHGENRÖSTER

Plum Compote

MAKES ABOUT
4 CUPS / 1KG

½ cup / 100g sugar

2.2 lb / 1kg prune plums, washed, halved, and pitted

Juice of 1 lemon

1 tsp ground cinnamon or 1 cinnamon stick

2 Tbsp Armagnac or Slivovitz

Zwetschgen are the classic plums used in both the German and Austrian sweet kitchen. They are small and oval and a gorgeous shade of dark blue. Zwetschgen are harvested in late summer and can be cooked into plum butter (page 39), stewed into compote, and baked into yeasted cakes (a recipe for which is in my book *Classic German Baking*). This compote is delicious with sweet, eggy Kaiserschmarrn (page 186), but can also be served under Topfenknödel (page 245), on top of Grießbrei (page 175) or Milchreis (page 170), alongside Böhmische Knödel (page 224), or simply with a dollop of yogurt.

Caramelizing the sugar before adding the prunes gives the compote a deeper, richer flavor, especially when paired with the splash of Armagnac at the end. If you prefer to skip the caramelization, just add the sugar with the plums and go from there. You can skip the Armagnac or Slivovitz if you want, but know that the spirits don't make the compote boozy, since you cook them off a bit, but they do add some complexity of flavor.

The compote keeps well in the refrigerator for about a week, or can be frozen or even canned. You can make Marillenröster (apricot compote—*Marille* is Austrian for "apricot") by replacing the plums with apricots and the Armagnac with apricot brandy or Cointreau.

1   Place the sugar in a large pot and set over medium-high heat. Let the sugar melt without stirring, though you can occasionally swirl the pot. When the sugar has melted, let it cook until it starts to turn golden brown. Don't let it burn. As soon as it has reached a rich gold color, quickly but carefully add the plums to the pot. Let the plums sizzle in the caramel for a minute or so, shaking the pot to help them settle. Add the lemon juice and shake the pot to distribute the juice. Add the cinnamon and stir. (If caramel from the bottom of the pot attaches itself to the wooden spoon, don't worry; just leave the spoon in the plums for a minute or two and it will melt as the plums cook.)

2   As soon as the liquid in the pot is bubbling, lower the heat, cover, and simmer for 8 to 10 minutes, stirring occasionally. Add the Armagnac, stir well, and simmer for another 3 minutes with the lid askew. The plums should be stewy, though not quite broken down, and submerged in their own liquid. Remove from the heat and set aside to cool, lid askew.

3   The compote can be eaten warm or cool. Refrigerated, it will keep for up to 1 week.

QUARKKEULCHEN

Quark Fritters with Potatoes and Raisins

MAKES 12 FRITTERS

14 oz / 400g starchy potatoes, like Russet, boiled and peeled

2 eggs

1 cup plus 3 Tbsp / 300g Quark (page 30)

¼ cup / 50g sugar

½ tsp salt

¼ cup / 30g all-purpose flour, plus more if potatoes are freshly boiled

Grated zest of ½ lemon

¼ cup / 40g raisins

Clarified butter or vegetable oil for frying

Applesauce for serving, optional

Cinnamon-sugar (page 16) for serving, optional

My mother-in-law is from the beautiful town of Meissen, near Dresden in Saxony. One of her specialties is classic Saxonian Quarkkeulchen, plump little patties of mashed potatoes, Quark, and raisins that are pan-fried until golden brown on both sides and served with applesauce. They are surprisingly filling and, unsurprisingly, appeal to most children. Quarkkeulchen are a classic recipe to use up leftover boiled potatoes, which most German households always have in supply. When I make them, I mash the potatoes with a fork because I like leaving a bit of texture in the patties, but if you prefer you can mash them until completely smooth. You can, of course, cook the potatoes freshly for this recipe; you just may need slightly more flour in the batter as the potatoes will be less dry than if they'd been cooked the day before. When fully mixed, the batter should hold its shape when spooned into the hot pan.

I think Quarkkeulchen benefit from being fried in clarified butter, but you can use vegetable oil, too. Any leftovers can be munched on cold the next day with a cup of coffee. You can substitute a gluten-free flour blend for the flour.

1   Place the boiled potatoes in a large bowl, then mash them coarsely with a fork or a potato masher or grate them on a box grater. Whisk in the eggs, Quark, sugar, and salt. Whisk in the flour and zest, making sure that everything is well-incorporated. Fold in the raisins. The batter should hold its shape when spooned into the pan; if necessary, add a spoonful or two of flour to the batter and mix well.

2   Pour a tablespoon or two of butter into a seasoned cast-iron or nonstick skillet. Place over medium-high heat. Using a large spoon, scoop four 3-inch / 7.5cm rounds of batter into the skillet. Cook for about 4 minutes, adjusting the heat so that the fritters don't burn. When the first side is golden brown, flip the fritters and cook the other side until brown, another 4 minutes or so.

3   Remove the fritters and place on a serving plate. Repeat with the remaining batter, adding more butter to the pan as necessary.

4   Serve the fritters with applesauce and/or cinnamon-sugar.

MARILLENKNÖDEL

Fresh Apricot Dumplings

MAKES 6 DUMPLINGS

1 cup / 250g Quark (page 30)

6 small apricots

6 sugar cubes or 3 tsp
  Demerara sugar

Grated zest of 1 lemon

4 Tbsp / 55g unsalted butter,
  at room temperature

1 egg yolk

¾ cup / 75g wheat farina
  (Cream of Wheat)

2 Tbsp granulated sugar

1 tsp pure vanilla extract

¼ tsp salt

Scant ½ cup / 50g all-purpose
  flour, plus more for
  forming

⅓ cup / 40g unseasoned
  bread crumbs

Confectioners' sugar
  for serving

From the culinary archives of the Austro-Hungarian Empire comes forth what I believe to be the crown jewel of dumplings: the marvelous Austrian fruit dumpling. Imagine a tender and delicate Quark-enriched dough flavored with lemon zest and vanilla, encasing a sugar-stuffed apricot (or small prune plum, if in season), then simmered until plump and pillowy, rolled in toasted, buttered bread crumbs, and dusted with a fine shower of confectioners' sugar. To eat, you sink the tines of your fork through the crisp coating, into the tender dumpling, and break open the sweet-tart fruit. Feed these to a table of hungry people and they will feel like royalty.

In Austria, these can either be served as the star of a light meal (preceded by a bowl of soup or followed by a big green salad) or as dessert. This recipe, which comes from Nicole Stich, a Munich-based food blogger, is easily doubled or even tripled, something I found out during an epic afternoon Marillenknödel party hosted by my dear friend Stephen Bitterolf, a half-Austrian Riesling importer, at his un-air-conditioned Brooklyn apartment over a decade ago. I set up an assembly line on the kitchen counter while the Riesling flowed copiously and made batches of dough, splitting apricots, poaching dumplings, toasting bread crumbs, and sifting confectioners' sugar, over and over again.

The dough for the dumplings is rather soft and delicate, so try to handle it as little as possible. If you keep your counters and hands well-floured during the shaping, you should be fine. To make Zwetschgenknödel, simply replace the apricots with prune plums.

1   Place the Quark in a fine-mesh sieve and let drain into the sink for at least 15 minutes, but ideally closer to 1 hour.

2   Wash the apricots and dry them, then cut them open along their seams halfway, still leaving them hinged together, and remove their pits. Fill their centers with either a sugar cube or ½ tsp of Demerara sugar and set aside.

3   Bring a large pot of salted water to a boil, then turn down the heat to a light simmer.

CONTINUED

4 In a large bowl, use a wooden spoon to cream together the strained Quark, the zest, 2 Tbsp of butter, the egg yolk, wheat farina, granulated sugar, vanilla, and salt. When the mixture is well-combined and fluffy, fold in the flour until just combined. Don't overmix. Turn the dough onto a well-floured surface and, with well-floured hands, form the dough gently into a thick log.

5 Cut the log into six equal pieces. With floured hands, gently pat each piece into a small round, then place a sugar-filled apricot in the middle of the dough and gently wrap the dough around the apricot. Form a neat little dumpling (re-flour your hands as necessary) and make sure that the apricots are completely encased by the dough.

6 Carefully slip the dumplings into the simmering water and watch to make sure none stick to the bottom of the pot, stirring very gently if needed. Let them simmer on low heat for 12 to 14 minutes.

7 Meanwhile, melt the remaining 2 Tbsp of butter in a small skillet over medium heat, then add the bread crumbs. Cook, stirring, until the bread crumbs are golden brown and fragrant, between 3 and 5 minutes. They can burn easily, so keep an eagle eye on them. Remove from the heat but leave the bread crumbs in the pan.

8 Using a spider, remove the dumplings from the pot, draining well, then gently place them in the pan with the buttered bread crumbs and roll them around until each one is evenly covered. (Do this in batches.) Place the dumplings on a serving plate and dust generously with confectioners' sugar. Serve immediately.

GERMKNÖDEL

Giant Steamed Dumplings with Plum Butter and Poppyseeds

MAKES 4 DUMPLINGS

FOR THE DUMPLINGS

½ cup / 125ml whole milk,
   lukewarm

½ oz / 15g fresh yeast or
   1½ tsp instant yeast

1¾ cups plus 2 Tbsp / 300g
   all-purpose flour, plus more
   for dusting

1½ Tbsp / 20g unsalted butter,
   melted, plus more for
   brushing if steaming

¼ cup plus 1 Tbsp / 30g
   confectioners' sugar

1 tsp vanilla extract

2 egg yolks

Grated zest of ½ lemon

¼ tsp salt

4 Tbsp Pflaumenmus (page 39)

FOR SERVING

8½ Tbsp / 120g unsalted
   butter, melted

⅓ cup plus 1 tsp / 50g
   poppyseeds, ground

¼ cup / 25g confectioners'
   sugar

Oh, the mighty Germknödel. If the crown jewel of dumplings is the Austrian Marillenknödel (page 189), then the Germknödel is the plump and well-fed emperor of the dumpling kingdom. There may be nothing more impressive, nearly bordering on preposterous, than a puffy dome of steamed sweetened dough stuffed with a rich dollop of tangy Pflaumenmus, poured over with melted butter, topped with ground sweetened poppy seeds, and, finally, a generous shower of confectioners' sugar.

These dumplings are cozy, indulgent treats and best eaten in cold, dark months. There's a reason every Austrian ski hut serves them to ravenous diners whose appetite has been sharpened by the snow and ice. While they are an Austrian classic, Germknödel have become so beloved in Germany that you can even find industrially produced ones in the freezer section of almost every grocery store. It goes without saying that homemade ones are far superior.

Germ, which is Austrian dialect for "yeast" (Hefe in German), indicates that this dumpling isn't one made of leftover bread or boiled potatoes. For these dumplings, you make a rich yeast dough flavored with vanilla and lemon zest, as if you were making sweet rolls or a braided bread. Then you divide the dough into pieces, roll them out into rounds, pop a bit of Pflaumenmus into each one, and then let them rise before steaming them into puffy mounds. You can either steam them over simmering water or in a panful of simmering sweetened milk, which will give them a delectable bottom crust. Either way, the topping is essential: Ground poppyseeds and confectioners' sugar add texture, sweetness, and a mystically delicate flavor, while a generous pour of melted butter helps the dumpling go down easily. Some people serve Germknödel doused in silky Vanillesoße (page 238), then topped with ground poppyseeds.

If you want to steam the dumplings over water, you'll need a pot with a steamer insert and a lid. To grind poppyseeds, you will need a hand-cranked poppyseed grinder or a spice grinder. Don't use unground poppyseeds. Only grinding poppyseeds unlocks their mysterious flavor. If you can find fresh yeast, this is a wonderful recipe to use it in. But you can also substitute instant yeast. Do not use active dry yeast.

If you leave out the poppyseed filling, shape these into slightly smaller rounds (divide this recipe into 8 portions instead of 4), steam them in milk, and serve them with a fruit compote like Zwetschgenröster (page 186), you'll have made Dampfnudeln.

CONTINUED

GERMKNÖDEL
continued

1 If using fresh yeast: Pour the lukewarm milk into a large bowl. Crumble in the fresh yeast and whisk to dissolve. Whisk in ⅓ cup plus 1 Tbsp / 50g of flour until smooth, then cover with a cloth and set aside for 15 minutes. In a separate bowl, whisk together the butter, confectioners' sugar, vanilla, egg yolks, zest, and salt. Whisk until frothy. Pour the remaining flour into the bowl with the yeast mixture and, stirring, pour in the egg mixture.

2 If using instant yeast: Place the instant yeast, flour, confectioners' sugar, and salt in a large bowl and whisk to combine. In a separate bowl, whisk together the lukewarm milk, butter, vanilla, egg yolks, and zest. Pour the egg mixture into the flour mixture.

3 Stir with a wooden spoon until a shaggy dough comes together, then knead in the bowl to absorb all the flour. Scrape the dough onto a very lightly floured work surface and knead until the dough is smooth, about 5 minutes. Resist adding additional flour to keep the dumplings as supple as possible.

4 Place the dough into a clean bowl and cover with a cloth. Place in a warm spot and let rise for about 45 minutes.

5 When the dough is puffy and risen, divide it into four pieces that each weigh 4½ oz / 130g. Roll each piece into a ball, then flatten to a circle about 5 inches / 13cm in diameter. Using your fingers, push a little well in the middle of each circle.

6 Spoon a tablespoon of Pflaumenmus into each well. Gently pull on the sides of each dough round to stretch it out a little, then pull the sides to the middle and pinch the seam closed to form a dumpling, without any Pflaumenmus squeezing out. When you've closed the dumpling, place it seam-side down on your work surface and use your hands to smooth the dumpling a few times and simultaneously turn it on its axis to seal the bottom as well as possible. Repeat with the remaining dough and jam. Cover the dumplings with a dish towel and let them rise for 30 minutes.

CONTINUED

GERMKNÖDEL
continued

7   To steam over water: Cut a piece of parchment paper to fit a steamer insert. Brush the parchment paper evenly with melted butter and place it in the steamer. Bring some water in a lidded pot to a boil. (Make sure the water level is below the insert.) When the water is boiling, gently transfer the dumplings, so as not to deflate them, onto the parchment-lined steamer insert (depending on the size of your pot, you may have to steam the dumplings in two stages). Place the insert gently over the pot of simmering water and cover. Keep the water at a simmer and steam for about 25 minutes, until the dumplings are puffy and have a dull sheen to them.

8   To steam in milk: Place 1 cup / 125ml of milk in a wide saucepan and add 2 Tbsp sugar and 1 Tbsp of butter. Set over medium heat. As soon as the milk starts to bubble, gently slip the dumplings, so as not to deflate them, into the simmering milk. Cover the pan and turn the heat to low. Let the dumplings steam for about 25 minutes. The milk will slowly evaporate as the dumplings cook. Keeping the heat low will ensure that it doesn't burn or evaporate too quickly. Ideally, the milk-steamed dumplings will develop a thin bottom crust.

9   When the dumplings have finished cooking, remove the lid and turn off the heat. Carefully transfer each dumpling to a serving plate. Spoon the melted butter equally over each dumpling. Sprinkle each dumpling equally with ground poppyseeds and confectioners' sugar and serve immediately with two forks to tear the dumpling apart rather than cutting it with a fork and knife.

VEGETABLES, POTATOES & DUMPLINGS

In German, the word for a starchy side dish like potatoes, noodles, or dumplings is Sättigungsbeilage, a term that originated in the German Democratic Republic. Roughly translated, it means "a satiating side that fills you up," which tells you a lot about the German mindset when it comes to these dishes. The goal of side dishes, traditionally and still today, was to provide satiety more than anything else. Even my German husband, born in the mid-1970s, thinks of starchy sides primarily as a way to quell his hunger. If, at dinnertime, there isn't quite enough rice or pasta or potatoes to go around, even with other food present, he feels a bit anxious. Just in case you were wondering, yes, there's a German word for that feeling, which I learned from my friend Lu Nelson, a Canadian who has lived in Berlin for twenty years: Sättigungsbeilagenpanik!

Perhaps unsurprisingly, potatoes dominate this chapter. As Nika Standen Hazelton put it in her wonderful Time-Life cookbook, *The Cooking of Germany*, "once [Germans] accepted [the potato as an edible tuber], they proceeded to apply to its use more ingenuity and inventiveness than had any of their neighbors." Fried potatoes, boiled potatoes, mashed potatoes, grated potatoes, bread made from potatoes, cake made with potatoes, potato dumplings, and potato noodles; the sheer number of traditional German dishes based on the potato is astonishing.

German cooked-vegetable dishes largely break down into two camps— they are usually either creamy or sour. The creamy roux, or Mehlschwitze, used to thicken a pot of vegetables was also an ingenious way to stretch the ingredients a little further and to add a few more calories onto everyone's plate. But those delicate flour-based sauces also paired well with the heartier flavors of German cooking and provided a copious sauce to help all those potatoes on the side go down. Cabbage, on the other hand, whether it's green or red or a gorgeously ruffled Savoy, is always good when paired with the sharp, strong flavors of vinegar and bacon.

RAHMSPINAT

Creamed Spinach

SERVES 4 AS A SIDE

1 lb / 500g frozen spinach

1 cup / 250ml water

1 Tbsp unsalted butter

1½ tsp all-purpose flour

¼ cup / 65ml vegetable stock

⅓ cup plus 1 Tbsp / 100g sour
    cream

Freshly ground black pepper

Freshly grated nutmeg

This classic side dish features heavily in the comfort meal fantasies of many German children (and former children). One classic German meal features Rahmspinat with a fried egg on top and potatoes on the side. There is much discourse over the best kind of potato dish to go with this meal. A dear friend, who was born in Kassel but grew up in West Berlin, always insisted on Bratkartoffeln (page 211), but others say they are too rich here. Salzkartoffeln (page 209) get many votes, especially because it's nice to crush the boiled, peeled potatoes together with the creamy spinach with your fork. This would be my choice. But the most passionate voices are those who insist that creamy Kartoffelpurée (page 210) is best with Rahmspinat and fried eggs.

I use frozen whole-leaf spinach exclusively. (Fresh spinach is not always easy to find in Berlin, and I'm happy to skip the onerous washing process.) The key, I find, is not to overcook it. You can, of course, use fresh spinach, if you prefer. I chop the spinach by hand because I like the slightly rougher texture in the finished dish. If you want a creamier finish, you can use a food processor to puree the cooked spinach instead.

While the spinach is draining, you make a very small portion of roux with vegetable stock, which becomes the bulk of the flavoring of the final dish. If you substitute the stock with water or milk, be sure to add enough salt to your taste. Sour cream instead of heavy cream gives the finished dish a subtle fresh tang, which I love, and makes it slightly less rich. You can substitute a gluten-free flour blend for the flour.

1   Place the frozen spinach in a small pot with the water. Cover and place over high heat. Bring to a boil and cook for 5 minutes, then drain. Let cool for 10 minutes before squeezing out excess water. Chop finely. (If you want a creamier dish, puree the spinach in a food processor.)

2   Place the butter in a small saucepan over medium heat. Melt and add the flour. Cook, whisking, until the mixture has turned golden and bubbles. Whisk in the stock until smooth. Let cook for about 1 minute until thickened.

3   Stir the chopped spinach into the sauce and lower the heat. Stir in the sour cream, then season with pepper to taste and several scrapes of nutmeg. Taste for seasoning and adjust if necessary. Serve immediately.

KOHLRABIGEMÜSE

Creamed Kohlrabi

SERVES 4 TO 6
AS A SIDE

3 medium kohlrabi, peeled
2 cups / 500ml vegetable broth
2 Tbsp unsalted butter
3 Tbsp all-purpose flour
¾ cup / 200ml whole milk
¾ tsp salt
Freshly ground black pepper
30 scrapes of whole nutmeg

Kohlrabi is a relatively new vegetable on American plates, but in Germany it's a classic. While I usually serve it raw to my children before dinner on a plate of other crudités (the best way to get them to eat vegetables, I find), cooked kohlrabi is a delicately toothsome dish. The kohlrabi, cut into batons, are first cooked in broth, then stirred into a creamy white sauce flavored with nutmeg. It's very soothing, best served with boiled potatoes to crush into the sauce and something hearty like Buletten (page 119) or pan-fried sausages. Raw kohlrabi's crunch really appeals to me, but I love cooked kohlrabi, too—it becomes sweet and tender—and the velvety sauce is delicious. If the kohlrabi still have leaves attached, set aside a few of the nicest ones to mince and fold into the sauce at the end. Incidentally, this preparation can also be used for other cruciferous vegetables like cauliflower or Brussels sprouts. Just remember to blanch them first.

You can substitute a gluten-free flour blend for the flour.

1   Cut the kohlrabi into ½-inch / 1.3cm slices, then cut the slices into ¼-inch / 6mm batons. Set aside.

2   Bring the broth to a boil in a medium saucepan. Add the kohlrabi and simmer, covered, for about 10 minutes, until tender. Drain, saving the cooking liquid.

3   In a medium saucepan, melt the butter over medium-high heat. Scatter in the flour and cook, stirring, for a minute or two. Whisk in ¾ cup / 200ml of the reserved broth, then whisk in the milk. Continue to cook, whisking, until the sauce has thickened, 3 to 5 minutes. Add the salt, the pepper to taste, and the nutmeg. If the sauce is too thick, loosen it with a bit more of the vegetable broth.

4   Fold in the drained kohlrabi, adjust the seasoning to your taste, and serve.

WIRSINGGEMÜSE

Creamed Savoy Cabbage

SERVES 6

2 Tbsp unsalted butter

1 onion, halved and slivered

¾ tsp salt

1 small head of Savoy cabbage
(1.5 to 1.8 lb / 750 to 850g),
cored, quartered, and
sliced into thin strips

6½ Tbsp / 100ml water

⅛ tsp sugar

1 cup / 250ml heavy cream

30 scrapes of whole nutmeg

Freshly ground black pepper

Usually, German recipes for cooked cabbage skew sour, as with Sauerkraut, or sweet-sour, as with Rotkohl (page 202). This stewed Savoy cabbage is an exception. It is cooked with onions and a bit of cream and nutmeg, taming and sweetening the faint bitter flavor that Savoy can sometimes have. It's delicious served with hearty Semmelknödel (page 222) or Kaspressknödel (page 105), but also makes a wonderful side to Buletten (page 119) or Maultaschen (page 155).

1   Melt the butter in a 10- to 12-inch / 25 to 30cm sauté pan with a lid or a large pot over medium heat and add the onion and ½ tsp of salt. Cook, stirring occasionally, until the onion is tender and fragrant, about 5 minutes.

2   Add the cabbage to the pot. Stir well and raise the heat to medium-high. Cook for 3 to 4 minutes, stirring occasionally, then pour in the water. Add the remaining ¼ tsp of salt and the sugar. As soon as the water starts to bubble, cover the pot and let cook for 10 minutes.

3   Remove the lid, stir well, and add the cream, nutmeg, and pepper. Stir again, and as soon as the cream starts to bubble, cover the pot and cook for another 10 minutes. The cabbage should be tender and creamy.

4   Taste and adjust the seasoning. Set aside until ready to serve.

ROTKOHL

Braised Red Cabbage with Apples and Onions

SERVES 8 TO 10,
WITH LEFTOVERS

2 Tbsp lard or goose fat
  (preferable) or vegetable oil

2 medium onions, peeled and
  finely chopped

2 tsp salt, plus more as needed

2 cooking apples, peeled,
  cored, and cut into
  ½-inch / 1cm dice

2 Tbsp sugar, plus more as
  needed

1 medium head (about 2.8 lb
  / 1.3kg) of red cabbage,
  halved, cored, and thinly
  shredded

½ cup / 125ml red wine

10 cloves

10 juniper berries

1 bay leaf

1 cup / 250ml beef broth

¼ cup / 60ml apple cider
  vinegar or red wine
  vinegar, plus more
  as needed

½ cup / 125ml apple juice

Red currant or lingonberry
  preserves, optional

Braised red cabbage is perhaps, besides Sauerkraut, Germany's most quintessential vegetable dish. And it more than deserves this illustrious status. One humble head of cabbage can end up feeding about ten people as a side, and its gloriously purple tangle is always a visual highlight on a table filled with brown gravy and yellow potatoes. But most important, of course, is its flavor—tangy and complex, sweet-sour and spiced. It is the perfect foil to all those rich meats and dark gravies, and a lovely balance to soft and yielding potato dishes in all their forms. It is the classic side to Rinderrouladen (page 149), Schweinebraten (page 137), roasted goose (page 134), and Sauerbraten (page 152).

Rotkohl cooked in goose fat or lard is particularly delicious. It's worth your time to seek them out. Home cooks in Germany all make their Rotkohl slightly differently, but the goal is having a final dish that balances sweet and sour, with the spices playing a supporting role without overpowering everything else. Braised red cabbage improves with time, so, if possible, you should make this ahead of time and reheat it at least once before serving. In fact, German cooks insist that this dish should only be eaten after being reheated at least once. Braised red cabbage can also be frozen once it's completely cooled.

This dish is best made with red cabbage that you've cooked from scratch, but if you live near a German grocery store, you have probably seen 1-pound jars of cooked red cabbage stocked on the shelves. If you're in a rush, here's a little secret for you: You can, just like many German home cooks, doctor these jars of braised cabbage to make them taste nearly as good as homemade. If using a jar of cabbage, start the recipe below, then add the cabbage after step 2. Mix well, then lower the heat. Add a splash of apple cider or red wine vinegar, ½ teaspoon each of salt and sugar, some freshly ground black pepper, half of the quantities of cloves, half of the juniper berries, and the bay leaf and mix well. Then lower the heat, cover, and cook the cabbage, stirring occasionally, for 20 to 25 minutes. Season to taste and serve.

CONTINUED

1   Place the cooking fat in a large, heavy bottomed pot and melt over medium heat. Add the onions and 1 tsp of salt and cook, stirring, for a few minutes. Add the apple. Cook until fragrant and soft, 5 to 8 minutes.

2   Sprinkle in the sugar and cook until it melts and starts to caramelize, stirring occasionally.

3   Add the cabbage and turn up the heat to medium-high. Stir well. Let the cabbage wilt and cook for 5 to 10 minutes, stirring occasionally.

4   Pour in the wine and bring to a simmer. Add the remaining 1 tsp of salt, the cloves, juniper berries, and bay leaf, stirring to combine. Pour in the broth, vinegar, and apple juice. Bring to a boil over high heat, then lower the heat and cover. Braise the cabbage for about 1 hour 30 minutes, stirring occasionally.

5   Taste the cabbage for seasoning, adding a pinch more salt or sugar or a splash of vinegar to achieve a good balance of sweet-sour and savory. You can also add a spoonful or two of red currant or lingonberry preserves if you'd like a fruitier flavor. Stir well. Braised cabbage improves with time, so if possible, you should make this ahead of serving and reheat it at least once before serving. Once completely cooled, braised red cabbage can be frozen for several months.

BAYRISCH KRAUT

Braised Green Cabbage with Onions and Bacon

SERVES 4 TO 6 AS A SIDE

2 Tbsp vegetable oil, lard,
    or goose fat
3.5 oz / 100g smoked bacon
    or Schinkenspeck, minced
1 Tbsp sugar
2 medium onions, peeled and
    finely chopped
½ tsp salt, plus more
    as needed
Freshly ground black pepper
2 lb / 1kg green cabbage
    (approximately half of one
    large cabbage), outer leaves
    discarded, cored, and thinly
    sliced
1 tsp caraway seeds
1½ cups / 350ml beef
    or vegetable broth
3 Tbsp apple cider vinegar
1 bay leaf

Bayrisch Kraut, or Bavarian cabbage, is a traditional way of cooking a fresh head of green cabbage in a bit of broth and its own sweet juices. It is wonderful served either with a plump grilled sausage, alongside a pile of mashed potatoes (page 210), or with slices of Böhmische Knödel (page 224) for pure comfort. It also would be a lovely alternative side to Schupfnudeln (page 95).

You build the flavors of the dish by frying bacon or Schinkenspeck and onions together with salt and sugar, then you add thinly sliced cabbage and plenty of caraway seed, which is cabbage's flavor soulmate and has digestive properties. The cabbage braises until the cooking liquor is sweet and aromatic and the cabbage is tender. It's an easy, simple dish that's a great candidate for weeknight suppers. Some versions of Bayrisch Kraut include an apple (peeled, cored, and chopped) for sweetness and flavor.

In the recipe below, I add a relatively small amount of broth to braise the cabbage. If you want a more abundantly saucy dish, the better to serve with a starchy side like potatoes or dumplings, you can increase the broth quantity to 2 cups / 500 ml, then bind the sauce with a cornstarch slurry at the very end of cooking: Whisk 1½ tsp of cornstarch into 2 Tbsp of water until completely smooth, then whisk the slurry into the cooking liquor until completely dissolved, bring to a simmer, cook for a minute or two until thickened, then serve.

1   Place the cooking fat in a large pot over medium-high heat, then add the bacon. Cook, stirring, for 3 to 5 minutes, then sprinkle in the sugar. Stir and let cook until the sugar has melted and is just starting to caramelize, 2 to 3 minutes. Add the onions, salt, and pepper and stir well. Cook, stirring occasionally, for 5 to 8 minutes, until the onions are glassy and fragrant.

2   Now add the sliced cabbage and the caraway seed to the pan. Mix briefly. Cover and let the cabbage cook for a few minutes, then stir and cover again. After about 5 minutes, the cabbage should be getting somewhat softer and easier to stir. Mix well to distribute the onions and bacon, then pour in the broth and add the vinegar and bay leaf.

3   As soon as the broth starts to boil, turn the heat down. Cover and braise for 45 minutes, stirring occasionally, until tender.

4   Taste for seasoning, adding more salt if desired. Remove from the heat and serve.

WEINSAUERKRAUT

Wine-Braised Sauerkraut

SERVES 4 TO 6

2 Tbsp lard or vegetable oil

⅓ cup / 1.7 oz / 50g minced
    Speck, optional

1 large onion, minced

1.4 lb / 650g Sauerkraut

1¼ cups / 300ml white wine

1 bay leaf

10 juniper berries

¾ tsp salt

1 Tbsp sugar, or a little less
    for a more sour taste

Freshly ground black pepper

1 large starchy potato, like
    Russet, peeled

There may be no other recipe more closely associated with German cooking than Sauerkraut, even though it is consumed widely throughout Eastern and central Europe. Sauerkraut is lacto-fermented cabbage, made by massaging or pounding shredded cabbage together with salt until it's submerged in its own juices and then fermented for weeks. It was the main method of preserving cabbage for centuries, providing a good source of vitamins, fiber, and probiotics for the long, hard winters.

Germans usually braise Sauerkraut before eating it, with flavorings like juniper berries, bay leaf, caraway seeds, and wine. Many traditional recipes thicken it before serving, to bind up all the juices into a creamier sauce. Those thickeners can range from a roux to grated potatoes (as I've used here). Sauerkraut shows up in countless regional specialties, typically accompanying hearty meat dishes that require a punchy side to stand up to their richness, but also next to Schupfnudeln (page 95).

The key, I find, to getting braised Sauerkraut right is to make sure to balance its aggressive sourness with sweetness. I've indicated a tablespoon of sugar here, but you can and should learn to cook Sauerkraut to your own taste. If you prefer Sauerkraut without Speck, you can leave it out. Instead of using white wine, you can braise it with apple juice as they do in Hessen. You can also use beer, as Thuringians do. If you don't like the soft shreds of potato that I add at the end, skip them and instead make a roux in the pot after you've cooked the onions by whisking flour into the cooking fat and letting it cook for a few minutes, then thinning it out (always whisking) with the cooking liquid and folding the Sauerkraut into the sauce to cook.

1   Place the lard in a large pot over medium-high heat. When it has melted, add the Speck, if using, and onions and cook over medium heat for 5 to 7 minutes, stirring occasionally, until the onion is translucent and fragrant.

2   Add the Sauerkraut, loosening it with a fork, and mix well. Raise the heat for a minute or two, then pour in the wine and add the bay leaf, juniper berries, salt, sugar, and pepper to taste. Mix well. Bring to a boil, let cook for 2 to 3 minutes, then turn the heat down to a simmer and cover the pot. Cook gently for 25 minutes.

3   Grate the potato with the large holes of a box grater. After 25 minutes of cooking, mix the grated potato into the Sauerkraut. Cover again and cook for 10 to 15 minutes, until the potatoes are completely tender. Remove from the heat and serve.

EINGEBRANNTE ERDÄPFEL

Stewed Potatoes with Caraway and Sour Cream

SERVES 4 TO 6 AS A SIDE

4 Tbsp / 55g unsalted butter

1 medium yellow onion,
    finely diced

2 lb / 900g waxy potatoes like
    Yukon Gold, peeled and
    sliced ⅛-inch / 3mm thick

1 tsp caraway seeds

1 tsp sea salt, plus more as
    needed

1½ cups / 350ml beef
    or vegetable broth

1 bay leaf

1 Tbsp all-purpose flour

2 Tbsp white wine vinegar
    or apple cider vinegar

Freshly ground black pepper,
    optional

¼ to ⅓ cup / 60 to 80g sour
    cream

Minced chives or flat-leaf
    parsley for garnish

Einbrenn is the Austrian word for roux, which is the thickening agent for this humble yet delicious Austrian potato dish. (Erdapfel is Austrian for "potato"; literally translated it means "earth apple.") Thinly sliced potatoes are cooked in a creamy, lightly herbal broth and stretched into a warm and comforting dish that is reminiscent of potato salad but is as rib-sticking as a wintry stew. A perfect example of the hearty, rustic fare traditionally served up by home cooks, this dish can be padded with bits of leftover roast meat or sliced sausages, or lightened with thinly sliced pickles folded in at the end to underline the sour note. I like serving this alongside Buletten (page 119) or sausages.

The bay leaf, caraway, and vinegar are nonnegotiable elements of the dish, giving it a surprisingly sophisticated flavor, but you can swap out the broth for water (simply adjust the seasoning at the end) and even skip the sour cream, if you absolutely must. You can substitute a gluten-free flour blend for the flour.

1   Melt 3 Tbsp of the butter in a deep, wide pan over medium heat. Add the onion and cook, stirring occasionally, for 5 minutes, until fragrant and glassy.

2   Add the potatoes, caraway, and salt to the pan. Stir well to combine. Add the broth and tuck in the bay leaf. When the broth comes to a boil, turn the heat down, cover the pan, and simmer for 15 minutes.

3   Melt the remaining 1 Tbsp of butter in a small pan over medium heat. Whisk in the flour and cook, whisking, until the flour is no longer raw and the mixture is a pale golden brown. Whisk in ¼ cup / 60ml of the broth from the potatoes until smooth, then scrape this mixture into the pan of potatoes. Add the vinegar and stir well to combine.

4   Cover again and simmer for 5 to 10 more minutes, until the potatoes are completely tender and the sauce is silky. Taste for seasoning and add pepper if you desire. Just before serving, gently stir in the sour cream and top with herbs.

BUTTERMILCHGETZEN

Potato-Buttermilk Casserole

Vegetable oil or clarified
  butter
⅔ cup / 3.5 oz / 100g minced
  Speck or bacon, optional
1 lb 13 oz / 800g starchy
  potatoes, peeled and
  uncooked
1 yellow onion, peeled
10.5 oz / 300g starchy
  potatoes, like Russet,
  boiled, cooled, and peeled
¾ cup / 200ml buttermilk
1 tsp whole caraway seeds
1 tsp salt
Freshly ground black pepper

This traditional recipe from the Ore Mountains in Saxony gives new life to any leftover boiled potatoes you might have on your hands. Combined with grated raw potatoes, crisp cubes of Speck, fragrant caraway, and a generous pour of buttermilk, then baked until crisp, Buttermilchgetzen is a cozy casserole that manages to be both hearty and light. The buttermilk gives the casserole a deliciously sour note, while the grated cooked potatoes bind and give it body.

Traditionally, Getzen was served as the main course, with salad on the side. It could, however, also be served as a side to a roast, for example. It's a great candidate for a potluck dish as it's easily made in advance and transportable.

I think the Speck is essential here, but it is possible to make the Getzen vegetarian: Mince the onion instead of grating it and fry it in the oil or clarified butter until browned and fragrant. Mix this into the potato mixture in place of the Speck. Add ½ tsp more salt to the dish before baking.

1 Preheat the oven to 400°F / 200°C. Grease the bottom and sides of a 9 by 13-inch / 22 by 33cm baking pan.

2 If using the Speck, place 1 Tbsp of oil in a small sauté pan over medium heat and add the Speck. Cook, stirring occasionally, until the fat has rendered and the Speck is fragrant and crisp, about 5 minutes. Set aside.

3 Using the grater of a food processor or the large holes of a box grater, shred the uncooked potatoes. Place in a large bowl. Shred the onion and add to the bowl. Grate the boiled potatoes into the bowl using the large holes of a box grater.

4 Add the buttermilk, caraway, salt, and pepper to taste to the potatoes. Scrape the Speck into the bowl, if using. Mix well.

5 Scrape the mixture into the prepared pan, smoothing the top. Place in the oven and bake for 1 hour, until the top has browned and crisped. Serve immediately.

BOILED POTATOES

At some point in the process of writing this cookbook, I wondered if I shouldn't just throw in the towel on *Classic German Cooking* and call it *Classic German Potatoes* instead. There are about as many potato dishes in Germany as there are Germans. In fact, I own several vintage German cookbooks that focus exclusively on the potato! But rather than indulge in my fit of pique, I've attempted to pare down the myriad recipes available to focus only on the most essential. The four recipes below—for boiled peeled potatoes, boiled potatoes, parsleyed potatoes, and mashed potatoes—are at the top of that list. Salzkartoffeln (boiled peeled potatoes) are the beloved side dish for most of the meat dishes in this book, as well as a few of the vegetarian ones, while Pellkartoffeln (boiled unpeeled potatoes) are the starting point for everything from potato salad (pages 61 and 62) to Rösti (page 215) to Bratkartoffeln (page 211). Petersilienkartoffeln (parsleyed potatoes) elevate the humble side at celebration meals. Kartoffelpurée, mashed potatoes flavored with nutmeg and light on butter, can be deployed almost anywhere, but will be especially important to kids.

SALZKARTOFFELN
Boiled Peeled Potatoes

SERVES 4 AS A SIDE

2.2 lb / 1kg waxy potatoes
1 Tbsp sea salt

1 Peel the potatoes and rinse well. Depending on the size, cut into halves or quarters. Place in a large pot and just cover with cold water. Add the salt.

2 Place the pot over high heat and bring to a boil. Cover and turn the heat to low. Simmer until the potatoes are just tender, about 15 minutes. Drain the potatoes well, then return them to the empty pot and cover. Let them steam for another 5 minutes before serving.

PELLKARTOFFELN
Boiled Potatoes

SERVES 4 AS A SIDE

2.2 lb / 1kg waxy potatoes
1 Tbsp sea salt

1 Wash and scrub the potatoes, but do not peel them. Place them in a large pot and just cover with cold water. Add the salt.

2 Place the pot over high heat and bring to a boil. Cover and turn the heat to low. Simmer until the potatoes are just tender, 15 to 20 minutes. Drain the potatoes well, then return them to the empty pot and cover. Let them steam for another 5 minutes before serving. In my house, each eater peels their own potato at the table and leftover potatoes are left unpeeled until their application in another recipe.

CONTINUED

BOILED POTATOES
continued

PETERSILIENKARTOFFELN
Parsleyed Potatoes

SERVES 4 AS A SIDE

2.2 lb / 1kg waxy potatoes
1 Tbsp sea salt
Handful of flat-leaf parsley, minced
2 Tbsp unsalted butter

1   Wash and scrub the potatoes, but do not peel them. Place them in a large pot and just cover with cold water. Add the salt.

2   Place the pot over high heat and bring to a boil. Cover and turn the heat to low. Simmer until the potatoes are just tender, 15 to 20 minutes. Drain the potatoes well, then return them to the empty pot and cover. Let them steam for another 5 minutes.

3   Peel the potatoes while still hot; if you like, you can cut them in half. Melt the butter in a large pan. Add the parsley, then immediately add the potatoes to the pan and gently stir until they are all coated with butter and parsley. Serve immediately.

KARTOFFELPURÉE
Mashed Potatoes

SERVES 4 TO 6 AS A SIDE

2.2 lb / 1kg starchy potatoes
1 Tbsp plus ½ tsp sea salt, plus more as needed
1¼ cups / 310ml whole milk
2 Tbsp unsalted butter
15 scrapes of whole nutmeg
Freshly ground black pepper, optional

1   Peel the potatoes and rinse well. Depending on the size, cut into halves or quarters. (The pieces should be 2 to 3 inches / 5 to 7.5cm.) Place in a large pot and just cover with cold water. Add 1 Tbsp of salt.

2   Place the pot over high heat and bring to a boil. Cover and turn the heat to low. Simmer until the potatoes are completely tender, about 15 minutes. Drain the potatoes well, then return them to the empty pot.

3   Place the pot over low heat and add the milk. Using a potato masher, start mashing the potatoes as you mix in the milk. Add the butter and continue to mash. Season with ½ tsp of salt, the nutmeg, and pepper, if using, then continue to mix and mash. When the potatoes are smooth and airy, adjust the seasoning as desired and serve. Some prefer their mashed potatoes with more texture; simply stop mashing when you've achieved the texture you like.

BRATKARTOFFELN

Fried Potatoes with Onions and Bacon

SERVES 2 TO 4

¼ cup / 30g minced
    Schinkenspeck or bacon
2 to 3 Tbsp vegetable oil
1 medium onion, diced
5 medium cold waxy boiled
    potatoes, like Yukon Gold,
    peeled and sliced into ¼ to
    ½ inch / 6mm to 1.3cm
    slices
Salt and freshly ground
    black pepper
1 Tbsp unsalted butter
Small handful of flat-leaf
    parsley, minced

One of my oldest sense memories is walking down Bambergerstraße, the street my mother lived on for many years, past one of the blocklike buildings built in the postwar reconstruction period, and smelling the very particular savory scent of onions frying in lard or butter coming from a lace-curtained window on the ground floor. I loved that street and my mother's apartment very much, and I loved that smell of frying onions. It was different from the cooking smells in my parents' kitchens, but it was still so familiar and cozy. It was such a German smell.

Another German thing is always having leftover boiled potatoes knocking around the kitchen. One of the most popular ways to use up leftover boiled potatoes in Germany is to make Bratkartoffeln, a frying pan full of fried potatoes with aromatic onions and small bits of Schinkenspeck. I used to imagine that when I walked past that kitchen with the lace curtains, the cook inside was making Bratkartoffeln for lunch. Bratkartoffeln are a typical side for lots of classic German dishes, but they are also the basis of Bauernfrühstück (page 28) and in fact are often just served as the main meal.

It's worthwhile to track down Schinkenspeck for this recipe (and others); it is leaner than bacon and more authentic. There are several German butchers in the United States that do a mail-order business. But in a pinch, you can use bacon instead.

It took me several tries to get this recipe just right, but now, in my opinion, it is perfect. The key is cooking the onions and bacon first, then removing them from the pan to fry the potatoes. Also, don't skip the butter and parsley at the end; they tie up the flavors and make these Bratkartoffeln sing. The recipe can be doubled; just make sure to use a slightly larger skillet (or cook it in two batches).

1   Place the Schinkenspeck in a 10-inch / 25cm nonstick or well-seasoned cast-iron skillet over medium-high heat (if the pork is particularly lean, add 1 Tbsp of oil) and cook for 1 minute, then add the onions and cook, stirring occasionally, until the pork bits are crisp and the onions are well-browned (don't let them burn) and fragrant, about 10 minutes. Scrape out into a bowl and set aside.

CONTINUED

BRATKARTOFFELN

continued

2   Wipe out the pan just to make sure there are no errant pieces of onion remaining and add 2 Tbsp of oil. Place back over medium-high heat and add the sliced potatoes, shaking once to distribute them evenly. Don't worry if the potatoes aren't all in one layer. Cook the potatoes for about 5 minutes without stirring or touching the pan, then shake the pan to move the potatoes around. You can flip them with a spatula, too. Season with salt and pepper.

3   Cook for another 10 minutes or so, periodically shaking the pan and flipping the potatoes, until they are golden brown and crisp in spots.

4   Add the butter and toss well. Scrape in the reserved bacon and onion and toss well. Cook for a few more minutes, then remove from the heat. Stir in the parsley, adjust the seasoning, and serve.

RÖSTI

Swiss Pan-Fried Potato Cake

SERVES 4 TO 6 AS A SIDE,
OR 2 TO 3 AS A MAIN

6 or 7 medium (about 2.2 lb /
   1kg) waxy potatoes, like
   Yukon Gold, boiled and
   cooled
2 small (or 1 large) yellow onions
Salt
40 scrapes of whole nutmeg
Freshly ground black pepper
2 Tbsp unsalted butter
2 Tbsp vegetable oil

Swiss Rösti—one large potato pancake cooked in a skillet and cut into wedges—is one of Switzerland's finest culinary inventions. Unlike German potato pancakes, Rösti is made with potatoes that have already been boiled (ideally, the day before, so that they are cold and slightly dried out) and is cooked in a skillet as one large pancake rather than fried into individual patties. Grated onions and freshly grated nutmeg, plus salt and pepper, are the classic flavorings.

To cook Rösti, my cast-iron crepe pan with very low sides is my favorite pan to use—it's easier to invert the Rösti than in a regular cast-iron pan. But you can use a regular well-seasoned cast-iron pan or a nonstick pan, too. (A stainless steel pan isn't great as the potatoes will likely stick.) The goal is to pack the entire potato batter into the pan as compactly and evenly as possible so that it cooks into one solid cake that is golden brown on both sides, with some deliciously crisp bits here and there.

Serve Rösti as a side to Geschnetzeltes (page 130) or as a main course with some herbed Quark (page 33) and Beet Salad (page 48).

1   Peel the potatoes and grate into a large bowl using the largest holes of a box grater. Peel the onions and grate into the same bowl.

2   Season with 1½ tsp of salt, or more to taste, and the nutmeg, plus plenty of pepper. Stir well to distribute the seasonings and onion throughout the potato mixture, which will become more compact.

3   Place 1 Tbsp of butter and 1 Tbsp of oil in a large skillet and melt over medium-high heat. Scrape the potato mixture into the pan and, using the back of a spoon or spatula, pat into one large, even cake.

4   Cook over medium-high heat for 6 to 8 minutes. The bottom should be golden brown—you can check by using a small knife to loosen the edges of the cake and peer at the underside. Place a large pot lid over the pan and flip the cake onto the lid. Place the pan back on the heat and add the remaining 1 Tbsp of butter and 1 Tbsp of oil to the pan. Slide the potato cake back into the pan and cook the other side for about 8 minutes, until golden brown.

5   Remove the pan from the heat and cut the Rösti into wedges in the pan (if using a nonstick pan, be sure to use a wooden spatula to cut) before serving.

KARTOFFELKLÖßE

Potato Dumplings

Kartoffelklöße (Kloß is the Prussian term for dumpling; in the south and in Austria, the term is Knödel) are plump orbs of grated or mashed, or grated and mashed, potatoes bound together with little else than a bit of starch, then poached until pillowy and soft. They're often stuffed with a crisp, buttery crouton as a little surprise (and, according to widespread kitchen lore, to help them cook faster), and they are fantastic for mopping up lots of dark gravy. In fact, a classic dish on the kids' menu of traditional German restaurants is simply a potato dumpling or two served in a puddle of brown gravy.

Kartoffelklöße are considered special occasion food, usually served at Sunday lunches or holiday meals, particularly with roast goose and gravy (page 134), Sauerbraten (page 152), or Rouladen (page 149). There are many variations on them, but I've decided to include just two here. The first, Thüringer Kartoffelklöße, are made with a mixture of grated raw potatoes and mashed cooked potatoes. The consistency of the finished dumplings is delightful, a toothsome balance between pillowy, sticky, chewy, and yielding. The second, also known as Seidenklöße, or silken dumplings, are made with mashed cooked potatoes, egg yolks, and potato starch. Their consistency is finer and smoother. (Seidenklöße can also be filled with a pitted prune stuffed with a sugar cube, poached as below, and served topped with melted butter and cinnamon-sugar as a sweet meal or dessert.) Leftover potato dumplings can be sliced and fried in a bit of butter to revive them, though I like Seidenklöße at room temperature, too.

Stuffing either dumpling with toasted croutons is traditional: Cut two slices of sandwich bread into ¼ inch / 6mm cubes, toast the cubes in some melted butter until crisp and golden brown all over, then salt them and set them aside. When shaping the dumplings, place 1 or 2 croutons in the middle of each dumpling before finishing shaping them. Any leftover croutons can be saved for soup.

THÜRINGER KLÖßE

MAKES 8 DUMPLINGS

2 lb / 900g starchy potatoes,
   like Russet, peeled

1¼ tsp salt, plus more
   as needed

50 scrapes of whole nutmeg,
   plus more as needed,
   optional

1   Take a third of the peeled potatoes and cut them into halves or quarters. Place in a small pot with cold water to cover by an inch, salt it generously, and set over high heat. Bring to a boil, then lower the heat, cover, and simmer for about 20 minutes, until tender. Drain completely, return the potatoes to the pot, and set aside for a few minutes to dry out.

2   Over a medium bowl, grate the remaining potatoes on the small holes of a box grater, making sure to catch all the liquid. You can also use a food processor fitted with a small shredder. Place a cheesecloth or a cotton towel over another bowl and pour the potatoes and all of the liquid into the cloth, scraping the bowl with a rubber spatula. Gather up the cloth, twisting the sack closed, and squeeze out the liquid in the potatoes, making sure to catch all of it in the bowl below. Keep squeezing until no more liquid emerges from the grated potatoes. When you have finished squeezing, the potatoes in the cloth should be dry to the touch. Set the bowl with the liquid aside for 10 minutes.

3   Using a potato ricer or potato masher, mash the cooked potatoes until completely smooth.

4   The water from the grated potatoes will have separated from the natural starch, which will be at the bottom of the bowl. Carefully pour off the water, leaving the starch behind in the bowl. Place the grated potatoes into the bowl with the starch and add the mashed, cooked potatoes. Season with the salt and nutmeg, if using. Using your hands, mix until well-combined. If desired, taste a small piece for seasoning, adding more salt and nutmeg if necessary. The mixture should hold its shape when pressed together and should not be too sticky.

5   Bring a large pot of well-salted water to a boil. While the water is coming to a boil, shape the dough into 2-inch / 5cm round dumplings, filling them, if desired, with a couple of croutons. The dumplings should be smooth and firm. When the water boils, lower the heat to a bare simmer and gently place the dumplings in the water. Cover and let simmer over very low heat for 20 to 25 minutes. Using a spider or slotted spoon, remove the dumplings from the water and let them drain well. Place the dumplings in a serving bowl or plate and serve.

SEIDENKLÖßE

MAKES 12 DUMPLINGS

2.2 lb / 1kg starchy potatoes,
    like Russet
1 Tbsp coarse salt for boiling
    potatoes
1½ tsp salt
50 scrapes of whole nutmeg
2 egg yolks
½ cup / 90g potato starch

1   Place the potatoes, unpeeled, in a large pot and cover with cold water by an inch. Add the coarse salt. Place over high heat, bring to a boil, then lower the heat, cover, and simmer for about 25 minutes, until cooked through. Drain completely, return the potatoes to the pot, cover, and let sit off heat to steam for 5 minutes.

2   Peel the potatoes and place in a large bowl. Add the 1½ tsp of salt and the nutmeg. Mash until completely smooth. Mash in the egg yolks until well-combined. Stir in the potato starch until completely absorbed. At this point, the potato mixture should no longer be sticky.

3   Shape the mixture into twelve 2-inch / 5cm round dumplings and set aside.

4   Bring a large pot of salted water to a boil. As soon as it boils, lower the heat to a very low simmer. Gently place half of the dumplings into the pot. Cover and poach over very low heat for 20 minutes. Remove the dumplings from the pot with a slotted spoon or spider and drain well. Repeat with the remaining dumplings. When finished, place the dumplings in a serving bowl or plate and serve.

SEMMELKNÖDEL

Bread Dumplings

MAKES 8 DUMPLINGS

6 (about 9.5 oz / 270g) stale
   Kaiser or hard white rolls,
   very thinly sliced, or the
   equivalent amount of stale
   white sandwich bread, cut
   into ¼-inch / 6mm cubes
1 cup / 250ml whole milk,
   plus more as needed
1 Tbsp unsalted butter
1 large yellow onion, finely
   minced
1 tsp salt, plus more for the pot
Handful of flat-leaf parsley,
   minced
2 eggs
Freshly ground black pepper

Semmel is the southern German and Austrian word for everyday plain white rolls, and Semmelknödel are dumplings made from stale rolls. They are a specialty of southern Germany and Austria, where the Bohemian influence looms large in the culinary canon. In that region, grocery stores and bakeries even sell large bags of pre-diced "Knödelbrot" to save home cooks the step of having to cube the rolls themselves. Semmelknödel are the traditional accompaniment to things like Schweinebraten (page 137), Gulasch (page 126), and Pilzgulasch (page 110).

Serviettenknödel are a variation on Semmelknödel, in which the raw dumpling mixture is rolled up in a kitchen towel (which is where the word "Serviette" comes in) or aluminum foil, then poached in simmering water. After it has finished cooking, you unroll the dumpling roll and cut it into slices. (An oven-baked version of Semmelknödel is on page 110. If you would prefer to try the traditional method, prepare the recipe below and, instead of step 4, scrape it out onto a kitchen towel or piece of aluminum foil. Shape the mass into a log that is uniformly 2 inches / 5cm wide, and roll it up tightly in the towel or foil, then tie the ends if using the towel or twist the aluminum foil. Lower into a pot of simmering water and poach over low heat for 20 minutes. Remove from the pot, drain well, then open and cut into slices to serve.)

The size of dumpling I indicate here will make dumplings large enough to satisfactorily accompany a dinner portion of meat and sides. My husband can eat two in one sitting, and I can eat one. But you can also shape the mixture into smaller dumplings and serve them in beef broth (page 66), for example, as a starter. Any leftover Semmelknödel can be refrigerated for 3 to 4 days. To reheat them and transform them into a beloved dish in its own right called Knödelgröstl, slice the leftover dumplings into a few thick slices, then pan-fry them in a little butter. If you like, you can scramble some eggs in the pan with the dumpling slices. To gild the lily, fry some onions and Speck in the butter before you add the sliced dumplings.

If you add some diced Schinkenspeck or bacon to the onion in step 2, then you will have made Speckknödel. If, instead of using stale white rolls, you use an equivalent amount of stale soft pretzels, you will have made Brezenknödel.

1   Place the bread in a large bowl. Heat the milk until hot but not boiling and pour over the bread. Toss briefly and set aside.

2   Melt the butter in a small sauté pan over medium heat and cook the onion with ½ tsp of salt until translucent and soft, 8 to 10 minutes, stirring frequently. Toward the end of cooking, add the parsley and mix well. Cook for another minute. Remove the pan from the heat and scrape into the bowl of bread cubes. Stir to distribute.

3   Beat the eggs together in a small bowl, then add them to the bread with the remaining ½ tsp of salt and the pepper to taste. Using your hands, mix, toss, and gently knead until all the ingredients are fully combined. The mixture should be uniformly moist but hold its shape when formed into a ball. If it feels too dry, you can add a splash or two of milk. Refrigerate for 30 minutes.

4   When ready to cook, bring a large pot of salted water to a boil. Using your hands, moistened with cold water, divide the bread mixture into eight equal portions and roll firmly and evenly into balls. The cold water should help smooth the surface of the dumplings. Once you've finished shaping a dumpling, run your wet hands over the surface making the "dumpling shaping" movement a few more times to smooth the surface. Set aside and repeat with the remaining mixture and more water. (At this point, you can freeze the uncooked dumplings, if desired.) When the water starts to boil, lower the heat and carefully place the dumplings in the water. You may need to cook them in two batches so as not to crowd them. Cover and let the dumplings poach for about 15 minutes. The water should not boil.

5   When the dumplings are finished, fish them out of the water with a slotted spoon or spider, drain them on a piece of paper towel, and transfer them to a platter or serving bowl. Serve immediately. If using frozen dumplings, put them frozen in the simmering water and let them cook, over the lowest heat, for about 20 minutes.

BÖHMISCHE KNÖDEL

Bohemian Steamed Dumplings

MAKES 2 (8-INCH / 20CM)
LOAVES, SERVING 4 TO
6 AS A SIDE

¾ oz / 20g fresh yeast or
    2 tsp instant yeast
½ tsp sugar or honey
¾ cup / 200ml lukewarm
    water
2½ cups / 400g all-purpose
    flour, plus more for
    kneading
1 egg
1 tsp salt
Unsalted butter

The first time I ate Böhmische Knödel, I was at my husband's grandmother's house in Bavaria at Christmastime. She and her husband, a hunter in Lederhosen and a feathered hat, lived in a little wooden house at the edge of the snowy woods, with chickens and goats and beehives in the garden. Despite my fluent German, I only understood about half of what he said in his thick Bavarian accent.

For lunch that Christmas Day, my mother-in-law, Kerstin, put venison that her stepfather had hunted in a buttermilk brine, then braised it for hours until it fell off the bones. To sop up the rich gravy, Kerstin made an enormous Bohemian dumpling, a pillowy yeasted dough simmered in salted water until it was majestically large, which we then cut into thick, velvety slices at the table. The dumpling slices were perfect for soaking up the gravy. Bohemian dumplings, as their name reveals, are originally from Czechia and beloved in Austria and southern Germany.

The dumpling is best made with fresh yeast, which gives it the most pillowy texture and delicious flavor. If you cannot find fresh yeast, you can substitute 2 tsp of instant yeast (just skip the first step and simply mix all the dry ingredients including the yeast together). But I don't recommend using active dry yeast. Traditionally, the Bohemian dumpling is cut into slices with a thread, so as not to deflate its puffy heft, but a serrated knife gently applied does the trick, too. Bohemian dumplings are delicious with any dish with plenty of sauce, like Gulasch (page 126), Pilzgulasch (page 110), Schweinebraten (page 137), or even Sauerbraten (page 152).

Leftovers, if there are any, can be sliced and pan-fried in a little butter until golden brown on both sides, then served with leftover gravy or sautéed mushrooms and onions. Alternatively, they can also be served with Plum Compote (page 186) or any other fruit compote for a sweet meal.

1   If using fresh yeast: Crumble the yeast into a small bowl and whisk in the sweetener and 3 Tbsp plus 1 tsp / 50ml of lukewarm water until the yeast dissolves. Cover and set aside for 10 minutes. Place the flour, egg, and salt into a large bowl. Scrape in the foamy yeast mixture and pour in the remaining lukewarm water.

2   If using instant yeast: Mix the yeast, sugar (if using honey, add with the wet ingredients), salt, and flour together in a bowl. Then pour in the lukewarm water and egg.

3   Mix together with a wooden spoon until a shaggy dough comes together. Knead briefly in the bowl until all the flour is incorporated, then scrape the dough out onto a lightly floured work surface and knead until smooth, about 8 minutes. After a minute or two, you should not have to add any additional flour. You want to add as little additional flour as possible to keep the dumpling supple.

4   Shape the dough into a ball and place it back in the bowl. Cover with a towel and set aside for about 45 minutes at room temperature, until the dough is puffy and risen.

5   Remove the dough from the bowl and divide into two equal pieces. Shape the dough into two oval loaves about 6 inches / 15cm inches long and 3½ inches / 8cm wide at the widest point. Cover with a towel.

6   Fill a very large pot (the dumplings will grow substantially as they cook) with salted water and bring to a boil. As soon as it boils, lower the heat to a simmer and carefully, so as not to deflate the dumplings, slip them into the hot water. Immediately cover the pot and let the dumplings simmer for about 20 minutes, until they have doubled in size.

7   Using a spider, gently remove the dumplings from the pot, letting them drain briefly in the spider, then place them on a wooden cutting board.

8   Using a serrated knife or a thin piece of string placed under the dumpling and then pulled together and up, cut the dumpling into ½-inch / 1.3cm slices and serve immediately. Leftovers can be cooled to room temperature, then refrigerated overnight and pan-fried to reheat them.

DESSERTS

Germany's famous cakes, tortes, and cookies are rarely served after a full meal in Germany. They usually occupy the afternoon Kaffeezeit meal that is served with coffee or tea. Most classic German desserts are little portions of spoonable creams or puddings that are accompanied by a bit of berry sauce or fruit compote. It makes a lot of sense. After a traditional German meal, you may not have room for much more than a few spoonfuls of something light and creamy, but you still want *something* a little special to end the meal.

Germans famously have quite a sweet tooth. Haribo, known worldwide for its gummy candies, is a German company and its Gummibärchen are a near-daily treat and reward for German children. Germans are among the biggest consumers of chocolate in Europe. Germans are the ones who first started making chocolate bunnies and eggs for Easter. German marzipan from Lübeck, often wrapped in a chocolate coating, is so popular that there are snack-size bars for sale at the checkout of most grocery stores. German even has a specific word just for eating sweets: naschen. *Zeit Magazin*, the magazine supplement of the weekly newspaper *Die Zeit*, once published a delightful list of many regional German words for naschen, including schleckern, schnackern, schnösen, and schnuppen. Yes, I'd like to schnuppen some of that chocolate bar, wouldn't you? Just another example of the German language's endless potential for amusement.

German desserts run the gamut from kitsch to relative elegance. They include Spaghetti Eis, which is vanilla ice cream extruded through a Spätzle press to resemble spaghetti, then topped with strawberry "tomato" sauce and grated coconut "cheese"; Wackelpudding (wobbly pudding), which is woodruff-flavored Jell-O, often served with the omnipresent vanilla sauce; and Westfälische Götterspeise, "Westphalian food of the gods," a layered trifle of canned fruit, whipped cream, grated chocolate, and toasted pumpernickel crumbs. Though these desserts all have their loyal fans, many have, over time, fallen from public favor for one reason or another, appearing only rarely in canteen displays or at an annual holiday meal.

In this chapter, I included the greatest hits of German desserts that I think deserve a permanent spotlight. They range from simple stovetop puddings to molded desserts, from pillowy dumplings to baked fruit. For other sweet dishes that can be served as dessert, see the Sweet Main Courses chapter (page 168). And don't forget Quarkspeise (page 31)!

SCHOKOLADENPUDDING MIT VANILLESOßE

Chocolate Pudding with Vanilla Sauce

SERVES 4 TO 6

3.5 oz / 100g semisweet
    chocolate (about 50% cacao
    solids), chopped
2 cups / 500ml whole milk
1 Tbsp sugar
¼ tsp salt
¼ cup / 30g cornstarch
1 egg yolk
Vanilla Sauce (page 238)
    for serving
Whipped cream for serving

I hesitated to include chocolate and vanilla pudding in this book, worrying that they might be too basic, but the truth is that both Schokopudding, as it's colloquially known in German, and Vanillepudding are deeply beloved and popular treats in Germany. When I polled people about whether to include them, a majority was emphatically in favor.

This chocolate pudding, made as directed below, is not too sweet and has a rich chocolate flavor. It is essential, I find, that you serve it with a topping of creamy-sweet Vanillesoße, a classic pairing here in Germany. The vanilla sauce tempers the bittersweet chocolate and elevates each bite. If the pudding is too deep in chocolate flavor for you, you can use milk chocolate instead, but then I'd skip the vanilla sauce. For a very German presentation, you can also make a batch each of chocolate and vanilla pudding and, once cooled, layer them in serving cups. Alternatively, you can always dollop the portions of chocolate pudding with whipped cream, either sweetened or not.

If you use a darker chocolate than one with 50% cacao solids, you may need to add a spoonful of sugar or two to the milk before proceeding with the recipe.

1   Place the chocolate, 1¾ cups / 400ml of milk, the sugar, and salt in a medium pot over medium heat and heat, stirring, until the chocolate has melted.

2   In the meantime, whisk together the remaining ¼ cup / 100ml of milk with the cornstarch and egg yolk in a small bowl until smooth and no lumps remain.

3   When the chocolate has completely melted, whisk the cornstarch mixture into the chocolate milk. Turn the heat up a little and keep whisking until the mixture starts to thicken. Cook for about 3 minutes, whisking all the while, until the whisk leaves traces in the pudding.

4   Remove from the heat and immediately scrape the hot pudding into a serving bowl or into individual serving cups. Place plastic wrap directly against the surface of the hot pudding to prevent a skin from forming. (If you like pudding skin, skip this step.)

5   Cool to room temperature, then refrigerate for a few hours.

6   Serve topped with a few spoonfuls of Vanillesoße or a dollop of whipped cream or layer the pudding with Vanillepudding (page 230).

VANILLEPUDDING

Vanilla Pudding

SERVES 4 TO 6

2 cups / 500ml whole milk

1 vanilla bean, split lengthwise
  and scraped

3 Tbsp sugar

¼ tsp salt

¼ cup / 30g cornstarch

1 egg yolk

The yin to chocolate pudding's yang, this is a simple cornstarch pudding, with an egg yolk added for extra-silky richness. This vanilla pudding is delicious when layered with Schokopudding (page 228), or with a dollop of whipped cream to gild the lily, but I like it best topped with a puddle of barely sweetened, freshly cooked berries, like raspberries or strawberries.

Some old-fashioned German pudding recipes call for the remaining egg white to be beaten to stiff peaks, then folded into the hot pudding at the end. This makes the pudding lighter and fluffier. The heat from the pudding cooks the egg white, so don't worry too much about salmonella; still, I'd do this only with eggs from provenances I trust. But to me, vanilla pudding is best when kept simple and straightforward. (I save the egg white for my morning eggs.)

1 Place 1¾ cups / 400ml of milk in a saucepan. Add the vanilla bean and the scrapings as well as the sugar and salt to the saucepan. Place over medium heat and stir occasionally, taking care not to let the milk boil.

2 In a small bowl, whisk the cornstarch into the remaining ¼ cup / 100ml of milk, then whisk in the egg yolk until completely smooth.

3 When the edges of the milk in the saucepan are starting to bubble, very slowly pour in the cornstarch mixture, whisking constantly. Continue to whisk and regulate the heat so that the pudding doesn't scorch. Cook for about 3 minutes, until the whisk leaves traces in the pudding.

4 Scrape the pudding into a serving bowl or individual serving cups. Place plastic wrap directly against the surface of the pudding to prevent a skin from forming. Cool to room temperature, then refrigerate for a few hours.

5 Serve topped with a berry sauce, like on page 239, or layered with Schokoladenpudding (page 228).

HERRENCREME

Vanilla-Rum Cream with Chocolate

SERVES 6 TO 8

2 cups / 500ml whole milk

1 vanilla bean, split lengthwise and scraped

3 Tbsp sugar

¼ tsp salt

¼ cup / 30g cornstarch

1 egg yolk

2 Tbsp rum or Armagnac

1 cup / 250ml whipping cream

1.5 oz / 45g grated dark chocolate (70% cacao solids), plus more for garnish

Shortly before I finished writing this book, I went out for coffee with Robert Rieger, a photographer who lives in my neighborhood. Robert is originally from Westphalia, and when I told him a little about the cookbook, he asked me breathlessly if I had included a recipe for Herrencreme, a Westphalian dessert that consists of vanilla pudding mixed with rum, whipped cream, and chocolate shavings. The look on his face when I told him I hadn't was enough to change my mind. Consider Herrencreme the grown-up riposte to regular chocolate or vanilla pudding. You make it by stirring a bit of rum (though Armagnac or cognac are also a good match here) into a batch of vanilla pudding, then folding in billows of whipped cream and a scattering of dark chocolate shavings.

Traditionally, Herrencreme was served at weddings in the Münsterland region of Westphalia. Its name, "gentlemen's cream," is an anachronism, coming from a time when dark chocolate was considered more to men's tastes than to women's. In this recipe, I recommend using dark chocolate with 70% cacao solids to balance the sweetness of the pudding and stand up to the rum. I think it's best if portioned into individual serving cups or glasses, rather than one large serving bowl. A few extra shavings of chocolate on top, which you can do with a vegetable peeler just before serving, are the perfect finish.

1   Place 1¾ cups / 400ml of milk in a saucepan. Add the vanilla bean and the scrapings as well as the sugar and salt to the saucepan. Place over medium heat and stir occasionally, taking care not to let the milk boil.

2   In a small bowl, whisk the cornstarch into the remaining ¼ cup / 100ml of milk, then whisk in the egg yolk until completely smooth.

3   When the edges of the milk in the saucepan are starting to bubble, very slowly pour in the cornstarch mixture, whisking constantly. Continue to whisk and regulate the heat so that the pudding doesn't scorch. Cook for about 3 minutes, until the whisk leaves traces in the pudding. Remove from the heat and whisk in the rum.

4   Immediately scrape into a bowl. Place plastic wrap directly against the surface of the pudding to prevent a skin from forming. Cool completely.

CONTINUED

HERRENCREME
continued

5   When the pudding has fully cooled, whip the cream until stiff. Remove the plastic wrap and loosen the pudding by whisking it until smooth and creamy. Whisk in the whipped cream until completely incorporated and perfectly creamy. Fold the grated chocolate into the pudding.

6   Spoon into individual serving cups or a large serving bowl. Refrigerate until ready to serve, at least 1 hour and up to 12 hours. Just before serving, cut shavings of dark chocolate with a vegetable peeler to arrange on top of the pudding.

ZITRONENCREME

Puckery Lemon Cream

SERVES 8 TO 10

4 sheets gelatin

4 lemons

½ cup / 100g sugar

Pinch of salt

½ cup plus 2 Tbsp / 150g
  whole-milk yogurt or sour
  cream

1¼ cups / 300ml whipping
  cream, chilled

Throughout my childhood, my mother lived in an apartment in Berlin's Bavarian Quarter, and her neighbor Christa across the landing became a close friend. Christa's daughter Julia and I were just a year apart and had so much to say to each other that Christa eventually placed a bench on the landing for us to use. And for many years, we were invited to their Christmas.

Christa's Christmas Eve was the most archetypal German Christmas celebration you could ever imagine. We got dressed to the nines. We weren't allowed in the living room until a bell tinkled at exactly 6:00 p.m., at which point the door would swing open and our eyes would grow wide upon seeing the room glowing with candlelight, a boys' choir singing in dulcet tones on the stereo, and in the center of the room a towering tree hung with polished red apples, glass balls, carved wooden angels, and real candles—lit with real flames! The presents under the tree could be opened only once a riddle was solved for each individual present, so festivities went late into the night. Dinner was a resplendent roasted goose, red cabbage, and dumplings served on Christa's exquisite heirloom china. Dessert, served in a cut crystal bowl, was a creamy-smooth lemon cream, a perfectly light and sweet-sour end to the rich meal.

Christa's secret was that she made the lemon cream from a grocery store packet, but doctored it by adding two or three times as much lemon juice. But Zitronencreme is a very classic German recipe that has been around for a long time. Traditionally, it was always made with eggs, but I ended up falling for this more modern version—yes, adapted from a grocery store packet!—which uses gelatin and yogurt. It is smooth and creamy, with just the right balance of sweet and sour. You can either serve this in one beautiful bowl at the table and spoon out portions or you can fill the cream into individual cups and chill until set. I usually leave the cream unadorned, but if you're the crafty type, you could decorate the top with some sugared, candied lemon peel or slices, or even some beautiful edible flowers.

CONTINUED

ZITRONENCREME
continued

1   Place the gelatin in a small bowl and cover with cold water. Set aside for about 5 minutes, until softened.

2   Grate the zest of 2 lemons into a small pot. Roll all of the lemons firmly against your countertop to loosen their juices. Halve and juice the lemons and place the juice in the pot with the zest. Add the sugar and salt. Set the pot over medium-high heat. Stir occasionally until the sugar has completely dissolved. Turn the heat down to low.

3   Squeeze out the gelatin and stir into the very hot lemon juice. Stir to dissolve completely—but do not let the mixture simmer or boil; remove from the heat if necessary—then pour through a fine-mesh sieve into a liquid measuring cup or a bowl with a spout. Set aside for 10 minutes.

4   Place the yogurt in a medium bowl. Whisk in the lemon mixture until completely smooth. Refrigerate for 15 to 20 minutes.

5   While the mixture is chilling, whip the cream with electric beaters until stiff. Slowly pour the lemon mixture into the whipped cream, then fold together with a rubber spatula until the lemon mixture and cream are completely smooth and well-combined. Scrape into a serving bowl or into individual serving cups. Refrigerate for a minimum of 3 hours and up to 12 hours. Serve cold.

ROTE GRÜTZE MIT VANILLESOßE

Red Berry Pudding with Vanilla Sauce

SERVES 6

¼ cup / 30g cornstarch

¼ cup / 60ml water

2 cups / 500ml prune or
cherry juice, no sugar
added

¼ cup / 50g sugar

Optional flavorings: grated
lemon zest, halved vanilla
bean, cinnamon stick

2 cups / 200g raspberries

2 cups / 200g red currants,
stemmed

2 cups / 200g sour cherries,
pitted

Vanilla Sauce (recipe follows)
for serving

My favorite German dessert of all time is this one: rote Grütze, or "red porridge," is a chilled pudding made of berries and fruit juice, served with homemade vanilla sauce. The recipe comes from northern Germany, though it also shows up in Scandinavia. The texture is gorgeous: velvety, nubby, and silky all at once. A cold jug of vanilla sauce with it is wonderful; the cold, creamy sauce offsets the tartness of the pudding. To keep it very simple, just pour cold heavy cream over the rote Grütze.

This recipe, for me, is like Proust's madeleine. When I was ten, I moved to Berlin to live with my mother. I'd been in Berlin for only a few weeks when my mother and stepfather were invited to their friends' for dinner. When they came home, it was late, but I was still awake and called out to my mother. I was feeling tender and lonely; my father in Boston was far away and Berlin still felt strange and new. She came into my dark bedroom holding a ceramic bowl that Muck and Jürgen had given her to take home to me. They had filled it with rote Grütze with vanilla sauce on top. I took a bite, the cold, sweet-tart pudding a delightful surprise. I fell asleep feeling better, a little less lonely. To this day, when I eat rote Grütze, I think of that night.

1   Put the cornstarch in a small bowl and whisk in the water to make a smooth slurry. Set aside.

2   Pour the fruit juice into a heavy 4-quart / 4L pot and add the sugar. If using a flavoring, add whichever one you like now. Set over medium heat and stir until the sugar has dissolved. Add the fresh fruit to the pot and bring just to a boil.

3   Give the slurry another whisk and pour it into the pot just as the fruit mixture starts to boil. The Grütze will start to thicken almost immediately. Bring it back to a boil, then remove the pot from the heat. If you used either the vanilla bean or cinnamon stick, remove it now.

4   Pour the hot pudding into a large serving bowl or into individual dishes, place plastic wrap directly against the surface to prevent a skin from forming, and let it cool completely before refrigerating overnight.

5   Serve cold with a jug of vanilla sauce for pouring over.

VANILLESOßE

Vanilla Sauce

MAKES ABOUT 2 CUPS /
500ML, SERVING 6

2 Tbsp plus 1 tsp sugar
2 cups / 500ml whole milk
¼ tsp salt
½ vanilla bean, split and
   scraped
2 Tbsp cornstarch
2 egg yolks
Up to ¼ cup / 60ml heavy
   cream, optional

This cool and creamy vanilla sauce is one of the most essential recipes in the German sweet kitchen. It can be paired with steamed dumplings or bread puddings for lunch; with puddings and strudels for dessert; and is such an integral part of the German food canon that you can also buy it, ready-made, at the grocery store. Homemade is nicest, of course, because then you can use the highest-quality milk and eggs and a real vanilla bean for the best flavor.

Most Vanillesoße recipes include egg yolks for color and flavor but not as many as one would use in a French crème anglaise. Instead, a bit of cornstarch adds body without additional richness. One should be able to pour Vanillesoße generously over each portion; it is, after all, acceptable as part of a main meal. If you prefer a slightly thinner sauce, you can add a bit of heavy cream to the sauce after it has cooled completely and whisk until combined.

1   Place the sugar, 1⅔ cups / 400 ml of the milk, the salt, and split vanilla bean with its seeds in a medium saucepan. Place over medium-high heat. Stir briefly with a wooden spoon.

2   While the milk is heating up, add the remaining milk to a bowl and whisk the cornstarch into the milk until no lumps remain, then whisk in the egg yolks. Set aside.

3   When the milk in the pot starts to bubble, turn the heat down to medium-low and remove a ladleful, then drizzle it slowly into the bowl with the cornstarch slurry as you whisk the mixture to temper the egg yolks. When the hot milk has been fully whisked into the cornstarch, slowly pour the cornstarch mixture into the pot of hot milk, whisking constantly.

4   Raise the heat to medium, continuing to whisk, and cook for a few minutes longer. The mixture should slowly thicken. The traditional German way to see if the sauce is ready is to stir the sauce with a wooden spoon, then remove the spoon from the pot and blow gently on the back of the sauce-coated spoon. If the sauce is ready, it will form the shape of the petals of a rose.

5   Pour the finished Vanillesoße into a bowl and let cool, whisking occasionally to keep a skin from forming, to room temperature. The sauce will keep for up to 3 days in the refrigerator. Remove the vanilla bean before serving.

BAYERISCHE CRÈME

Bavarian Cream with Raspberry Sauce

SERVES 10

FOR THE CREAM
4 sheets gelatin
4 egg yolks
⅓ cup / 70g sugar
2 cups / 500ml whole milk
1 cup / 250ml heavy cream
½ tsp vanilla extract

FOR THE RASPBERRY
    SAUCE
3 cups / 300g fresh or frozen
    raspberries
Juice of ½ lemon
1 Tbsp sugar

Bavarian cream is a molded custard, meaning that it holds its shape once unmolded, and is made with gelatin, eggs, milk, and cream. It differs from Italian panna cotta because it includes egg yolks, which give the cream a richer flavor and creamier texture. It is classically served with a tangy raspberry puree. One theory is that Bavarian cream developed out of the original regional recipe of Bavarian Rahmsulz and was given the French name *crème bavaroise* when Antonin Carême codified it in his nineteenth-century cookbooks. In the classic pastry kitchen, Bavarian cream is used as a component in structurally complicated desserts. Mercifully for you and me, it is easily made at home and makes for an elegant, simple dessert.

Bavarian cream is best made a day before serving, as it needs time to both chill and set. You can pour the cream into individual dessert cups or one large bowl, but to underline its retro appeal, a fluted mold would be nicest. Invert it just before serving, bring it to the table to the inevitable oohs and aahs, then cut it into slices and plate them with the ruby-red sauce.

1   Place the gelatin in a small bowl and cover with cold water. Set aside.

2   Place the egg yolks in a medium bowl and add the sugar. Place over a water bath and whisk for 4 to 5 minutes, until pale and light. Set aside.

3   Heat the milk in a medium saucepan over medium heat until it just boils, then whisk very gradually into the egg yolk mixture. Whisk in the cream and vanilla.

4   Squeeze out the gelatin, then whisk into the cream mixture until fully dissolved. Pour the mixture into individual ramekins or one large bowl or mold. If you plan to unmold the Bavarian cream, rinse the mold out with cold water before pouring in the cream mixture. Place in the refrigerator and chill for at least 6 hours, ideally 12 hours or overnight.

5   To make the sauce, place the raspberries in a bowl and add the lemon juice and sugar. Mix well. Let macerate at room temperature for a few hours.

6   When ready to serve, unmold the creams onto individual serving plates or one large serving platter or bowl. Spoon the raspberry sauce alongside. Serve immediately.

ERRÖTENDES MÄDCHEN

Raspberry Buttermilk Pudding

SERVES 8 TO 10

6 sheets gelatin

2 cups / 200g fresh or frozen
    raspberries, plus more for
    serving, optional

¼ cup plus 2 Tbsp / 75g sugar

⅛ tsp salt

⅓ cup / 90g lingonberry
    preserves, plus more for
    serving, optional

2 cups / 500ml buttermilk

½ cup / 125ml heavy cream,
    plus more for serving,
    optional

Errötendes Mädchen ("blushing maiden") is a quivering raspberry-buttermilk dessert that hails from the north of Germany. It's rarely seen anymore, but it is a lovely and refreshing finish to a meal, especially in summer. Its rosy color comes from raspberries and tart lingonberry preserves mixed with buttermilk, which also give the sweet cream a hint of sweet-sour complexity.

Traditionally, errötendes Mädchen was a molded dessert, poured into a pudding mold and then unmolded before serving. But I like to keep gelatin-based desserts as wobbly as possible, because I think the mouthfeel is nicer when you eat them. So I think it's easiest to just pour this into individual serving cups before it sets and to leave the dessert unmolded. If you do decide to go the old-fashioned route, unmold the dessert over a sink or counter, in case you have any drippage. Folding a bit of whipped cream into the mixture before it sets gives the buttermilk cream richness and flair, but you could skip it for a somewhat lighter result.

You can find lingonberry preserves at Ikea or at specialty grocery stores. In a pinch, you can substitute fresh or frozen cranberries, adding a few additional spoonfuls of sugar as cranberries will be tarter than lingonberry preserves.

1   Place the gelatin in a small bowl and cover with cold water. Let soak for about 5 minutes, until softened.

2   While the gelatin is soaking, place the raspberries in a small saucepan with the sugar, salt, and preserves over medium-high heat. Stir and bring to a boil. Let simmer for a few minutes, until the raspberries have completely broken down and the sugar has dissolved. Pour through a fine-mesh sieve into a bowl and press out as much of the raspberry pulp as possible. Discard the seeds.

3   As soon as the raspberries are strained, squeeze out the gelatin and immediately add it to the hot raspberry mixture. Stir until completely dissolved. Whisk in a bit of the buttermilk to temper the hot raspberry mixture, then whisk in the remaining buttermilk. Refrigerate for 20 minutes.

4   In a separate bowl, whip the cream until stiff, then whisk together with the raspberry mixture until just combined but no white streaks remain. Pour the raspberry cream into individual dessert cups or into a pudding mold that you have rinsed with cold water just before filling. Refrigerate for a minimum of 4 hours and up to 12 hours before serving.

5   If serving in dessert cups, serve as is. If using a pudding mold, run a thin knife around the edge of the pan before unmolding. If the pudding won't budge, dip the bottom of the mold in hot water for a moment before unmolding. If desired, decorate each dessert cup or the entire unmolded pudding with small dollops or rosettes of additional whipped cream and a spoonful of preserves or single raspberries.

REIS TRAUTTMANSDORFF

Creamy Molded Rice Pudding with Raspberry Sauce

SERVES 8

1 cup / 200g short-grain rice
2½ cups / 625ml whole milk
⅓ cup / 70g sugar
⅛ tsp salt
2-inch / 5cm piece of lemon
    or orange peel
3 sheets gelatin
1 tsp vanilla extract
1¼ cups / 300ml heavy cream
Vegetable oil
Raspberry Sauce (page 239)

Reis Trauttmansdorff, a molded rice pudding enriched with piles of whipped cream and stabilized with sheet gelatin, is the elegant European counterpart to cinnamon-dusted bowls of rice pudding. If you love rice pudding like I do, I think you will love this dessert. It was named for an eighteenth-century Austrian diplomat named Ferdinand von Trauttmansdorff, who purportedly had a raging sweet tooth. But beyond that, not much is known about his relationship to this dish.

I love its high-low appeal. At first glance, what could be simpler than rice pudding? Well, this rice pudding, flounced up with peaks of whipped cream and silky gelatin, molded in a fluted pan and then unmolded with a flourish at the table, with a bowl of shimmering berry sauce alongside, is a whole other ball game. It's a showstopping end to a special meal. Once unmolded, you can slice the pudding into portions.

1   Place the rice, milk, sugar, salt, and citrus peel in a medium pot. Place over medium-high heat and bring to a boil, stirring frequently. As soon as the milk starts boiling, turn the heat down to low, cover, and cook until tender and creamy, 18 to 20 minutes, stirring occasionally.

2   Remove the pot from the heat and let sit for 10 minutes. In the meantime, soak the gelatin in cold water until soft.

3   Scrape the rice into a mixing bowl and remove the citrus peel. Stir in the vanilla. Squeeze out the gelatin and add to the rice. Stir well to dissolve. Let cool completely, stirring occasionally.

4   In a separate bowl, whip the cream with electric beaters until you get firm peaks. Fold the cream into the cooled rice.

5   Using a brush or your fingers, oil a Bundt pan or pudding basin with just a few drops of oil. Remove any excess with a paper towel. Scrape the rice mixture into the pan or basin and smooth the top. Place in the refrigerator and chill for a minimum of 4 hours and up to 24 hours.

6   Before serving, run a very thin knife around the edge of the pan or basin and invert over a serving dish. Slice into portions and serve each with a spoonful of raspberry sauce.

GRIEßFLAMMERI

Farina Pudding with Fruit Sauce

SERVES 6 TO 8

3 eggs, separated

3¼ cups / 750ml whole milk

⅓ cup / 70g sugar

¼ tsp salt

¾ cup plus 1½ Tbsp / 150g wheat farina (Cream of Wheat)

½ cup / 125ml freshly squeezed orange juice (2 or 3 oranges)

Raspberry Sauce (page 239) or Zwetschgenröster (page 186)

If the warm and creamy Grießbrei (page 175) in the sweet main courses chapter is the cozy nursery food that almost every German associates with childhood comforts, then Grießflammeri is its gussied-up older sister. The word "flammeri" comes, amusingly enough, from the English word "flummery," an old-fashioned molded pudding. Grießflammeri is made by cooking farina in a higher ratio to milk (for a sturdier result), then stirring in egg yolks for richness and folding in beaten egg whites for loft. The pudding firms up as it chills, so you can either pour it into individual serving cups or put it in a mold and later, after unmolding it, slice it into portions. You can flavor the pudding with vanilla extract or citrus zests or juice. In this recipe, I've used orange juice, which gives it just a hint of acidity and flavor. The high temperature of the freshly cooked farina will be enough to cook the eggs; still, you should only make this with very fresh eggs, ideally from a trusted provenance.

No matter how you end up serving it, I think it's crucial to pass a fruit sauce along with the Flammeri. A raspberry sauce (page 239) is classic here, but you could also do a mix of berries, or even an apricot or plum compote (page 186) that you've pureed until smooth. The acidity and brightness of the sauce is the perfect pairing with the smooth and creamy Flammeri.

1 Place the egg whites in a very clean bowl and whip them with electric beaters until stiff peaks form.

2 Place the milk, sugar, and salt in a medium saucepan and bring just to a boil over medium heat. Whisking constantly, pour in the wheat farina. Bring back to a boil, then take the pot off the heat and let it sit, covered, for 2 to 3 minutes.

3 Working quickly, whisk in the egg yolks until completely combined, then whisk in the orange juice. Finally, fold in the egg whites until completely combined and no streaks remain.

4 Rinse a pudding mold or Bundt or Gugelhupf cake pan with cold water and gently scrape in the farina mixture. Smooth the top and let cool completely before refrigerating. The pudding should be refrigerated for at least 4 hours before serving. It can be made 1 day in advance.

5 To serve, spoon fruit sauce onto a large serving dish. Unmold the pudding onto the sauce. Cut into slices and serve each slice with a bit of sauce.

TOPFENKNÖDEL MIT BUTTERBRÖSEL

Quark Dumplings with Toasted Bread Crumbs and Blueberry Compote

MAKES 10 DUMPLINGS

FOR THE DUMPLINGS

2 Tbsp / 30g unsalted butter,
    at room temperature

½ tsp salt

Zest and juice of ½ lemon

¼ cup / 50g granulated sugar

2 eggs

1⅓ cups plus 1½ Tbsp / 350g
    Quark

⅔ cup / 70g unseasoned bread
    crumbs

2 Tbsp potato starch

FOR THE BLUEBERRY
    COMPOTE

3½ cups / 430g fresh or frozen
    wild blueberries

⅓ cup / 70g granulated sugar

Juice of 1 lemon

Grated zest of 1 lemon,
    optional

2 Tbsp crème de cassis

1 Tbsp cornstarch

FOR THE TOPPING

1½ Tbsp unsalted butter

½ cup / 50g unflavored fine
    bread crumbs

1 Tbsp vanilla sugar
    (see headnote)

Pinch of salt

These delicate Austrian Quark dumplings (Topfen is the Austrian word for Quark) topped with crunchy buttered bread crumbs and served on a warm pool of blueberry compote are a special occasion dessert that will knock your socks off. If you live near some elderberry trees, you can also make the compote with those berries, which you gather in late summer. Alternatively, you can serve these Quark dumplings with plum compote (Zwetschgenröster, page 186) instead. Apricot compote would also make a lovely pairing.

As you'll note, the dumpling batter has a larger ratio of Quark than other Quark-based dumplings, and no flour, just bread crumbs and potato starch to bind it. Since there is no stuffing to the dumpling, it can afford to be a richer batter. It's helpful to use an ice cream scoop to portion the dumplings, but if you don't have one, of course you can just use your hands to roll them. I wet my hands with cold water to help shape the batter without it sticking too much. The crowning glory of this dish are the vanilla-scented, butter-toasted bread crumbs, which add the most delicious toasty flavor, a delicate crunch, and a scent of sophistication.

To make vanilla sugar, place 1 cup / 200 grams of sugar and 1 vanilla bean in the bowl of a small food processor. Blend until the vanilla bean is completely broken down and incorporated in the sugar. Store in a clean jar with a lid. Alternatively, you can just sink a vanilla bean into a bag of sugar and let it perfume it on its own, but it may take a few days for the sugar to truly take on the flavor, so this should be done well before you start this recipe.

One organizational note: While the batter and compote can be made in advance, these dumplings must be cooked and served à la minute, which means that you, the cook, must leave your diners at the table while you prepare the dumplings. If you are the lucky home cook with an eat-in kitchen, then you don't have to go very far. If your dining table is in a different room from your kitchen, get your guests to clean up the dinner dishes while you cook the dumplings, then they can help you bring in the dessert plates as the dumplings emerge from their bread crumb bath. (To help future you, you can portion the compote out onto dessert plates before dinner—then all you must do is cook the dumplings and roll them in bread crumbs before plating them.)

CONTINUED

TOPFENKNÖDEL MIT BUTTERBRÖSEL
continued

1   First, make the dumpling batter: Place the butter in a mixing bowl. Add the salt, lemon zest and juice, and granulated sugar. Using a handheld mixer or a whisk, beat until combined. Add the eggs, beating well after each addition. Beat in the Quark, bread crumbs, and potato starch until smooth. Cover the bowl with plastic wrap and refrigerate for at least 1 hour and up to 3 hours.

2   While the batter is resting, make the blueberry compote: Place the blueberries in a small saucepan and add the sugar, lemon juice, and zest, if using. Mix, then place over high heat and bring to a boil. Lower the heat to medium and let bubble, stirring, for about 5 minutes. Meanwhile, whisk the crème de cassis and cornstarch together in a small bowl until completely smooth. Whisk the slurry into the bubbling blueberries, mixing well. Let bubble for another minute. The compote should be stewy and slightly thickened. Remove from the heat and set aside.

3   Make the topping: Melt the butter in a small pan over medium heat and add the bread crumbs and vanilla sugar. Stirring constantly, cook the bread crumbs until golden brown, fragrant, and crunchy. Remove from the heat and set aside.

4   Bring a large pot of salted water to a boil. Using wet hands or a large ice cream scoop, portion the batter into ten round dumplings. Gently slip the dumplings into the boiling water. When the water comes to a boil again, lower the heat and simmer the dumplings, uncovered, for about 10 minutes. The dumplings will float at the top of the pot when ready. Remove the dumplings from the pot with a spider or slotted spoon and let drain for a moment on a paper towel.

5   To serve, spoon some fruit compote onto each plate, then top with one or two dumplings. Sprinkle them with the bread crumb mixture and serve immediately.

BRATÄPFEL MIT VANILLESOßE

Almond-Stuffed Baked Apples with Vanilla Sauce

MAKES 5 BAKED APPLES

2 Tbsp raisins

2 Tbsp rum, optional

3 oz / 90g almond paste

1 Tbsp honey

½ tsp ground cinnamon

2 Tbsp toasted slivered
    almonds

Grated zest of ½ lemon

3 Tbsp unsalted butter,
    at room temperature

5 large cooking apples

Vanillesoße (page 238)
    for serving

German baked apples are all about their luxurious filling—a gorgeously sticky blend of rum-soaked raisins, aromatic almond paste, crunchy toasted almond slivers, honey, cinnamon, and grated lemon zest. You can use any apple that gets soft and somewhat frothy during baking. Make sure to choose large apples that can accommodate the generous filling so that you end up having a good amount of fruit to spoon up! Serve homemade vanilla sauce with the baked apples, though a scoop of vanilla ice cream would also be lovely.

Be sure to purchase almond paste and not marzipan, which is often doctored with additional sugar and flavorings. You can find almond paste in well-stocked grocery stores or online. If it's fresh, you should be able to pluck it into pieces with your hands. If it's not fresh anymore, you will have to grate it with a box grater. To make your own, there is a recipe in my cookbook *Classic German Baking*.

1 Soak the raisins in the rum (or hot water) for an hour. Drain and set aside.

2 Preheat the oven to 400°F / 200°C.

3 Grate or crumble the almond paste into a small bowl. Add the raisins, honey, cinnamon, almonds, zest, and butter. Using your fingers, knead together until smooth and well-combined. Set aside.

4 Wash and dry the apples. Holding a paring knife at an angle, cut out the stem and the top part of the core of each apple. Then, with a melon baller or very sturdy little spoon, core each apple, leaving the bottom intact. Each apple should have a cavity large enough for one-fifth of the filling.

5 Divide the filling among the apples. If any apple doesn't sit properly, slice off just a thin piece of the bottom to make it level. Place the apples in a baking pan.

6 Bake for about 25 minutes, until the apples are tender and the filling is golden brown.

7 Remove from the oven and let cool for 10 minutes before serving with a puddle of vanilla sauce per person.

BIBLIOGRAPHY

Gropman, Gabrielle Rossmer and Sonya Gropman, *The German-Jewish Cookbook,* Brandeis University Press, 2017

Hawes, James, *The Shortest History of Germany,* Old Street Publishing, 2017

Hazelton, Nika Standen, *The Cooking of Germany,* Time-Life Books, 1969

Heinzelmann, Ursula, *Beyond Bratwurst: A History of Food in Germany,* Reaktion Books, 2014

Hess, Reinhard, *Deutschland: Kochen und Verwöhnen mit Originalrezepten,* Gräfe und Unzer Verlag, 2006

Kahane, Kitty and Brit Hartmann, *Kittys Berlin Kochbuch,* Jacoby & Stuart, 2009

Morgenstern, Lina, *Illustriertes Kochbuch,* Heinrich Killinger Verlag, 1905

Plachutta, Ewald, Mario Plachutta, and Christian Wagner, *Die gute Küche,* Verlag Orac, 1993

Ruckser, Elisabeth, *Aus Omas Kochbuch,* Servus bei Benevento Publishing, 2017

Sälzer, Sabine and Gudrun Ruschitzka, *Die echte deutsche Küche,* Gräfe und Unzer Verlag, 1993

Schinharl, Cornelia, *Gut gekocht!,* Franckh-Kosmos Verlags-GmbH, 2010

Schwarzer, Horst and Annette Wolter, *Das Große Kochbuch,* Deutscher Bücherbund GmbH & Co, 1981

Seiser, Katharina and Meinrad Neunkirchner, *Österreich vegetarisch,* Christian Brandstätter Verlag, 2021

Siebeck, Wolfram, *Die Deutschen und ihre Küche,* Rowohlt Berlin, 2007

Wechsberg, Joseph, *The Cooking of Vienna's Empire,* Time-Life Books, 1968

Wiener, Sarah, *Herdhelden,* Gräfe und Unzer Verlag, 2011

Willinsky, Grete, *Kochbuch der Büchergilde,* Büchergilde Gutenberg, 1958

ACKNOWLEDGMENTS

First, thank you to the entire Ten Speed Press team. I feel so fortunate to have found such a good home for both *Classic German Baking* and *Classic German Cooking*. Thanks to Aaron Wehner, publisher; Dervla Kelly, acquiring editor; Ashley Pierce, production editor; Mari Gill and Faith Hauge, production designers; and Phil Leung, production manager. Big thanks to Sasha Tropp, copyeditor, and Heather Rodino, proofreader, whose work immeasurably improved my own. My fervent gratitude especially to Molly Birnbaum, editor in chief, and Lizzie Allen, designer, for their kindness, collaborative spirit, and calming presence, even from afar.

Thank you to my agent and dear friend, Brettne Bloom at The Book Group. I'm so lucky to have you in my corner.

Thank you to the talented team that brought these classic dishes to life so beautifully: photographer Elena Heatherwick and assistant Marco Kesseler, and food stylist extraordinaire Xenia von Oswald and assistant Shin Hye Hong. Thank you also to Celia Dunsire, Angus Dunsire, and the most delightful shoot mascot, Miss Winifred (Winnie) Heatherwick Dunsire. Writing a book can be a lonely business, and having all of you around for a week of making visual magic felt like a cosmic reward.

Thank you to Sally Fuls at Berlin's Königliche Porzellan-Manufaktur. I was honored to include some of KPM's most beautiful pieces in this book. For the remaining props, my gratitude goes to Christa von Gossler, Adelheid Humbert, the Joly and Joly-Nelson families, Letizia Weiss, and Ann Wertheimer. Thank you also to Ann, Christa, and Letizia for letting us shoot in your homes.

My gratitude to the intrepid recipe testers who worked their way through everything so conscientiously: Andrea Davis, Debbie Fine, Hinnerk Gölnitz, Maximiliane Krauss-Waller, Liz McClure, Sue Mildrum, Sara Saljoughi, Gemma Saylor, Kate Schirg, and especially Kate and Nathan Schmidt, who went above and beyond.

Thank you to my mother, Letizia Weiss, not only for all the physical gifts over the years that have popped up throughout this book (antique mustard pot, family linens, delicate porcelain), but for the support of all things great and small in my life.

Thank you to my father, Richard Weiss, for his enthusiasm and encouragement of all of my work, for weighing in on the recipe selection, and for showing up for dinner again and again. Thank you to both my father and my stepmother, Susan Ernst, for testing recipes.

A heartfelt thank-you to all my friends and family who tested recipes, came over for meals, and shared their family recipes and most beloved food memories. Special thanks go to Kerstin Beuchel, Andreas Braunsdorf, Christie Dietz, Christa von Gossler, Joana Gröning and Julian Rönsch, Lena Häusler, Joan Klakow, Kim Klakow and Susanne Kaufhold, Kathrin Kuna, Françoise Joly, Jürgen Marsch and Muck Marsch-Ziegler, Tina and Christoph Müller-Stüler, Lu, James, Basil, and Balthazar Nelson, Jane Joo Park, Robert Rieger, Lena Schimmelbusch, and Maja Welker. And a grateful salute to the dearly departed Florian von Buttlar, whose affection for Bratkartoffeln and Rahmspinat mit Spiegelei remains with me always.

Thank you to Marguerite Joly, whose encouragement, cherished friendship, and hungry family were integral to completing the project.

Thank you to my husband, Max, whose love and support nourished me throughout the writing of this book, and to our two darling boys, Hugo and Bruno. I hope the recipes in this book capture many of the taste memories of our family. Cooking for you is one of the great joys of my life.

INDEX

A

Abendbrot, 13, 45

almonds
  Bratäpfel mit Vanillesoße (Almond-Stuffed Baked Apples with Vanilla Sauce), 248
  Kaiserschmarrn mit Zwetschgenröster (Torn Souffléd Pancake with Plum Compote), 183–84
  Kirschenmichel (Sour Cherry Bread Pudding), 176–77
  Scheiterhaufen (Apple Bread Pudding), 178

apples, 15
  Apfelkren (Horseradish Applesauce), 148
  Apfelküchle (Apple Fritters with Cinnamon-Sugar), 35–36
  Apfelpfannkuchen (Apple Pancakes), 182
  Bratäpfel mit Vanillesoße (Almond-Stuffed Baked Apples with Vanilla Sauce), 248
  Heringssalat mit Rote Beete (Pickled Herring Salad with Potatoes and Beets), 58
  Kohlrabisalat mit Apfel (Kohlrabi-Apple Salad), 55
  Matjes Hausfrauen Art (Herring in Cream Sauce with Apples and Onions), 162
  Quarkauflauf (Oven-Baked Quark Soufflé with Fruit), 180
  Rotkohl (Braised Red Cabbage with Apples and Onions), 202–4
  Scheiterhaufen (Apple Bread Pudding), 178
  Schupfnudeln mit Apfel-Sauerkraut (Potato Noodles with Apple Sauerkraut), 95–96
  Westfälisches Blindhuhn (White Bean Stew with Bacon, Green Beans, Apples, and Pears), 84–85

Apricot Dumplings, Fresh (Marillenknödel), 189–90

asparagus
  Spargel mit Kratzete und Hollandaise (White Asparagus with Herbed Pancakes and Hollandaise Sauce), 114–15
  Spargelsalat (White Asparagus Salad), 56

B

bacon, 21
  Bauernfrühstück (Farmer's Breakfast: Meat and Potato Hash), 28–29
  Bayrisch Kraut (Braised Green Cabbage with Onions and Bacon), 205
  Bratkartoffeln (Fried Potatoes with Onions and Bacon), 211–12
  Buttermilchgetzen (Potato-Buttermilk Casserole), 208
  Erbseneintopf (Thick Pea Stew), 83
  Graupensuppe (Beef Barley Soup), 87
  Kartoffelsuppe (Potato-Sausage Stew), 78–79
  Kohlrouladen (Stuffed Cabbage Rolls), 139–41
  Krautsalat (Shredded Cabbage Salad), 52
  Linsensuppe mit Pflaumen (Lentil Soup with Sausage and Prunes), 80
  Rinderrouladen (Braised Beef Rolls with Mustard and Pickles), 149–51
  Schupfnudeln mit Apfel-Sauerkraut (Potato Noodles with Apple Sauerkraut), 95–96
  Westfälisches Blindhuhn (White Bean Stew with Bacon, Green Beans, Apples, and Pears), 84–85
  Wirsingeintopf (Savoy Cabbage Stew), 86

Barley Soup, Beef (Graupensuppe), 87

Bauernfrühstück (Farmer's Breakfast: Meat and Potato Hash), 28–29

Bayerische Crème (Bavarian Cream with Raspberry Sauce), 239

Bayrisch Kraut (Braised Green Cabbage with Onions and Bacon), 205

beans
  Bohnensalat (Green Bean Salad), 57
  Westfälisches Blindhuhn (White Bean Stew with Bacon, Green Beans, Apples, and Pears), 84–85

beef
  Buletten (Savory Meat Patties), 117
  Gefüllte Paprika (Stuffed Peppers), 123–25
  Graupensuppe (Beef Barley Soup), 87
  Gulaschsuppe (Paprika Beef Soup), 73
  Kohlrouladen (Stuffed Cabbage Rolls), 139–41
  Königsberger Klopse (Meatballs in Lemon-Caper Sauce), 120–22
  Maultaschen (Swabian Meat and Spinach Dumplings), 155–61
  Rinderbrühe (Clear Beef Broth), 66–68
  Rinderrouladen (Braised Beef Rolls with Mustard and Pickles), 149–51
  Sauerbraten (Spiced Braised Beef), 152–54
  Tafelspitz (Austrian Boiled Beef with Horseradish Sauce), 147–48
  Wiener Saftgulasch (Austrian Beef Stew), 126–28

beets
  Heringssalat mit Rote Beete (Pickled Herring Salad with Potatoes and Beets), 58
  Rote Beete Salat (Red Beet Salad), 48

Blueberry Compote, Quark Dumplings with Toasted Bread Crumbs and (Topfenknödel mit Butterbrösel), 245–47

Böhmische Knödel (Bohemian Steamed Dumplings), 224–25

Bohnensalat (Green Bean Salad), 57

bouillon cubes or paste, 15

Bratäpfel mit Vanillesoße (Almond-Stuffed Baked Apples with Vanilla Sauce), 248

Bratkartoffeln (Fried Potatoes with Onions and Bacon), 211–12

bread, 15
  Kaspressknödel (Pan-Fried Cheesy Bread Dumplings), 105–6
  Kirschenmichel (Sour Cherry Bread Pudding), 176–77
  Reicher Ritter (Plum-Stuffed French Toast), 38
  Scheiterhaufen (Apple Bread Pudding), 178
  Semmelknödel (Bread Dumplings), 222–23

Serviettenknödel mit Pilzgulasch (Bread Dumplings with Mushroom Goulash), 110–13
Zwei Eier im Glass mit Schnittlauchbrot (Soft-Boiled Eggs with Chives and Buttered Bread), 26
breakfast, 25
Buletten (Savory Meat Patties), 117
butter, 16
Buttermilchgetzen (Potato-Buttermilk Casserole), 208

C
cabbage
Bayrisch Kraut (Braised Green Cabbage with Onions and Bacon), 205
Kohlrouladen (Stuffed Cabbage Rolls), 139–41
Krautsalat (Shredded Cabbage Salad), 52
Rotkohl (Braised Red Cabbage with Apples and Onions), 202–4
Wirsingeintopf (Savoy Cabbage Stew), 86
Wirsinggemüse (Creamed Savoy Cabbage), 201
Celery Root Cutlets with Remoulade (Sellerieschnitzel mit Remouladensoße), 108–9
cheese
Käsespätzle (Swabian Noodles with Mountain Cheese and Caramelized Onions), 93–94
Käsesuppe (Mountain Cheese Soup), 75
Kaspressknödel (Pan-Fried Cheesy Bread Dumplings), 105–6
Obatzda (Bavarian Cheese Spread), 40
See also Quark
cherries, 16
Kirschenmichel (Sour Cherry Bread Pudding), 176–77
Milchreis mit Kirschkompott (Warm Rice Pudding with Sour Cherry Compote), 170
Quarkauflauf (Oven-Baked Quark Soufflé with Fruit), 180
Rote Grütze mit Vanillesoße (Red Berry Pudding with Vanilla Sauce), 236
chicken
Hühnerfrikassee (Chicken Fricassee), 144–46
Paprika Geschnetzeltes (Sliced Chicken with Peppers and Paprika), 133

Chive Sauce, Creamy (Schnittlauchsoße), 148
Chocolate Pudding with Vanilla Sauce (Schokoladenpudding mit Vanillesoße), 228
cinnamon-sugar, 16
cod
Hamburger Pannfisch (Pan-Fried Cod and Potatoes in Mustard Sauce), 165–66
Hechtklößchen (Pike Dumplings in Cream Sauce), 163–64
cucumbers
Cremiger Gurkensalat (Creamy Cucumber Salad), 47
Gurkensalat (Cucumber Salad), 46
Cumberland Sauce, 138
currants
Cumberland Sauce, 138
Rote Grütze mit Vanillesoße (Red Berry Pudding with Vanilla Sauce), 236

D
desserts, 227
Bayerische Crème (Bavarian Cream with Raspberry Sauce), 239
Bratäpfel mit Vanillesoße (Almond-Stuffed Baked Apples with Vanilla Sauce), 248
Errötendes Mädchen (Raspberry Buttermilk Pudding), 240–41
Grießflammeri (Farina Pudding with Fruit Sauce), 244
Herrencreme (Vanilla-Rum Cream with Chocolate), 231–32
Reis Trauttmansdorff (Creamy Molded Rice Pudding with Raspberry Sauce), 243
Rote Grütze mit Vanillesoße (Red Berry Pudding with Vanilla Sauce), 236
Schokoladenpudding mit Vanillesoße (Chocolate Pudding with Vanilla Sauce), 228
Topfenknödel mit Butterbrösel (Quark Dumplings with Toasted Bread Crumbs and Blueberry Compote), 245–47
Vanillepudding (Vanilla Pudding), 230
Zitronencreme (Puckery Lemon Cream), 233–35
dumplings
Böhmische Knödel (Bohemian Steamed Dumplings), 224–25
Germknödel (Giant Steamed Dumplings with Plum Butter and Poppyseeds), 191–95

Grießklößchen (Semolina Soup Dumplings), 72
Hechtklößchen (Pike Dumplings in Cream Sauce), 163–64
Kartoffelklöße (Potato Dumplings), 216–21
Kaspressknödel (Pan-Fried Cheesy Bread Dumplings), 105–6
Marillenknödel (Fresh Apricot Dumplings), 189–90
Maultaschen (Swabian Meat and Spinach Dumplings), 155–61
Seidenklöße (Silken Dumplings), 221
Semmelknödel (Bread Dumplings), 222–23
Serviettenknödel mit Pilzgulasch (Bread Dumplings with Mushroom Goulash), 110–13
Thüringer Klöße (Potato Dumplings), 218
Topfenknödel mit Butterbrösel (Quark Dumplings with Toasted Bread Crumbs and Blueberry Compote), 245–47

E
eggs, 16
Bauernfrühstück (Farmer's Breakfast: Meat and Potato Hash), 28–29
Eier in Senfsoße (Eggs in Creamy Mustard Sauce), 90
Eierstich (Egg Soup Custard), 71
Zwei Eier im Glass mit Schnittlauchbrot (Soft-Boiled Eggs with Chives and Buttered Bread), 26
Eier in Senfsoße (Eggs in Creamy Mustard Sauce), 90
Eierkuchen (Thin Pancakes), 181
Eierstich (Egg Soup Custard), 71
Eingebrannte Erdäpfel (Stewed Potatoes with Caraway and Sour Cream), 207
elderberries, 2, 7
equipment, 23
Erbseneintopf (Thick Pea Stew), 83
Erdäpfelgulasch (Austrian Potato Paprika Stew), 101
Erdäpfelkas (Potato Cheese), 43
Errötendes Mädchen (Raspberry Buttermilk Pudding), 240–41

F
farina, 16
Grießbrei (Warm Farina Pudding), 175
Grießflammeri (Farina Pudding with Fruit Sauce), 244

farina (*cont.*)

Grießschnitten mit Zimt-Zucker (Pan-Fried Custardy Farina Squares with Cinnamon-Sugar), 173–74

Marillenknödel (Fresh Apricot Dumplings), 189–90

Quarkauflauf (Oven-Baked Quark Soufflé with Fruit), 180

fish

Hamburger Pannfisch (Pan-Fried Cod and Potatoes in Mustard Sauce), 165–66

Hechtklößchen (Pike Dumplings in Cream Sauce), 163–64

Heringssalat mit Rote Beete (Pickled Herring Salad with Potatoes and Beets), 58

Matjes Hausfrauen Art (Herring in Cream Sauce with Apples and Onions), 162

Flädle (Sliced Soup Pancakes), 69

French Toast, Plum-Stuffed (Reicher Ritter), 38

fritters

Apfelküchle (Apple Fritters with Cinnamon-Sugar), 35–36

Quarkbällchen (Quark Fritters), 34

Quarkkeulchen (Quark Fritters with Potatoes and Raisins), 187

fruit

Grießflammeri (Farina Pudding with Fruit Sauce), 244

Quarkauflauf (Oven-Baked Quark Soufflé with Fruit), 180

Quarkspeise (Creamy Fruit Quark), 31

See also individual fruits

G

Gänsebraten (Roast Goose), 134–36

Gefüllte Paprika (Stuffed Peppers), 123–25

gelatin, 17

Germknödel (Giant Steamed Dumplings with Plum Butter and Poppyseeds), 191–95

Geschmelzte Zwiebeln (Caramelized Onions), 161

gluten-free flour, 17

Goose, Roast (Gänsebraten), 134–36

Graupensuppe (Beef Barley Soup), 87

Grieß, 16

Grießbrei (Warm Farina Pudding), 175

Grießflammeri (Farina Pudding with Fruit Sauce), 244

Grießklößchen (Semolina Soup Dumplings), 72

Grießschnitten mit Zimt-Zucker (Pan-Fried Custardy Farina Squares with Cinnamon-Sugar), 173–74

Gulasch, 126

Erdäpfelgulasch (Austrian Potato Paprika Stew), 101

Gulaschsuppe (Paprika Beef Soup), 73

Serviettenknödel mit Pilzgulasch (Bread Dumplings with Mushroom Goulash), 110–13

Szegediner Gulasch (Pork and Sauerkraut Stew), 129

Wiener Saftgulasch (Austrian Beef Stew), 126–28

Gurkensalat (Cucumber Salad), 46

H

Hamburger Pannfisch (Pan-Fried Cod and Potatoes in Mustard Sauce), 165–66

Hechtklößchen (Pike Dumplings in Cream Sauce), 163–64

herbs, 17

Herrencreme (Vanilla-Rum Cream with Chocolate), 231–32

herring

Heringssalat mit Rote Beete (Pickled Herring Salad with Potatoes and Beets), 58

Matjes Hausfrauen Art (Herring in Cream Sauce with Apples and Onions), 162

Hollandaise, 114–15

Horseradish Applesauce (Apfelkren), 148

Hühnerfrikassee (Chicken Fricassee), 144–46

K

Kaiserschmarrn mit Zwetschgenröster (Torn Soufléd Pancake with Plum Compote), 183–84

Kartoffelklöße (Potato Dumplings), 216–21

Kartoffeln mit Frankfurter Grüne Soße (Potatoes with Creamy Green Herb Sauce), 98–99

Kartoffelpuffer (Potato Pancakes), 102–3

Kartoffelpurée (Mashed Potatoes), 210

Kartoffelsuppe (Potato-Sausage Stew), 78–79

Käsespätzle (Swabian Noodles with Mountain Cheese and Caramelized Onions), 93–94

Käsesuppe (Mountain Cheese Soup), 75

Kaspressknödel (Pan-Fried Cheesy Bread Dumplings), 105–6

Kirschenmichel (Sour Cherry Bread Pudding), 176–77

Knödel

Böhmische Knödel (Bohemian Steamed Dumplings), 224–25

Germknödel (Giant Steamed Dumplings with Plum Butter and Poppyseeds), 191–95

Kaspressknödel (Pan-Fried Cheesy Bread Dumplings), 105–6

Marillenknödel (Fresh Apricot Dumplings), 189–90

Semmelknödel (Bread Dumplings), 222–23

Serviettenknödel mit Pilzgulasch (Bread Dumplings with Mushroom Goulash), 110–13

Topfenknödel mit Butterbrösel (Quark Dumplings with Toasted Bread Crumbs and Blueberry Compote), 245–47

kohlrabi, 55

Kohlrabigemüse (Creamed Kohlrabi), 200

Kohlrabisalat mit Apfel (Kohlrabi-Apple Salad), 55

Kohlrouladen (Stuffed Cabbage Rolls), 139–41

Königsberger Klopse (Meatballs in Lemon-Caper Sauce), 120–22

Kopfsalat mit Joghurt-Dressing (Butter Lettuce Salad with Yogurt Dressing), 51

Kräuterquark (Herbed Quark), 33

Krautsalat (Shredded Cabbage Salad), 52

L

lemons, 18

Königsberger Klopse (Meatballs in Lemon-Caper Sauce), 120–22

Zitronencreme (Puckery Lemon Cream), 233–35

Lentil Soup with Sausage and Prunes (Linsensuppe mit Pflaumen), 80

Lettuce Salad, Butter, with Yogurt Dressing (Kopfsalat mit Joghurt-Dressing), 51

Linsensuppe mit Pflaumen (Lentil Soup with Sausage and Prunes), 80

Liptauer (Austrian Cheese Spread), 42

M

Marillenknödel (Fresh Apricot Dumplings), 189–90

Matjes Hausfrauen Art (Herring in Cream Sauce with Apples and Onions), 162

Maultaschen (Swabian Meat and Spinach Dumplings), 155–61

meat, 117. *See also individual meats*

Meatballs in Lemon-Caper Sauce (Königsberger Klopse), 120–22

Milchreis mit Kirschkompott (Warm Rice Pudding with Sour Cherry Compote), 170

milk, 18

mushrooms
Hühnerfrikassee (Chicken Fricassee), 144–46
Serviettenknödel mit Pilzgulasch (Bread Dumplings with Mushroom Goulash), 110–13
Zürcher Geschnetzeltes (Swiss Veal Strips and Mushrooms in Cream Sauce), 130–32

N

noodles
Käsespätzle (Swabian Noodles with Mountain Cheese and Caramelized Onions), 93–94
Schupfnudeln mit Apfel-Sauerkraut (Potato Noodles with Apple Sauerkraut), 95–96
Norddeutscher Kartoffelsalat (Creamy Potato Salad), 61

nutmeg, 18

O

Obatzda (Bavarian Cheese Spread), 40

onions
Bayrisch Kraut (Braised Green Cabbage with Onions and Bacon), 205
Bratkartoffeln (Fried Potatoes with Onions and Bacon), 211–12
Geschmelzte Zwiebeln (Caramelized Onions), 161
Käsespätzle (Swabian Noodles with Mountain Cheese and Caramelized Onions), 93–94
Matjes Hausfrauen Art (Herring in Cream Sauce with Apples and Onions), 162
Rheinische Zwiebelsuppe (Onion and Sausage Soup), 76
Rotkohl (Braised Red Cabbage with Apples and Onions), 202–4
Wiener Saftgulasch (Austrian Beef Stew), 126–28

P

pancakes
Apfelpfannkuchen (Apple Pancakes), 182
Flädle (Sliced Soup Pancakes), 69
Kaiserschmarrn mit Zwetschgenröster (Torn Souffléd Pancake with Plum Compote), 183–84
Kartoffelpuffer (Potato Pancakes), 102–3

Pfannkuchen / Eierkuchen (Thin Pancakes), 181
Rösti (Swiss Pan-Fried Potato Cake), 215
Sauerkrautpuffer mit Kräuterschmand (Sauerkraut-Potato Pancakes with Herbed Sour Cream), 104
Spargel mit Kratzete und Hollandaise (White Asparagus with Herbed Pancakes and Hollandaise Sauce), 114–15

paprika, 18
Erdäpfelgulasch (Austrian Potato Paprika Stew), 101
Gulaschsuppe (Paprika Beef Soup), 73
Paprika Geschnetzeltes (Sliced Chicken with Peppers and Paprika), 133

Pears, White Bean Stew with Bacon, Green Beans, Apples and (Westfälisches Blindhuhn), 84–85

peas
Erbseneintopf (Thick Pea Stew), 83
Hühnerfrikassee (Chicken Fricassee), 144–46

Pellkartoffeln (Boiled Potatoes), 209

pepper, black, 15

peppers
Gefüllte Paprika (Stuffed Peppers), 123–25
Paprika Geschnetzeltes (Sliced Chicken with Peppers and Paprika), 133

Petersilienkartoffeln (Parsleyed Potatoes), 210

Pfannkuchen (Thin Pancakes), 181

Pflaumenmus (Roasted Plum Butter), 39

Pike Dumplings in Cream Sauce (Hechtklößchen), 163–64

plums, 20
Germknödel (Giant Steamed Dumplings with Plum Butter and Poppyseeds), 191–95
Pflaumenmus (Roasted Plum Butter), 39
Reicher Ritter (Plum-Stuffed French Toast), 38
Zwetschgenröster (Plum Compote), 186

pork
Buletten (Savory Meat Patties), 117
Gefüllte Paprika (Stuffed Peppers), 123–25
Kohlrouladen (Stuffed Cabbage Rolls), 139–41
Königsberger Klopse (Meatballs in Lemon-Caper Sauce), 120–22

Maultaschen (Swabian Meat and Spinach Dumplings), 155–61
Schweinebraten (Herbed Pork Roast), 137–38
Szegediner Gulasch (Pork and Sauerkraut Stew), 129
Wirsingeintopf (Savoy Cabbage Stew), 86
See also bacon; sausage; Schinkenspeck; Speck

potatoes, 7–8, 20, 197
Bauernfrühstück (Farmer's Breakfast: Meat and Potato Hash), 28–29
Bratkartoffeln (Fried Potatoes with Onions and Bacon), 211–12
Buttermilchgetzen (Potato-Buttermilk Casserole), 208
Eingebrannte Erdäpfel (Stewed Potatoes with Caraway and Sour Cream), 207
Erbseneintopf (Thick Pea Stew), 83
Erdäpfelgulasch (Austrian Potato Paprika Stew), 101
Erdäpfelkas (Potato Cheese), 43
Graupensuppe (Beef Barley Soup), 87
Gulaschsuppe (Paprika Beef Soup), 73
Hamburger Pannfisch (Pan-Fried Cod and Potatoes in Mustard Sauce), 165–66
Heringssalat mit Rote Beete (Pickled Herring Salad with Potatoes and Beets), 58
Kartoffelklöße (Potato Dumplings), 216–21
Kartoffeln mit Frankfurter Grüne Soße (Potatoes with Creamy Green Herb Sauce), 98–99
Kartoffelpuffer (Potato Pancakes), 102–3
Kartoffelpurée (Mashed Potatoes), 210
Kartoffelsuppe (Potato-Sausage Stew), 78–79
Norddeutscher Kartoffelsalat (Creamy Potato Salad), 61
Pellkartoffeln (Boiled Potatoes), 209
Petersilienkartoffeln (Parsleyed Potatoes), 210
Quarkkeulchen (Quark Fritters with Potatoes and Raisins), 187
Rheinische Zwiebelsuppe (Onion and Sausage Soup), 76
Rösti (Swiss Pan-Fried Potato Cake), 215
Salzkartoffeln (Boiled Peeled Potatoes), 209
Sauerkrautpuffer mit Kräuterschmand (Sauerkraut-Potato Pancakes with Herbed Sour Cream), 104

potatoes (*cont.*)

Schupfnudeln mit Apfel-Sauerkraut (Potato Noodles with Apple Sauerkraut), 95–96

Schwäbischer Kartoffelsalat (Swabian Potato Salad), 62

Seidenklöße (Silken Dumplings), 221

Thüringer Klöße (Potato Dumplings), 218

Westfälisches Blindhuhn (White Bean Stew with Bacon, Green Beans, Apples, and Pears), 84–85

Wirsingeintopf (Savoy Cabbage Stew), 86

Prunes, Lentil Soup with Sausage and (Linsensuppe mit Pflaumen), 80

puddings

Errötendes Mädchen (Raspberry Buttermilk Pudding), 240–41

Grießbrei (Warm Farina Pudding), 175

Grießflammeri (Farina Pudding with Fruit Sauce), 244

Herrencreme (Vanilla-Rum Cream with Chocolate), 231–32

Kirschenmichel (Sour Cherry Bread Pudding), 176–77

Milchreis mit Kirschkompott (Warm Rice Pudding with Sour Cherry Compote), 170

Reis Trauttmansdorff (Creamy Molded Rice Pudding with Raspberry Sauce), 243

Rote Grütze mit Vanillesoße (Red Berry Pudding with Vanilla Sauce), 236

Scheiterhaufen (Apple Bread Pudding), 178

Schokoladenpudding mit Vanillesoße (Chocolate Pudding with Vanilla Sauce), 228

Vanillepudding (Vanilla Pudding), 230

Q

Quark (Fresh Cheese), 18, 30

Erdäpfelkas (Potato Cheese), 43

Kräuterquark (Herbed Quark), 33

Liptauer (Austrian Cheese Spread), 42

Marillenknödel (Fresh Apricot Dumplings), 189–90

Quarkauflauf (Oven-Baked Quark Soufflé with Fruit), 180

Quarkbällchen (Quark Fritters), 34

Quarkkeulchen (Quark Fritters with Potatoes and Raisins), 187

Quarkspeise (Creamy Fruit Quark), 31

Topfenknödel mit Butterbrösel (Quark Dumplings with Toasted Bread Crumbs and Blueberry Compote), 245–47

R

Rahmspinat (Creamed Spinach), 198

raspberries

Bayerische Crème (Bavarian Cream with Raspberry Sauce), 239

Errötendes Mädchen (Raspberry Buttermilk Pudding), 240–41

Reis Trauttmansdorff (Creamy Molded Rice Pudding with Raspberry Sauce), 243

Rote Grütze mit Vanillesoße (Red Berry Pudding with Vanilla Sauce), 236

Reicher Ritter (Plum-Stuffed French Toast), 38

Reis Trauttmansdorff (Creamy Molded Rice Pudding with Raspberry Sauce), 243

Remouladensoße (Remoulade), 108

Rheinische Zwiebelsuppe (Onion and Sausage Soup), 76

rice

Gefüllte Paprika (Stuffed Peppers), 123–25

Milchreis mit Kirschkompott (Warm Rice Pudding with Sour Cherry Compote), 170

Reis Trauttmansdorff (Creamy Molded Rice Pudding with Raspberry Sauce), 243

Rinderbrühe (Clear Beef Broth), 66–68

Rinderrouladen (Braised Beef Rolls with Mustard and Pickles), 149–51

Rösti (Swiss Pan-Fried Potato Cake), 215

Rote Beete Salat (Red Beet Salad), 48

Rote Grütze mit Vanillesoße (Red Berry Pudding with Vanilla Sauce), 236

Rotkohl (Braised Red Cabbage with Apples and Onions), 202–4

S

salads, 45

Bohnensalat (Green Bean Salad), 57

Cremiger Gurkensalat (Creamy Cucumber Salad), 47

Gurkensalat (Cucumber Salad), 46

Heringssalat mit Rote Beete (Pickled Herring Salad with Potatoes and Beets), 58

Kohlrabisalat mit Apfel (Kohlrabi-Apple Salad), 55

Kopfsalat mit Joghurt-Dressing (Butter Lettuce Salad with Yogurt Dressing), 51

Krautsalat (Shredded Cabbage Salad), 52

Norddeutscher Kartoffelsalat (Creamy Potato Salad), 61

Rote Beete Salat (Red Beet Salad), 48

Schwäbischer Kartoffelsalat (Swabian Potato Salad), 62

Spargelsalat (White Asparagus Salad), 56

salt, 20

Salzkartoffeln (Boiled Peeled Potatoes), 209

sauces

Apfelkren (Horseradish Applesauce), 148

Cumberland Sauce, 138

Hollandaise, 114–15

Raspberry Sauce, 239

Remouladensoße (Remoulade), 108

Schnittlauchsoße (Creamy Chive Sauce), 148

Vanillesoße (Vanilla Sauce), 238

Sauerbraten (Spiced Braised Beef), 152–54

Sauerkraut, 20, 206

Sauerkrautpuffer mit Kräuterschmand (Sauerkraut-Potato Pancakes with Herbed Sour Cream), 104

Schupfnudeln mit Apfel-Sauerkraut (Potato Noodles with Apple Sauerkraut), 95–96

Szegediner Gulasch (Pork and Sauerkraut Stew), 129

Wine-Braised Sauerkraut, 206

sausage, 117

Erbseneintopf (Thick Pea Stew), 83

Erdäpfelgulasch (Austrian Potato Paprika Stew), 101

Kartoffelsuppe (Potato-Sausage Stew), 78–79

Linsensuppe mit Pflaumen (Lentil Soup with Sausage and Prunes), 80

Rheinische Zwiebelsuppe (Onion and Sausage Soup), 76

Scheiterhaufen (Apple Bread Pudding), 178

Schinkenspeck, 21

Bayrisch Kraut (Braised Green Cabbage with Onions and Bacon), 205

Bratkartoffeln (Fried Potatoes with Onions and Bacon), 211–12

Graupensuppe (Beef Barley Soup), 87

Kartoffelsuppe (Potato-Sausage Stew), 78–79

Linsensuppe mit Pflaumen (Lentil Soup with Sausage and Prunes), 80

Schupfnudeln mit Apfel-Sauerkraut (Potato Noodles with Apple Sauerkraut), 95–96

Schnittlauchsoße (Creamy Chive Sauce), 148

Schokoladenpudding mit Vanillesoße (Chocolate Pudding with Vanilla Sauce), 228

Schupfnudeln mit Apfel-Sauerkraut (Potato Noodles with Apple Sauerkraut), 95–96

Schwäbischer Kartoffelsalat (Swabian Potato Salad), 62

Schweinebraten (Herbed Pork Roast), 137–38

Seidenklöße (Silken Dumplings), 221

Sellerieschnitzel mit Remouladensoße (Celery Root Cutlets with Remoulade), 108–9

Semmelknödel (Bread Dumplings), 222–23

semolina, 16
  Grießklößchen (Semolina Soup Dumplings), 72

Serviettenknödel mit Pilzgulasch (Bread Dumplings with Mushroom Goulash), 110–13

soups and stews, 65
  Eierstich (Egg Soup Custard), 71
  Erbseneintopf (Thick Pea Stew), 83
  Erdäpfelgulasch (Austrian Potato Paprika Stew), 101
  Flädle (Sliced Soup Pancakes), 69
  Graupensuppe (Beef Barley Soup), 87
  Grießklößchen (Semolina Soup Dumplings), 72
  Gulaschsuppe (Paprika Beef Soup), 73
  Kartoffelsuppe (Potato-Sausage Stew), 78–79
  Käsesuppe (Mountain Cheese Soup), 75
  Linsensuppe mit Pflaumen (Lentil Soup with Sausage and Prunes), 80
  Rheinische Zwiebelsuppe (Onion and Sausage Soup), 76
  Rinderbrühe (Clear Beef Broth), 66–68
  Serviettenknödel mit Pilzgulasch (Bread Dumplings with Mushroom Goulash), 110–13
  Szegediner Gulasch (Pork and Sauerkraut Stew), 129
  Westfälisches Blindhuhn (White Bean Stew with Bacon, Green Beans, Apples, and Pears), 84–85
  Wiener Saftgulasch (Austrian Beef Stew), 126–28
  Wirsingeintopf (Savoy Cabbage Stew), 86

sour cream, 21

Spargel mit Kratzete und Hollandaise (White Asparagus with Herbed Pancakes and Hollandaise Sauce), 114–15

Spargelsalat (White Asparagus Salad), 56

Spätzle, 93
  Käsespätzle (Swabian Noodles with Mountain Cheese and Caramelized Onions), 93–94

Speck, 21
  Bauernfrühstück (Farmer's Breakfast: Meat and Potato Hash), 28–29
  Buttermilchgetzen (Potato-Buttermilk Casserole), 208
  Erbseneintopf (Thick Pea Stew), 83
  Kohlrouladen (Stuffed Cabbage Rolls), 139–41
  Krautsalat (Shredded Cabbage Salad), 52
  See also Schinkenspeck

spinach
  Hechtklößchen (Pike Dumplings in Cream Sauce), 163–64
  Maultaschen (Swabian Meat and Spinach Dumplings), 155–61
  Rahmspinat (Creamed Spinach), 198

spreads
  Erdäpfelkas (Potato Cheese), 43
  Liptauer (Austrian Cheese Spread), 42
  Obatzda (Bavarian Cheese Spread), 40
  Szegediner Gulasch (Pork and Sauerkraut Stew), 129

T

Tafelspitz (Austrian Boiled Beef with Horseradish Sauce), 147–48

Thüringer Klöße (Potato Dumplings), 218

tomatoes
  Gefüllte Paprika (Stuffed Peppers), 123–25

Topfenknödel mit Butterbrösel (Quark Dumplings with Toasted Bread Crumbs and Blueberry Compote), 245–47

Turkey, Sliced, with Peppers and Paprika (Paprika Geschnetzeltes), 133

V

vanilla
  Herrencreme (Vanilla-Rum Cream with Chocolate), 231–32
  Vanillepudding (Vanilla Pudding), 230
  Vanillesoße (Vanilla Sauce), 238

veal
  Wiener Schnitzel (Breaded Veal Cutlets), 142–43
  Zürcher Geschnetzeltes (Swiss Veal Strips and Mushrooms in Cream Sauce), 130–32

vegetables
  frozen, 17
  as side dishes, 197
  See also individual vegetables

vegetarian meals, 89

W

Westfälisches Blindhuhn (White Bean Stew with Bacon, Green Beans, Apples, and Pears), 84–85

Wiener Saftgulasch (Austrian Beef Stew), 126–28

Wiener Schnitzel (Breaded Veal Cutlets), 142–43

Wirsingeintopf (Savoy Cabbage Stew), 86

Wirsinggemüse (Creamed Savoy Cabbage), 201

Y

yogurt
  Kartoffeln mit Frankfurter Grüne Soße (Potatoes with Creamy Green Herb Sauce), 98–99
  Kopfsalat mit Joghurt-Dressing (Butter Lettuce Salad with Yogurt Dressing), 51
  Zitronencreme (Puckery Lemon Cream), 233–35

Z

Zitronencreme (Puckery Lemon Cream), 233–35

Zürcher Geschnetzeltes (Swiss Veal Strips and Mushrooms in Cream Sauce), 130–32

Zwei Eier im Glass mit Schnittlauchbrot (Soft-Boiled Eggs with Chives and Buttered Bread), 26

Zwetschgenröster (Plum Compote), 186

Published in the United States by Ten Speed Press, an imprint of the Crown Publishing
Group, a division of Penguin Random House LLC, New York.
TenSpeed.com

Ten Speed Press and the Ten Speed Press colophon are registered trademarks of
Penguin Random House LLC.

Typeface: HAL's Timezone

Library of Congress Cataloging-in-Publication Data
Names: Weiss, Luisa, author. Title: Classic German cooking : the very best recipes
for traditional favorites / Luisa Weiss. Identifiers: LCCN 2023050596 (print) | LCCN
2023050597 (ebook) | ISBN 9781984861887 (hardcover) | ISBN 9781984861894 (ebook)
Subjects: LCSH: Cooking, German. | Cooking—Germany. | LCGFT: Cookbooks. Clas-
sification: LCC TX721 .W436 2024 (print) | LCC TX721 (ebook) | DDC 641.5943—dc23/
eng/20240102
LC record available at https://lccn.loc.gov/2023050596
LC ebook record available at https://lccn.loc.gov/2023050597

Hardcover ISBN: 978-1-9848-6188-7
eBook ISBN: 978-1-9848-6189-4

Printed in China

Editor: Molly Birnbaum | Production editor: Ashley Pierce
Designer and art director: Lizzie Allen | Production designers: Mari Gill and Faith Hague
Production manager: Phillip Leung
Food stylist: Xenia von Oswald | Food stylist assistant: Shin Hye Hong
Photo assistant: Marco Kesseler
Copyeditor: Sasha Tropp | Proofreader: Heather Rodino | Indexer: Ken DellaPenta
Publicist: Lauren Chung | Marketer: Joey Lozada

10 9 8 7 6 5 4 3 2 1

First Edition